# Reinventing

The above picture, taken in southern Brazil by photographer Peter Kloehn of New York City, is of an Umbanda altar on which are placed representations of the spirits believed to guide its members. Many of these supernatural beings are believed to incorporate in the leaders of the group when they enter into trance during rituals. This is when the spirits consult with and help the members of the group. The representation of Christian saints, *orixás* (deities) from Africa, and spirits of former slaves and other marginalized Brazilians on the same altar clearly depicts the syncretic mixing of the supernaturals venerated by the members of this group and is representative of the theme of *Reinventing Religions*.

# Reinventing Religions

*Syncretism and Transformation in Africa and the Americas*

Edited by Sidney M. Greenfield and André Droogers

ROWMAN & LITTLEFIELD PUBLISHERS, INC.
*Lanham • Boulder • New York • Oxford*

ROWMAN & LITTLEFIELD PUBLISHERS, INC.

Published in the United States of America
by Rowman & Littlefield Publishers, Inc.
4720 Boston Way, Lanham, Maryland 20706
http://www.rowmanlittlefield.com

12 Hid's Copse Road, Cumnor Hill, Oxford OX2 9JJ, England

Copyright © 2001 by Rowman & Littlefield Publishers, Inc.

*All rights reserved.* No part of this publication may be reproduced, stored in a retrieval system, or transmitted in any form or by any means, electronic, mechanical, photocopying, recording, or otherwise, without the prior permission of the publisher.

Cover photo is courtesy of Jualynne E. Dodson of the African Atlantic Research team of the University of Colorado, Boulder, and José Millet Batista, senior research associate of Casa del Caribe en Santiago de Cuba, March 2000.
    The cover photograph, taken in Santiago de Cuba, comes from practitioners of the tradition of Regla de Palo. It shows a section of an altar that was displayed in a priest's home. The altar is both recognition and reverence of the Native American's first occupation of the land and spiritual space in the Americas. The other elements displayed, such as the rock, pieces of tree leaves, and sticks from the earth, are derived from the African religious heritage in Cuba.

British Library Cataloguing in Publication Information Available

**Library of Congress Cataloging-in-Publication Data**

Reinventing religions : syncretism and transformation in Africa and the Americas / edited by Sidney M. Greenfield and André Droogers.
    p. cm
    Includes bibliographical references and index.
    ISBN 0-8476-8852-6 (alk. paper) — ISBN 0-8476-8853-4 (pbk. : alk. paper)
    1. Blacks—Religion—Congresses. 2. Syncretism (Religion)—Africa, Sub-Saharan—Congresses. 3. Syncretism (Religion)—Latin America—Congresses. 4. Afro-Brazilian cults—Congresses. I. Greenfield, Sidney M. II. Droogers, A. F.

BL2490 .R45 2001
200'.89'96—dc21

00-059199

Printed in the United States of America

∞™ The paper used in this publication meets the minimum requirements of American National Standard for Information Sciences—Permanence of Paper for Printed Library Materials, ANSI/NISO Z39.48-1992.

*To Ellie and Ineke,*
for their patience and support

# Contents

**Introduction: A Symposium**     9
    Sidney M. Greenfield and André Droogers

**1 Recovering and Reconstructing Syncretism**     21
    André Droogers and Sidney M. Greenfield

**2 A Yoruba Healer as Syncretic Specialist:
Herbalism, Rosicrucianism and the Babalawo**     43
    Frank A. Salamone

**3 Population Growth, Industrialization and the Proliferation
of Syncretized Religions in Brazil**     55
    Sidney M. Greenfield

**4 Ethnicity, Purity, the Market and Syncretism in
Afro-Brazilian Cults**     71
    Roberto Motta

**5 Religious Syncretism in an Afro-Brazilian Cult House**     87
    Sergio F. Ferretti

**6 The Presence of Non-African Spirits in an Afro-Brazilian Religion:
A Case of Afro-Amerindian Syncretism?**     99
    Mundicarmo M. R. Ferretti

| | | |
|---|---|---|
| 7 | **The Reinterpretation of Africa: Convergence and Syncretism in Brazilian Candomblé**<br>Sidney M. Greenfield | 113 |
| 8 | **Possession and Syncretism: Spirits as Mediators in Modernity**<br>Inger Sjørslev | 131 |
| 9 | **Joana's Story: Syncretism at the Actor's Level**<br>André Droogers | 145 |
| 10 | **Ragga Cowboys: Country and Western Themes in Rastafarian-Inspired Reggae Music**<br>Werner Zips | 163 |
| 11 | **Polyvocality and Constructions of Syncretism in *Winti***<br>Ineke van Wetering | 183 |
| 12 | **Seeking Syncretism: The Case of Sathya Sai Baba**<br>Morton Klass | 201 |

**Index** — 215

**About the Contributors** — 229

# Introduction

# A Symposium

Religion, in its broadest sense, is fundamental in the lives and meaning systems of most people, especially those of Africa. It also has been at the heart of most encounters between Africans and outsiders. This book is about syncretism, specifically religious syncretism. Its focus is on the religious beliefs and practices of those alive today who are the products of the contact, mixing or interpenetration between Africans, Euro-Americans and others during the last five centuries.

When the Portuguese first landed on the west coast of the African continent at the beginning of the European expansion in the fifteenth century, priests, intent on "saving the souls" of the natives (i.e., converting them), accompanied the troops and traders who formed the first European colonial settlement at the *feitoria* (factory), or port of trade at Elmina. For the next five centuries missionaries, often in advance of merchants and soldiers, played a leading part in the European conquest and colonization of the continent. But Europeans and their belief systems were not the only ones with their eyes on Africa. Islam has been extending its victory over Christianity on the southern shores of the Mediterranean Sea, across the Sahara Desert and down both coasts of the African continent for more years than Europeans and Christianity have been active on the continent. One might say that the "holy war" between the two world religions (Christianity and Islam) that dominated the lives and affairs of the nations and peoples of Europe and the Middle East from the time of the prophet Mohammed in the seventh century to the beginnings of the expansion and discoveries in the fifteenth has been and continues into the present to be played out, or perhaps we might say fought out, in Africa with Africans as the prize.

But the contest between religions for the "hearts and minds" of Africans (and we use that overworked Cold War phrase to imply that the beliefs at stake here also extended into the economic and social domains) was not limited to the Old World. Beginning shortly after the Portuguese first landed, Africans were taken by them, and then by nationals representing other European states to succeed the Portuguese as "world leaders," as slaves to work the plantations they founded in the tropics of the New World. The moral legitimacy for plantation slavery, and the slave trade on which it depended, of course, was to save the souls of those, like the captured Africans, who had not previously been exposed to and therefore had not accepted Jesus Christ as their savior.

For more than five centuries Africans on both sides of the Atlantic basin have been exposed to proselytizing European, Middle Eastern and other foreign religions and the cultural and social institutions in which they each developed. In all that time, however, the belief systems and religious practices of the peoples of much of the continent, and especially for our purposes those from West Africa, and their descendants across the Atlantic, have not disappeared. Rather, they have adapted to and accommodated with Christianity, Islam and other belief systems. Moreover, the traditions and practices of Africa have influenced the beliefs and behaviors of non-Africans, not only on the African continent, but in the Americas and in those parts of the Middle East to which Africans were brought as slaves.

Scholars, especially anthropologists, have been studying these contacts—between Africans and Europeans, and each with other people—at least since the early years of the twentieth century. They also have studied the social and cultural outcomes of those contacts that at times produced modified and/or new religious and other cultural forms—which came to be known as syncretisms. Prior to World War II and for a brief period thereafter, these contacts between social groups and the intermixing of their cultures were conceptualized within anthropology as the study of acculturation and were central to the discipline's research agenda. At that time the study of religion also was a primary anthropological concern. Beginning shortly after World War II and increasingly as research funds became more available from government and private sources for the study of development, modernization, and other primarily secular issues, however, anthropologists turned their attention away from topics such as religion and culture contact. Moreover, since the middle of the 1940s, anthropology has been organized increasingly along geographical lines. Departments hire Africanists, Asianists, Europeanists, Latin Americanists, etc. who participate in area studies programs and present the results of their research as often at meetings of African,

Asian, European, etc., studies associations as they do at anthropology conferences. As a result, comparison of religions and cultures across geographical areas has suffered. While there has been some continuing examination of contact between Europeans and Africans, and culture contact in general, like most other things, it too has become a specialty.

When we decided to organize the session of which this book is the product for the 1995 meeting of the American Anthropological Association (AAA), our intent was to bring together a group of scholars who were doing research on aspects of culture contact, primarily but not exclusively between Africans and Europeans, and the descendants of both, who also had focused their studies on religion. Our hope was that we might turn some attention back to the agenda of comparative studies of the contact between and interpenetration of cultures that had been so important in the anthropology of an earlier period.

In preparing their papers for the Washington symposium the contributors were asked specifically to use syncretism and/or revitalization, concepts once so important in the field, as organizing themes for the presentation, interpretation and analysis of their research data. As organizers and later as editors, we were not interested in either concept as such, but rather we wished to see if one or both might still be useful theoretical constructs.

## Assimilation and Multiculturalism

Up through the 1950s, most North Americans to study the once separate social groups and cultures that had in recent times become part of a modern national society—willingly or not—and the continuing contact between them and those who controlled the larger society and its institutions assumed that the "minority" groups would adapt inevitably to and be assimilated into the dominant group. The implication was that the minorities would cease to exist as separate groups, with their cultures, by means of the syncretic process, becoming absorbed—at least in part—into what was considered to be an open, dynamic and evolving national culture. The dominant imagery for this was the melting pot.

European scholars, perhaps because of their greater familiarity with colonial peoples, assumed in contrast that minority groups wished to preserve their differences, with the implication for the national society in which they lived being what later was to be called multiculturalism. In brief, most North American scholars were assimilationists while the Europeans were not. Anthropological theory, we have come to understand in retrospect, reflected this. As the reader will see in the next chapter, anthropologists who advocated assimilationism mostly organized their research in terms of a theory that at the time was part of a discourse with a political agenda, an assimilationist one. Again we have come to appreciate in retrospect that syncretism was employed most often to indicate which specific aspects of the traditions of which of the diverse social groups had been incorporated into the emerging national culture.

Since the 1960s, however, most North American anthropologists have changed their position and now accept the assumptions of their colleagues across the Atlantic. Moreover, Third World anthropologists, who have become a growing voice in theoretical discussions and whose experiences are mostly with oppressed groups in their respective emerging nations, also give preference to theories and concepts that oppose assimilation and assume the continuing existence and autonomy of minority groups and the preservation of their cultural differences. One consequence of this change in social philosophy has been the rejection of the theory that had won such wide acceptance amongst anthropologists, but which conceptualized culture contact and syncretism in terms of assimilation. As a result, as we also shall see in the next chapter, there has been a proliferation of new theoretical formulations in the discipline with each seeking a new view of what the world is like that presupposes, as part of a new political discourse, the continuing existence of social groups and the perpetuation of their cultural differences. Debate over the meaning of the concept of syncretism and how it is to be used reflects this. One of the insights that came out of this debate is that people are able to adapt and to change, and yet succeed in maintaining their identity. Several of the contributions in this book illustrate this view.

In the papers presented at the Washington symposium each of the authors defined (or redefined) syncretism—and not always explicitly—in terms of the theoretical perspective that had been used in collecting his or her research data. What soon became clear was that the participants often had employed different theoretical orientations that led them to see the interactions between groups and the resulting mixing of their cultures in different and at times contradictory ways. We have made no attempt in editing the papers to reconcile these several theories and their difffering ways of treating the concept of syncretism. Instead, we have written chapter 1 to provide the reader with an epistemological framework to help navigate the often murky and dangerous waters of the relationship between concepts and the differing theoretical orientations that give meaning to them. As will be seen, there is no single or even dominant paradigm in anthropology today. As a result, a concept such as syncretism, developed as part of one theoretical framework, may (and does in the papers that follow) have a totally different meaning when adopted and used within another framework. As organizers we neither expected nor asked to achieve theoretical unanimity at the symposium; nor did we expect to have it in the published volume. We do not believe this to be possible at the present time. It is our own form of academic multiculturalism, in the eclectic way. Our objective in the seminar, and in this volume, was and is not to come up with a new theory with another view of what the world is like, in terms of which syncretism might be redefined. Our more modest goal instead is to take a fresh look at syncretism and the processes that produce it and in this way hopefully to revive a research agenda that we believe has been too long neglected.

## A Reflexive Approach

Discussion during symposia held as parts of professional conferences—such as the AAA—is severely limited. The formal program is unable to accommodate lengthy periods of intensive interaction and exchange among the participating scholars. If such interaction is to occur, a setting must be arranged outside the formal conference structure. Appreciating this, we asked the participants to remain in Washington for an additional day after the AAA meeting ended. On that Monday we convened at the home of the daughter of one of the coeditors who lives in Washington. During that day-long session the diversity of theoretical positions represented in the papers became even more clear.

This led us to ask the participants to revise the draft paper they presented in Washington, making explicit the theoretical framework they had used both in the conduct of the research and in the analysis of the data. The participants also were asked to make explicit the kind of questions they were asking, both of informants in the field and of the data they collected, and to relate them to the theoretical framework they employed. Therefore, although the papers included in this volume may represent different theoretical positions, each is clear, in Thomas Kuhn's terms (elaborated in chapter 1), as to what the author assumes the world to be like and how the theory s/he has selected enables them to relate data to theory by means of concepts.

In anthropology, unlike the situation in the physical and biological sciences (also elaborated in chapter 1), the subject matter, the actors in the religious and other social settings studied, often have their own theories that explain for them aspects of their beliefs and behaviors. These views may, and often do, differ from the theoretical frameworks employed by the scholars who study them. After the often intense interchanges that occur during research, practitioners may be influenced by the researcher's discourse—and its theoretical foundations—while the reverse also many be true. The conference participants were asked also to address this issue where possible in the revised version of their paper.

## The Volume

As happens in projects such as this, some of the participants in the Washington seminar were unable to revise their manuscripts for publication, or chose—for a variety of reasons ranging from changes in their academic or personal responsibilities to involvement in new projects to loss of interest in this one—to withdraw from the venture. To the nine papers by the remaining contributors the editors have added chapter 1, a general discussion of the role of theory in science that focuses on the concept of syncretism. Its purpose, as has been noted, is to orient the reader in the often confusing and muddy waters of scholarly discussion. Also added were two papers by each of the editors, which although written for other occasions, were the result of their thinking about the issues raised both in Washington and in the preparation of the volume.

Three of the contributors—including one of the editors—are North Americans. Four others—including the other editor—are Europeans. The remaining three are from Brazil where most of the research reported on was conducted. Three more of the chapters are based on data collected in the West Indies, one on a group of which some members have emigrated to Holland and another on the teachings of a South Indian holy man that have been brought to Trinidad. One chapter is based on research conducted in Africa, specifically on the Yoruba whose influence has been significant both in Brazil and the West Indies. Six of the contributors are male; three are female.

Following the theoretical orientation in chapter 1, Frank A. Salamone, in "A Yoruba Healer as Syncretic Specialist," examines the curing practices of Prince Doctor, a Yoruba herbalist. Prince also is an anthropologist—he is doing graduate studies—a traditional Yoruba religious leader, or *Babalawo*—in training—and maintains that simultaneously he also practices (in his healing) Christianity, Islam and Rosicrucianism. While Prince Doctor is somewhat of an extreme example, Salamone explains that his position is not entirely unique among the Yoruba. In setting out the healer's world view, Salamone provides the reader with insights into Yoruba epistemology and the areas into which it has been extended. This analysis enables the author to provide insights into the process of creolization and the role of religious-based power in situations where political options are limited. Moreover, it presents a unique perspective on the incorporation of outside elements into a functioning religious system that enables the reader to see how the Yoruba mix religious and healing practices from diverse parts of the world in Nigeria today and how they use them to achieve their personal goals.

In chapter 3, "Population Growth, Industrialization and the Proliferation of Syncretized Religions in Brazil," Sidney M. Greenfield, using syncretism in the "objective" sense (see chapter 1), provides an interpretive overview of the development of popular religion in Brazil against the background of changes in demography and political economy in the twentieth century. His contention is that after the Roman Catholic Church lost its monopoly when Brazil became a republic in 1889, other religions, with their roots in Africa, Europe, Asia and the Americas, entered what, following Peter Berger, he calls a religious market place, to compete with it for followers. On the model of Roman Catholicism's traditional patron-client exchanges between a devotee and a saint, which Greenfield views as the defining practice of its popular form practiced in Brazil, each has come to offer alternative supernaturals—and ritual access to them—who offer to satisfy a growing number of requests for help by the members of a population that has increased tenfold during the past century without a commensurate and fairly distributed increase in their access to resources.

Greenfield's essay is followed in chapter 4 by Roberto Motta's "Ethnicity, Purity, the Market and Syncretism in Afro-Brazilian Cults." In the sense that Motta also uses syncretism "objectively" and organizes the paper using the market as a metaphor for the context in which religious competition takes place in Brazil, it may be read as a companion piece to the previous chapter. Motta provides the reader with an historically rooted typology of what he calls the mixed Indo-Afro-European religions in terms of what he calls the "Brazilian Paradox": that while "they [the religious groups] assert ethnicity and ethnic identity at one level, they seem simultaneously to negate and deny it at another. Whereas faithfullness to "authentic" Indian or African origins is proclaimed on the one hand, new converts are recruited without distinction as to their color, ethnicity, or national origin, on the other." Building on Gilberto Freyre's idea of the "fraternal association of values and sentiments" and "religion [as] the point of contact and fraternization" between the cultures and races, Motta proposes the concept of *identitophagy*, around which he develops a framework for understanding the variety of religions practiced in Brazil which also will help the reader place the specific groups examined in the four chapters to follow.

The two chapters to follow, one by Sergio F. Ferretti and the other by Mundicarmo M. R. Ferretti, are about the *Tambor de Mina*, a religious tradition practiced in the northeastern Brazilian state of Maranhão. In chapter 5, Sergio Ferretti uses syncretism in Herskovits' classic sense "as a reinterpretation of cultural traits" in his "Religious Syncretism in an Afro-Brazilian Cult House." He modifies Herskovits' view, however, in terms of recent thinking on 1) the reciprocal influence between the culture of subaltern classes and that of the dominant ones and 2) that encounters of religions are not always a dialogue between equals. He also employs Roberto Da Matta's affirmation that *relacionar*, to link together, is a basic Brazilian characteristic that tends to construct bridges, uniting separate trends by distinct traditions. Ferretti then offers a typology of different kinds of syncretisms, concluding that the specific center he studied is both syncretic and traditional: although Catholic and other elements have been incorporated along with African ones, the group, he claims, has not compromised the maintenance of its African tradition. Syncretism, he proposes, may be viewed as a strategy that enables marginalized groups to continue their traditional religious practices by incorporating them along with forms of the dominant group in a mixed religious practice. In this sense, Ferretti suggests, it may be interpreted as a strategy of adaptation and conflict avoidance in a society characterized by prejudice which privileges those who are white and their religious and other cultural practices. It also, he adds, enabled a religious center of an oppressed group to be a dynamic locus of cultural resistance that in this case has contributed to the preservation of an Afro-Brazilian identity.

In chapter 6, Mundicarmo M. R. Ferretti tells us about "The Presence of Non-African Spirits in an Afro-Brazilian Religion." We learn specifically how the members of the family of the King of Turkey, Ferrabrás of Alexandria, as written about in the *História do Imperador Carlos Magno e os Doze Pares de França (Stories of the Emperor Charlemagne and the Twelve Peers of France)* and made popular in Brazilian folk tales, came to be known by Amerindian names and worshipped on par with African spirits at the Casa das Minas. The author then reminds us that the many examples of non-African spirits worshiped in other religious centers throughout Brazil should not be interpreted without careful examination, as they often are, as examples of Afro-Amerindian syncretism.

In "The Reinterpretation of Africa: Convergence and Syncretism in Brazilian Candomblé," Sidney M. Greenfield again takes an "objective" approach to syncretism to look critically at present-day efforts to reject syncretism by some of the leader of Bahia's Candomblés who claim instead that their beliefs and practices are not mixed but rather a "pure" and "authentic" continuation of those of their Yoruba ancestors. Using recent studies of Yoruba culture history, Greenfield shows that the religious elements brought to Brazil which became the basis of Candomblé were but part of a larger, more complex system that was functionally integrated into a total society. Removed from that setting and placed within a new one on the other side of the Atlantic, Candomblé in Brazil was of necessity changed and modified—by practitioners who were a poor, marginal minority. It could not, Greenfield argues, therefore be a pure and authentic continuation of Yoruba tradition. Instead he suggests that there was a convergence of aspects of Yoruba beliefs and practices and the Catholicism of the Luso-Brazilians; as a result, followers of each found the religion of the other to be not only meaningful, but also made the adoption and/or incorporation of some of the salient practices of the other acceptable to them.

In "Possession and Syncretism: Spirits as Mediators in Modernity," Inger Sjørslev looks at the current popularity of the Afro-Brazilian religions Candomblé and Umbanda as phenomena of modernity. Syncretism in their beliefs and practice, she maintains, is related to power and agency. Her contention is that, in the identity politics within possession ritual, syncretism provides the instrument and the opportunity for creativity and adaptation to new challenges and interpretations of history and the present cultural and social context, in the sense that it lends flexibility to the individual positioning within these. The reflexivity that characterizes modern life is reflected in the sphere of the religious, and syncretism has entered "native" discourse both as an element in the current views on power and as a manifestation of the reflexive attitude to the past. In this respect, the role of syncretism also points to the question of ethnographic authority.

In the final contribution on Brazilian syncretism, André Droogers introduces the reader to Joana, a Brazilian woman in her forties. Her religious biography is described, including her experiences with syncretism. The reason this chapter is dedicated to a description of one person's religiosity is to show how syncretism operates at the actor's level. Much has been written on the structural side of the mixing of religious traditions, and usually believers are talked about in more general terms, taken as a category. The emphasis on individual religiosity does not mean that the social and cultural frameworks are ignored. During periods of crisis in her life Joana appeals to various social, cultural and especially religious repertoires that she has accumulated in the course of her life. In his analysis Droogers uses the "connectionist" concept of schema, as presented in chapter 1. Joana's case also illustrates the triangle of meaning-making presented there, particularly the way actors and social and symbolic structures are related.

Following up on the themes of power and agency, in chapter 10, "Ragga Cowboys: Country and Western Themes in Rastafarian-Inspired Reggae Music," Werner Zips begins with his personal journey to Jamaica and Reggae music, which he proceeds to deconstruct in terms of what he considers to be the logic underlying its mixing of "Western film topics, idioms, myths, practices and actual bodily comportment in Jamaican culture." Applying the theoretical framework developed by Pierre Bourdieu, he begins at what he calls the actor's level of (self) explanation and moves to the structural one that he asserts determines various practices of Jamaican artists and consumers with respect to Reggae music. Performers are assumed to embody *dispositions* that they need to promote their access to "capital" in a given field. These dispositions may be thought of as inscribed in what Bourdieu refers to as their *habitus* in such a way that they are viewed by the actors as "natural" and therefore unquestioned. This perspective, Zips contends, among other things, provides a restraint from the often uncritical acceptance of the mixing or syncretism of form as deviation from anything presupposed as original or "pure." It also "enables researchers at times to unveil patterns of domination that sometimes are not recognized by the actors themselves. If the latter are to become aware of the situation, they must be exposed to an analytic reflection of the inherent logic of their practices, including the ways in which they come to embody the structures and values of the dominant society. Only by such a reflexive stance is it possible to clarify how the general values of mainstream culture provide the "norms" that are reproduced in popular culture."

In chapter 11, "Polyvocality and Constructions of Syncretism in *Winti*," Ineke van Wetering examines the results of culture contact and exchange between Christianity—both Roman Catholic and Protestant—and *Winti* (Surinam Creole religion) as they manifest themselves in birthday anniversary celebrations held by Creole women to determine whether or not they may be considered syncretic. In Amsterdam, where the research was done, she tells us that Creole women, carrying on the role they held in Surinam, see themselves as guardians of "their culture" (*We Kulturu*)—its authenticity—which was brought from the one-time Dutch colony when it attained political independence in 1970. *Winti* culture and religion are accepted in the multicultural Netherlands as a marker of Creole identity: "Although the women who pursue such politics are fully aware that they live in a globalizing, modern world, accepting this as a "normal" state of affairs, even participating in it with gusto, they will insist that when all is said and done it is their own culture that matters." That culture, van Wetering observes, has been partly sacralized. Birthday celebrations as secular events, however, have their roots in sacred, covert culture. For the convergence of culture traits of African and European origin in *Winti,* the term "syncretism", she concludes, has descriptive value; it refers to what happens concretely. Moreover, she adds, there obviously is a shared culture, a sedimentation of historical experience that marks boundaries. Contrary to what some writers have postulated, she maintains, Creole women's rituals communicate a vision of a shared, integrated whole.

In the final chapter Morton Klass, in "Seeking Syncretism: The Case of Sathya Sai Baba," turns away from contacts between and the subsequent cultural interpenetrations of Africans, Europeans and Amerindians to provide a comparative perspective when he examines syncretism in the teachings of the South Indian holy man, Sathya Sai Baba, as they have been put into practice by devotees in the West Indian nation of Trinidad and Tobago. Sai Baba, Klass tells us, claims in an assertion "accepted by all his devotees whatever their original faith, ... that he is God—the only God there is or has ever been. ... Is this then," Klass asks, "another example of the phenomenon of *syncretism* . . . ? Or is it in fact perhaps something even more—is the religion of Sathya Sai Baba the *ultimate* syncretism, an assertion that all religions are "one," and that "oneness" is personified by Sathya Sai Baba?" His answer is that although the devotees (subjectively) "do indeed believe in the syncretic nature of their belief system . . . objectively," although they have proved particularly attractive to people of South Asian descent who live in a black West Indian nation, "the teachings . . . do not constitute syncretism."

We believe, as the reader will see from the chapters to follow, that syncretism is still a useful term for examining the results of contact between peoples and cultures. Revitalization, on the other hand, no longer seems to be of analytic utility. The meanings attributed to syncretism, however, as also will be clear, have become the subject of a lively debate based more on the theoretical orientation of the student than on the reality being studied. We may conclude, as Morton Klass observes at the end of his paper, that "Syncretism . . . has objective and subjective meanings; it is arguably universal and non-existent; and it may be found in the eye of the beholder or the mind of the believer. One begins to see why the term has precipitated frustration and confusion over the centuries since

Plutarch first foisted it upon us—and also why, despite all, it remains ever stimulating, ever useful."

*A Note on Orthography*
We wish to caution the reader that the word for the deities from Africa that also are venerated in the Americas may be spelled differently depending on language and the part of the world being discussed. *Òrìsà* and *orisa*, for example, are used in Nigeria, whereas in Brazilian Portuguese *orixá* is more common. Each of our authors has his or her own preferences. We have chosen not to change what they used in their original manuscript. We hope that this does not overly confuse the reader.

# Chapter 1

# Recovering and Reconstructing Syncretism

André Droogers and Sidney M. Greenfield

### Some Epistemological Considerations

In his now-classic study of *The Structure of Scientific Revolutions*, the late Thomas Kuhn asks how someone, ignorant of the history of science, would examine electrical or chemical (or other) phenomena if inclined to do so.[1] "What must the world be like," he queries in his closing argument, "in order that man may know it?"[2]

To anthropologists it is obvious that the answer is symbolic. That is, it calls for the formulation of a mental picture expressible in words that form images as to what the world is like. Many alternative images are possible, of course. The specifics of any one selected serve as the building blocks on which an understanding of the chemical, electrical or, for that matter, any other phenomena can be developed. And since people other than scientists also are curious about the world around them, they too must develop a mental image or symbolic model that will enable them to explore, analyze and eventually gain an understanding of the events they experience and the phenomena they encounter. Science, as we have become increasingly aware, is a cultural process. Acknowledging this enables us to treat the doing of science, or any other form of scholarship, as comparable to and illustrative of our understanding of other forms of cultural practice. Furthermore, it also will enable us to separate two categories of persons seeking to understand the world: 1) the scientists and scholars, and 2) at least some of those they (the social scientists) study.

To satisfy their curiosity about aspects of the world they encounter, actors in both categories then develop mental models that when elaborated and tested over time, as is the case in science, form a basis for understanding. Occasionally, both the scientist, more specifically the social scientist, and the people studied find themselves interested in the same events or phenomena. The images, models and theories of the scientist (and therefore their explanations) may or may not overlap with or be congruent with those of the people studied.

The simplest answer to Kuhn's "what must the world be like" question is to be found in metaphor.[3] By likening the world to something already known, the curious person (scientist or layperson) may use what knowledge he or she has about the known to think about the unknown and formulate questions about it. The answers to the questions provide further insights and understandings that may be explored in detail.

Kuhn reminds us that effective research

> scarcely begins before a scientific community thinks it has acquired firm answers to questions like the following: What are the fundamental entities of which the universe is composed? How do these interact with each other and with the senses? What questions may legitimately be asked about the entities and what techniques employed in seeking solutions?[4]

Far from being absolute, Kuhn acknowledges that the answers are arbitrary. They are derived from the particular image of what the world is like adopted by the members of a scientific community.

Kuhn then does something that shows keen anthropological insight. He moves from his initial discussion of an isolated individual asking about natural phenomena to a scientific community. Such a community is a social group formed around a shared image as to what the world is like and how one studies it. The consensus its members hold enables them to ask similar questions, the answers to which expand their collective understanding of their shared field or subject of interest.

Once a paradigm, defined as "an accepted model or pattern,"[5] is agreed upon, the individual members do "puzzle solving," posing questions the hypothesized answers to which can be tested. This requires agreement by the members of a scientific community as to terms, called concepts, that enable them to relate observed events, or data, to the conceptual categories of their paradigm.

Taken cumulatively, the answers to the many questions asked and puzzles solved fill in the blanks or unknowns in the paradigm or model. This in turn expands that scientific community's knowledge of what the world is like and hence its ability to explain the phenomena of interest to it.

Before proceeding, two points in Kuhn's presentation are worth emphasizing. First, the questions asked by scientists and scholars, along with the concepts used to formulate them, as previously stated, are not about some absolute reality, but rather are derived from and therefore the products of the specific model or paradigm around which a consensus has developed. Independent of a shared mental picture, concepts and the hypotheses they are used to formulate have neither meaning nor relevance.

Secondly, the techniques to solve the puzzles and the methods employed by the members of a scientific community to test and validate theories also are based on and derived from the images of their shared paradigm or model. In Kuhn's words: "The existence of the paradigm sets the problem to be solved; often the paradigm theory is implicated directly in the design of the apparatus able to solve the problem."[6]

Not all puzzles can be solved, however, and occasionally scientists encounter anomalies that cannot be explained in terms of their agreed-upon paradigm. If the anomalies are of a sufficient magnitude, they may bring the utility of the paradigm itself into question. With the consensus shattered, one or more members of the scientific community may propose an alternative image as to what the world is like that ideally will incorporate previous knowledge while also making it possible to account for the anomalies.

In the natural sciences, where a single paradigm has tended to dominate studies of particular subject matters, or disciplines, the proposal of a new imagery to deal with anomalies in any one invariably has led to conflict between members of the scientific community. This process of paradigm replacement is what Kuhn is referring to in his title by "scientific revolutions."[7]

While the natural sciences have been characterized as each having a single dominant paradigm (at any point in time), the social sciences and particularly anthropology have been and still are characterized by the opposite: the simultaneous presence of multiple different images of what the world is like. In contrast with the natural sciences, anthropology and specifically cultural anthropology might not even be considered a single discipline. It is a subject matter in which several, often contradictory, models of what the world is like compete with each other for supporters. Instead of a single community of scholars who share a consensus as to what the world is like and how it is to be conceptualized so as to formulate questions and solve puzzles by agreed-upon techniques, there are small groups, and at times even isolated individuals, each working in terms of an image of what the world is like that often has little relationship to the ones used by others. The diverse imageries are called theories. Each is often but a partial picture of the world that as yet has not been elaborated in terms of answers to specific questions. Anomalies, phenomena that bring into question any one of the numerous theories, are easily encountered.

Our intent here is not to review the numerous theories that have been proposed by anthropologists as candidates to be a disciplinary paradigm. We only wish to remind the reader that there have been several. Furthermore, each contains its own key images, called concepts, that enable its picture of the world to be related to empirical events or phenomena. Moreover, proponents of each tend to ask different questions, or, in Kuhn's terms, to formulate different puzzles to be solved by different methods and techniques.

This situation, as might be expected, lends itself to considerable confusion and misunderstanding. To complicate matters, scholars often do not make explicit in their writings the image of the world from which their research derives. They also often neglect to relate the concepts they use to the images or theories to which they subscribe. Instead, the practice tends to be to cite others who agree with them and select specific quotations to illustrate partial images applicable to specific, limited problems. Insiders familiar with the literature invariably can discern the theoretical imagery used in any particular study. Outsiders, including students, often cannot.

Furthermore, criticism of alternative images, and the studies based on them, is at a premium. Far too often theories, and their core images, are developed and defended by criticizing an alternative without necessarily making explicit what is being proposed in its place. Criticism often takes the form of attacks that may be personal rather than of theories and their applications. Arguments tend to be *ad hominem*, exacerbating the splits between the supporters of the competing theoretical positions. Given this general situation, the reader should not be surprised to be told that it is the case with respect to the subject of this book. In our summary review of the literature on syncretism, therefore, we make explicit the specific meaning attributed to the concept by diverse authors and how it relates to the image of what the world is like expressed in their theories.

## Syncretism in Anthropology

Syncretism as a concept was introduced into anthropology by Melville J. Herskovits as part of what, beginning in the second and third decades of the twentieth century, was conceptualized as the study of acculturation, contact between carriers of different cultures.[8] Herskovits was a student of Franz Boas who, along with others mostly at Columbia University, subscribed to and contributed to developing the distinctive image of what the world was like on which American—as then opposed to European—anthropology came to rest.

Boas, as Stocking and others have written, was reacting to the evolutionary perspective that had shaped anthropological thinking from the time it was separated off as a distinct field of inquiry in the writings of E. B. Tylor, L. H. Morgan and others in the late nineteenth century.[9]

Nineteenth-century evolutionary thinking, as Nisbet and others have observed, rested on the metaphor of a growing organism as the answer to the question what the world is like.[10] Building on a long history of its use in explaining human behavior, starting with the Greeks and extending through the Church Fathers followed by Enlightenment thinkers, the nineteenth-century founders of what was to become anthropology, like their fellow intellectuals of the period, conceptualized human society as an organism-like entity. As such, it was assumed to grow. Furthermore, its postulated component parts, called institutions, like the whole, also were assumed to grow naturally, directionally, immanently, continuously, necessarily, and to proceed from uniform causes.[11]

When he conducted his first field research as a student, Boas found what to him appeared to be a series of anomalies that could not be explained according to the prevailing evolutionary paradigm. His own further studies, and those of his students, led to the reporting of further anomalous data that was used first to question and then to reject the use of the organic growth metaphor for the study of culture. This, of course, forced Boas and his followers to seek a different answer to Kuhn's question as to what the world must be like. What they selected was to become an alternative paradigm. At first their writings were mostly explicit in their criticism of evolutionism; only later did they elaborate the new model that was to become the closest thing to a paradigm that was to unify anthropology, primarily in North America.

In reaction to the inevitable, directional growth of culture and its component parts assumed by evolutionists, Boas seems instead to have envisioned a world of distinct and self-contained groups of people, each a separate society that had its own language, institutions and way of life, or culture, that continued or changed depending upon a combination of specific internal and exogenous forces. Moreover, each was assumed to be isolated, or at least relatively isolated, from the others. These were the "primitive" peoples and cultures, conceived in a way that was later criticized in their turn by those who rejected the Boasian paradigm.

Each culture, with its economic, political, religious, kinship and other institutions, was further conceptualized as being composed of smaller parts called culture traits which combined to form patterns and complexes. All were assumed to be able to move almost independently from group to group and people to people across time and space. Like whole cultures, culture traits, patterns and complexes, along with the institutions they formed, were believed to have their own specific histories.

Based on the new imagery, Boasian anthropologists asked different questions than did their evolutionist predecessors, the answers to which could be obtained only by going to, living with and learning first hand from the peoples whose cultures soon were assumed to be the object of all inquiry. Boasian anthropology developed an historicist and empiricist cast. Detailed ethnographies of specific peoples came to be its primary goal and, according to its critics, often an end in itself.

Although they pictured a world of self-contained, autonomous and isolated peoples and cultures, Boasians recognized that there had been, and continued to be, contact between people across cultural boundaries. At one level the cumulative results of these contacts were the great civilizations of the west and the east. These, however, were the objects of study of scholars from other disciplines. Anthropology set itself off from economics, sociology, political science, history and the humanities by focusing on the remnants—those peoples and cultures that had not been absorbed into the world's great civilizations.

By the 1930s anthropologists planning to study small-scale, isolated peoples and cultures realized that their numbers were growing smaller. What later was to be called the process of globalization already was well under way. While a small number of students still were able to devote themselves to learning all they could about the Mbuti, the !Kung, the Yanomamö, the Samoans, the Australian Aborigines, the Jivaro or the Tiwi, others turned to explore the impact of contact between once separate and distinct peoples and representatives of western civilization.

Syncretism originally was proposed as a dimension of reinterpretation in the acculturation process, conceptualized to picture what happened to a once isolated people and their culture when they entered into (prolonged) contact with another, usually more powerful, often colonial or imperial culture.[12] The imagery was that when acculturation takes place, each people may take, from what it finds in the other certain forms, culture traits and/or their meanings, which they may reformulate in terms of their own understandings, behaviors and/or practices. The new forms that may result might be composed of elements from the other culture taken over wholesale or a mixing of aspects of its own traditions and those of the other. The mixing and the process, including the reinterpretation of form and meaning that led to the new merged form, both came to be referred to as syncretism.

Herskovits used the concept of syncretism extensively in his studies of the descendants of African slaves in the New World. It enabled him to explain the many cultural patterns practiced by contemporary "Negros" ranging from music and dance to religion. They were viewed as the products of the differential mixing (syncretism) and reinterpretation of culture traits that had their origins in Africa and/or Europe.

Although other anthropologists also found the concepts of syncretism and reinterpretation advantageous in analyzing the cultures of peoples they studied, Herskovits' work, perhaps because he was so prolific and influential in the field or perhaps because the people he studied were at the center of so much public discussion and debate, tends to be preeminent and to serve as the exemplar. It must not be forgotten, however, that the meaning and utility of syncretism as a concept, and its value in analyzing ethnographic data, like all concepts, was embedded in a paradigm, a particular view of what the world was like. It is of interest to note that this paradigm had little acceptance in American academia outside of anthropology. Anthropologists studying acculturation, however, were exposed to the writings of authors in other disciplines and in turn to their paradigms and theories. Some of these other images were to be absorbed into anthropology and later adopted.

We might note further that the concept of syncretism played a special role in what has been referred to as Boas' (and many of his followers) social agenda.[13] Concerned as they were with the treatment of minorities in a national society that turned increasingly xenophobic and exclusionary after World War I, in developing their paradigmatic framework for anthropology as a science, Boas and his students also formulated a discourse whose hoped-for goal was the fashioning of a national (American) society in which racial and ethnic minorities were to be integrated and assimilated. Syncretism, or a mixing into new forms of the culture traits and patterns of the several diverse peoples who made up the United States and their reinterpretation by minorities as they were assimilated and integrated into a new national way of life, was to be a part of the means for its attainment. In their scholarly research, however, those to subscribe to the Boasian paradigm tended to remain historicist and empiricist.[14]

## A Problematic Concept

It is unfortunate that neither Herskovits nor others in anthropology to use the term syncretism were aware, or perhaps they simply chose not to acknowledge, that the word already was used by scholars in other fields to refer to something other than what they wished to conceptualize. The term had a long history that predated its incorporation into the Boasian framework. Scholars in other fields, however, used it in terms of theories that differed both from each other and from that of Boasian anthropology.

Syncretism was first used by Plutarch to describe the temporary coming together of the quarreling inhabitants of Crete in the face of a common enemy. His image of what the world was like was of warring groups. The Greek word from which the English "syncretism" is derived refers to people joining together, in this case in battle. Erasmus later employed it metaphorically to refer to an agreement between people with seemingly disparate opinions. The new referent was ideas and beliefs. Seventeenth-century theologians then gave it a negative connotation by using it for what to them was the undesirable reconciliation of Christian theological differences. Syncretism for them became a threat to "true" religion. To this negative judgment a more neutral view was added in the second half of the nineteenth century when some students of the history of religions began to use the word to acknowledge the mixing of religious elements from diverse sources, including Christianity, that had occurred and continues to take place.[15]

Had Herskovits selected another word to stand for the mixing and reinterpretation of cultural traits and patterns in situations of culture contact, perhaps we would be spared much of the conflict and confusion found in the literature today. As has happened with other concepts not originally coined within anthropology but incorporated into a theory that then is subjected to criticism by proponents of yet another image of what the world is like, the term syncretism has been criticized and deconstructed to such a degree that many, as Baird[16] concluded a quarter of a century ago, have chosen to avoid its use.

## Syncretism Ignored

While the Boasian paradigm was dominant as anthropology developed into an academic discipline in the United States, another imagery, that gave rise to a contrasting theoretical framework, provided the basis for a discipline of the same name in Great Britain. Building on the writings of Emile Durkheim, A. R. Radcliffe-Brown elaborated and instilled in a generation of students what came to be known as structural-functional theory. Also rejecting the organic growth imagery of evolutionism, structural-functionalists retained the metaphor of the organism as their answer to the question of what the world—called society as opposed to Boasian culture—was like. This led them to turn their attention to how the parts of the "organism," its institutions, contributed to the functioning and the maintenance of the equilibrium of what were assumed to be the world's numerous discrete societies. Change in this framework was equated with dysfunction. It was assumed to upset the balance essential to the continuity and survival of the whole. A society's well-being was postulated to depend on the unimpeded "functioning" of its political, economic, religious, etc. systems. Needless to say, contact, especially contact that brought about change, was not a topic of great interest to followers of Radcliffe-Brown, at least in the beginning. Consequently, syncretism, although it might have been, was not a subject about which structural-functionalists had much to say.

We do not propose here to review the root images of the many theories that have been introduced into anthropology over the years and what, if anything, each contributed to the subject of syncretism. We could, for example, examine Modernization Theory, Marxism, Structuralism, Symbolic Anthropology and others to show, that in terms of their respective and divergent views of what the world is like, syncretism as conceptualized in the Boasian paradigm was not always meaningful nor important. This might help to explain, as noted earlier, why the topic, once so important on the research agenda of American anthropology, fell into disfavor.[17]

## Syncretism and Questions of Power

In his introduction to *Syncretism and the Commerce of Symbols*, Göran Aijmer argues "against the honoured Durkheimian position that societies can be studied as integrated wholes. . . . We have no *a priori* right," he tells us, "to define either society, or culture, as well integrated 'wholes.'" He proposes instead an image of a human social universe composed of groups that are "agglomerations of people around particular activities." The members of the groups produce symbols that employ "systemic correspondences for bringing a society together into a union under the acceptance of a source of dominance."[18] With this seemingly Hobbesean view of the sociopolitical order, Aijmer turns his attention to the symbols that in his view encode the strategies and social discourses that he proposes as the proper subject matter of anthropological investigation and analysis. That is, after assuming a social world characterized by dominance, hegemony, oppression, the marginality and suppression of disadvantaged groups, etc., he turns to syncretism asking: (1) "What happens when two cultural traditions are juxtaposed in such a way and under such circumstances that they are judged as competing by those continuous social groups who are the agents of the traditions?" and (2) "Under what conditions do people in one such continuous group pay attention to symbolism upheld by another group?"[19]

At one level these questions seem not to be very different from those Herskovits and other Boasian students of syncretism asked. What has changed is the image of what the world is like in which group contact is assumed to take place. Whereas Boasians, especially in their social agenda, saw syncretism as a mechanism by means of which diverse groups would be assimilated and incorporated into a single, unified national society with a culture of mixed traits fashioned from the contributions of each, Aijmer and other present-day thinkers assume a world of continuously diverse groups competing for dominance over each other and hegemony.[20] The world of meanings of others is acknowledged only in the process of mobilizing strategies to defend themselves from or to strive for dominance over them. This, of course, leads to a political view of syncretism.

In a previous attempt to recast syncretism, one of us asked that power be looked at. "To argue that power is a dimension of syncretism, is one thing; interpreting relations of power is another."[21] Two categories of models of power may be distinguished. The first is functionalist and sees diversity as being overcome by a new synthesis. The second is Marxist in which diversity and conflict are seen as prevailing and continuing. In the first set of models, syncretism reconciles the contradictions in the process of achieving cohesion, while in the second it "is interpreted as an instrument of oppression, creating a false unity and hiding social conflicts."[22]

Shaw and Stewart, employing the second model implicitly, carry the new thinking a step further—reversing the Boasian political goal of assimilation—when they propose the concept of "anti-syncretism."[23] Accepting what seems to be a modified Marxist and multiculturalist view of what the world is like, they see human beings as actors constantly defining themselves symbolically and redefining themselves with respect to others with whom they always are assumed to be in contact. This being the case, they ask: What use is the concept of syncretism "since all religions have composite origins and are continually reconstructed through ongoing processes of synthesis and erasure."[24] Based on the view of society as composed of social groups in unreconcilable conflict, they "recast the study of syncretism as the politics of religious synthesis."[25] They mean by this the study of the conflicts that in their view of the world inevitably occur between different groups as each revises its symbolic meanings while competing with the others for dominance. Shaw and Stewart define anti-syncretism as "the antagonism to religious synthesis shown by agents concerned with the defence of religious boundaries."[26] It is "frequently bound up with the construction of 'authenticity,' which is in turn often linked to notions of 'purity.'"[27]

## Yet Other Uses of the Term

Ambiguity and contradiction in the use of and meaning attributed to syncretism are compounded further when we remember that scholars are not the only ones to formulate models of what the world is like and use concepts to relate it to empirical events. Some religious practitioners continue to use the term syncretism consistent with the view of the seventeenth-century theologians mentioned above. For them the mixing syncretism implies is illegitimate and therefore to be condemned out of hand and carefully avoided. This position is commonly held in many branches of Christianity, especially among the clergy and theologians. It also is to be found in other religions presently striving to protect the basis for what has come to be referred to as their identity.[28] Syncretism here tends to be treated as are magic and popular religion. In all three cases value judgments are made by spokespersons for recognized religious groups with regard to the truth or heresy of the phenomenological referents for the terms. In this way they exercise their power.

In contrast with this "subjective" view that is presented in the discourses of religious practitioners, there is a logically opposed "objective" view of syncretism that is taken by scholars who study religious phenomena who often are assumed to have no interest in defending the religious truths of the faiths they investigate.

The existence of a "subjective" view, or multiple subjective views, however, need not preclude the use of the concept in what we are calling its objective sense.[29] One problem is that differences also abound on the "objective" side. Once scholars go beyond using the term to refer to the basic mixing of religious elements, there is a wide range of diverse approaches. One question that might be asked is whether syncretism is to be used solely for the mixing of religious phenomena or whether non-religious items, such as ideology, science or even culture itself, are to be treated as part of the syncretic process? Another is whether syncretism should refer to the end result of mixing or to a continuing process? Should the focus of investigation be only on the eventual outcome or on the process with the assumption that it always will be continuing to produce new syntheses?

Another source of confusion is the degree to which elements are mixed and how much of a state of integration is necessary to recognize them as something new. If stable and integrated religions are the result of the syncretic process, are they still to be called syncretic? If so, Buddhism, Christianity and Islam, to mention a few, are syncretic religions, though some of their followers would be surprised to hear this. The same question may be put in another way if we ask whether syncretism has to do with the origin of religion or with later "threats" to its integrity and identity. There are still other points of disagreement. For example, is the term to be reserved for conscious efforts to mix religious elements, or used also to refer to the unconscious merging of religious elements? Finally, syncretism in itself does not indicate whether the two (or more) religions involved in the mixing process are influencing each other equally, or whether the process is asymmetric, with one dominating the other.[30]

## An Attempt at a Synthesis from Divergent Theoretical Positions

We have not attempted to present in this essay an encyclopedic overview of anthropological theories,[31] nor do we propose to offer yet another view of the world that will lead to still other ways of conceptualizing syncretism that in turn will generate new questions to be asked. Instead, we review some recent thinking and make suggestions that in our judgment hold promise for the study of syncretism and for the analysis of contact between social, cultural and especially religious groups.

Our first suggestion is that we steer clear of making unilateral choices from dichotomous alternatives that we believe have plagued so many debates within anthropology. Discussion of theoretical perspectives long has suffered from oppositional thinking and focusing on one term in a pair of dichotomies. In our review of the literature on syncretism we already presented the example of structural-functionalists emphasizing harmony and cohesion while Marxists look for contradiction and conflict. Where structural-functionalists study the working of autonomous social mechanisms, action theorists prefer to do research on the role of persons in society. While members of this community of scholars drew attention to the importance of order, continuity and system, others emphasized indeterminacy,[32] the inchoate,[33] risk[34] and rupture. Whereas to some, symbols are instrumental primarily in so-called social dramas,[35] others[36] view symbols as vehicles of culture. Where cultural ecologists show the importance of habitat, others point to the decisive role of habitus.[37]

A striking development in recent theoretical discussions is a decrease in one-sided options and an effort to see the several sides of conflicting issues. Eclecticism, formerly a dirty word, seems to be becoming fashionable. If we are tolerant and both acknowledge and examine the competing theoretical frameworks, we may learn to appreciate the importance of the questions we might not ask had we not been sensitized to them.

## Praxis Theories

Praxis theories appear to us to be an important attempt to go beyond dichotomies.

The term praxis—or practice—refers to a range of thinking that in one way or another elaborates the aphorism first made by Berger and Luckmann that "*Society is a human product. Society is an objective reality. Man is a social product.*"[38] The concepts and methods used in the application of praxis theories vary widely and it is difficult as yet to identify a community of scholars contributing to this contender to paradigmatic status. Even if Bourdieu,[39] Giddens,[40] Moore,[41] Ortner,[42] Sahlins[43]—to mention only a few—do not speak the same language and do not necessarily refer to each other's publications, they all seem to be looking for some way to show that actors (individuals) are influenced by and subject to social and symbolic structures. In addition, they agree that these structures provide a repertory of meanings that can be used to interpret events. This may lead the actors to create new meanings that in turn modify or change the social and symbolic structures. It is to these transformations, which may be summarized in what we will call the triangle of praxis or of signification, meant in the sense of the process of meaning-making and not as meaning itself, that we are referring in the subtitle of this book.

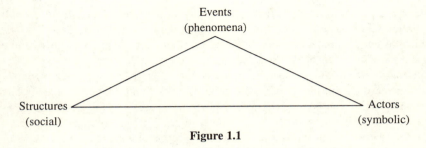

**Figure 1.1**

Praxis theory is necessarily reflexive—in that what is generalized about those studied must also be applicable to those who study them. It also is historical and processual and provides a context for the analysis of common events and everyday experiences. Another of its features is that asymmetrical relations, and hence power, easily can be identified. This combination of features that formerly were focal aspects of distinct theoretical frameworks is an indication of the eclectic nature of praxis approaches. Similarly, praxis theories, it seems to us, may be used eclectically no matter the emphasis and terminology used by individual writers. Further, it can be used to analyze both the researchers with respect to their own social and symbolic structures (i.e., scientific theories) and to the beliefs and structures of those they study.

## Cognitive Anthropology

Recent publications in what is called cognitive anthropology, we believe, contribute to the elaboration of a methodology for praxis theory.[44] If the relationship between actors and structures is a dialectical one, we may ask: How do actors produce, objectify and internalize structures? Put differently, how do structures prescribe the behaviors of individuals and how may they be changed by those who participate in them? If cultural knowledge is a prerequisite for social participation, how does this knowledge come into being? And how is it changed so as to in turn change society?

Individual experience through events, it appears, is the motor for what is called the production and reproduction of structures and their meanings. D'Andrade's notion of schema is useful here. He defines it as "the organization of cognitive elements into an abstract mental object capable of being held in working memory with default values or open slots which can be variously filled with appropriate specifics."[45] This is similar to Bourdieu's concept of habitus.[46]

The notion of connectionism[47] adds another dimension to the concept of schema by showing that the complexity of human thinking, which is viewed not only as open to the (so-called) sentential logic of serially organized verbal propositions, also—and much more importantly—is able simultaneously to consult parallel schemas as "collections of interconnected neuronlike units."[48] The schemas need not be complete; they may be what Bloch is referring to when he speaks of "chunked networks of loose procedures and understandings."[49] The networks are used to classify experiences through pattern recognition.[50] Moreover, different interpretations can be compared and integrated. Incomplete reconstructions can be repaired. Whereas serial or sentential logic recodes experience into symbols, parallel connectionist logic transforms experience in connections between neuron-like units.[51] The two forms of logic lead to two ways of learning with the serial one being more explicit and much quicker since it can be verbalized in terms of rules. The connectionist one, in contrast, leads to a more permanent result and, once learned, leads to more rapid and automatic execution.[52]

One consequence of connectionist logic is that it enables us to see culture as a process rather than as content.[53] Moreover, verbalization and expression in language, rules and other symbol systems are but a small part of the story: symbols are viewed as the result of the parallel activation of schemas and not as the causes of behavior.[54] Human beings hence are viewed as equipped to produce a culture that combines both continuity and rupture, interpretation and reinterpretation, tradition and innovation. In short, they can live with dichotomies and make sense of them. One implication of the connectionist model is that it may show us a way beyond the relativism of cultures so that people from different cultures might understand each other.

## Postmodernism

In its positive forms, postmodernism may contribute to reflexive praxis theory and research.

The distinction Rosenau makes between skeptic and affirmative postmoderns is useful if we are to be careful to avoid generalizations about a school of thought that itself denies the possibility of generalizations.[55] We believe that postmodernism is best seen as a form of reflexivity that has provided insights that should be taken seriously, but not overly so. The first lesson to be learned is that at least at present we be careful to avoid overgeneralizations based on all-embracing theories. A second insight is that the researcher is involved in the construction of knowledge. Consequently, it is advisable to pay special attention to the tools and literary styles that are available for use in research and its reporting. Third, we can learn from postmodernists to make fun, at least occasionally, of otherwise respectable, objective, measuring, rule-formulating science. Doing so softens the oppositional contrast between science and religion, which it seems would be pleasing to social scientists who study religion—whether or not they are believers. Skeptical postmodernists include religion in their criticism. Yet, without requesting their blessing we may say that postmodernism has altered the debate on the relation between religion and science.[56]

## Praxis Approaches and the Relationship Between the Local and the Global

A wave of recent publications on globalization has drawn attention to the limitations of terms such as westernization and modernization.[57] Their authors also criticize what they see as an excessive focusing by their colleagues on societies and states. The entire world, they contend, including the west, is subject to processes that involve more than modernization. Some states, for example, are subject to fragmentation whereas others may be absorbed into larger entities. The specifics of these global processes, however, rest in large part in their local manifestations. Relations between local events and these external processes must be studied, conceptualized and analyzed. In addition, deterritorialized social and cultural forms are emerging, both globally and locally, especially by means of the technology of electronic communication. The new forms result from a much more diffuse process not necessarily linked to a society or a power center. In a way globalization might be thought of as another example of the attempt to bridge old dichotomies: the global and the local are interwoven and interdependent to such a degree that Robertson speaks of glocalization.[58] Tradition and modernity are thought of as occurring simultaneously and to be interrelated. Furthermore, the national and the supranational link up in relations of interdependence. With regard to religion, globalization thinking emphasizes not just its privatization, as did modernization theory, but envisions new opportunities for it.[59]

## Economics, the State and Entrepreneurship

Globalization, of course, did not begin at the end of the twentieth century with electronic technology. The entry of proselytizing Christianity into Africa (and other parts of the world) that introduced new views of the universe, ritual behaviors and social practices provides one example. The simultaneous emergence and spread of the nation-state is another, while the expansion of the world economy is a third. All three resulted in the imposition of new structures that linked local level life to forces and structures imposed from the outside. The attention of scholars, it is interesting to see, first centered on the extra-local manifestations and processes as can be seen in the development of religious studies (from a European-Christian perspective) as a discipline and the appearance of economics and political science as academic fields. This may explain the opposition made between the local and extra-local with the assumption of influence of the latter on the former in modernization theory. Anthropology developed after these other disciplines. When anthropologists reported the results of their primarily local level studies, they most often presented the perspectives of their informants who usually viewed these influences as external impositions that introduced changes into local level life.

One dimension of the interdependence of the global and the local, if we return to our earlier discussion of power, is that religious, economic and/or governmental structures often become constraints on the choices available to local level actors. They initiate and may bring about changes in previous meaning systems and behavioral practices. The processes described above in which individuals cognitively internalize and then reconceptualize and transform structures are especially helpful here. Elsewhere, in another literature, this is referred to as entrepreneurship.

Joseph Schumpeter first introduced the term when trying to comprehend change in and the growth of economic structures.[60] He defined economic development (growth or directional change in the economy) as "the carrying out of new combinations." The individuals who made the new combinations he called entrepreneurs, and the process they engaged in became (for him and generations of economists, businesspeople and government leaders to come) entrepreneurship. One of us previously applied the term to broader social processes.[61] We suggest that the thinking proposed here for revising the study of contact between diverse peoples and social groups, and the new (syncretic?) structures and meanings that may be produced, also may be applied to the study of entrepreneurship. Likewise, thinking in terms of entrepreneurship may make possible a better understanding of the interdependence of the global, the national and the local.

The introduction of the world economy with its system of monetary rewards and markets into local communities, in addition to the often reported negative impact it has, also provides new, previously nonexistent, opportunities for local level actors. Material items and/or other aspects of previously held beliefs and behaviors (traditional culture) may be transformed into marketable commodities (new combinations) that can be sold outside the local community to the material benefit of one familiar with both local practices and demand at the national or global level. An example is to be found in the incorporation of musical elements from the once local level religious practices of *Candomblé* into Brazilian popular music and then marketed by performers and record companies in musical markets all over the world. Werner Zips, in his contribution to this volume, provides us with another example, using Jamaican Reggae music.

Another type of entrepreneurship occurs when, once isolated, local level people (minorities) become, willingly or otherwise, part of a national society. The modern nation-state, with its idea of a sovereign government that makes laws enforceable by police or other governmental agencies within its territory, provides opportunities for the making of new combinations. Which of the numerous, often religiously, linguistically and culturally diverse groups that inhabit the territory of a nation (especially a new nation) is to be, or to be recognized, in its government? The answer is of importance in that it will mean benefits for those who are and hardship to others, if indeed they survive. Where the electoral process determines who is to govern, the mobilization of the votes of members of local level groups often is led by political entrepreneurs who by redefining (reinventing?) themselves, their groups and their identities may gain access to power and resources of benefit to them and their followers. The symbols that emerge in contests for political power often may define the identity of individuals who through circumstances beyond their local-level control come to be members of groups that may not have existed even in the recent past. Alternatively, in some local groups unable to achieve electoral success, entrepreneurs still may be able to redefine themselves and their group so as to be able to enter into coalitions with other local level groups, perhaps from other regions. Such an alliance might strengthen the position of both groups politically, and in some contexts obtain for them benefits under programs initiated by competitors at the national or global level. Affirmative action programs may be viewed as an example of the latter. At times the deliberate mixing (syncretism?) of symbolic elements might be a winning strategy, while at other times an emphasis on authenticity and purity of tradition could work better.[62]

## The Actors of Syncretism

We already have noted that, unlike the situation in the physical and biological sciences, in anthropology the objects of study, the actors in the religious and other social settings studied, often hold their own views of what the world is like that explain for them aspects of their beliefs and behaviors. These views may, and often do, differ from the theoretical frameworks held by the scholars who study them. Following Victor Turner,[63] we refer to this multiplicity of meaning systems, both within the scholarly community and within and across the symbolic systems of those studied, as multivocality. Some years ago Kenneth Pike coined the terms emic and etic to refer to these usually contrasting explanatory models.[64] His distinction may be used to separate the two communities of actors involved in anthropological research.

In terms of the triangle of signification presented as figure 1.1 above, at least two perspectives are possible in all research situations. The scholars and the practitioners may differ in the way they comprehend the same set of facts. Each group also may contain individuals with differing perspectives. All may have their own political, economic and other convictions that influence their perception and interpretation of events. Some of those of the participants have been noted in the discussion of globalization and entrepreneurship.

In the field of religious studies two further subsets of actors may be distinguished. Religious leaders, at times in response to aspects of globalization and other changing circumstances, may develop public discourses that contribute to one or more of the entrepreneurial ventures outlined above. Their followers, in turn, may make their own interpretations and adaptations that may differ from those of their leaders.

Any distinction made between scholars and those they study may become blurred further when the former, for academic, political or even reasons of their own religious convictions, take sides in what seem to be the issues of the latter. Roger Bastide provided a case in point when he criticized Brazilian Umbanda as a deviation from African authenticity.[65] In addition to some scholars practicing the religions they study, some religious leaders have themselves become scholars who use their academic credentials to advance both their religious discourses and entrepreneurial ventures. The papers in this collection provide additional examples of how historical and ethnohistorical research on the origins of particular beliefs and behaviors are used to establish the superiority of one set of religious practice over those of another.

## Notes

1. Thomas S. Kuhn, *The Structure of Scientific Revolutions*, 2nd ed., enlarged. International Encyclopedia of Unified Science (Chicago: University of Chicago Press, 1970), 3-4.

2. Kuhn, *Structure*, 173.

3. See Roy D'Andrade, *The Development of Cognitive Anthropology* (Cambridge: Cambridge University Press, 1995); James Fernandez, *Persuasions and Performances, The Play of Tropes in Culture* (Bloomington: Indiana University Press, 1986); James Fernandez, ed., *Beyond Metaphor, The Theory of Tropes in Anthropology* (Stanford: Stanford University Press, 1991); Naomi Quinn, "The Cultural Basis of Metaphor," in *Beyond Metaphor: The Theory of Tropes in Anthropology*, James W. Fernandez, ed. (Stanford: Stanford University Press, 1991), 56-93; Naomi Quinn and Dorothy Holland, eds., *Cultural Models in Language and Thought* (Cambridge: Cambridge University Press, 1987).

4. Kuhn, *Structure*, 4-5.

5. Kuhn, *Structure*, 23.

6. Kuhn, *Structure*, 27.

7. Kuhn, *Structure*.

8. Melville J. Herskovits, *Acculturation: The Study of Culture Contact* (Gloucester, Mass.: Peter Smith, 1958 [original 1938]).

9. George W. Stocking, Jr., ed., *The Shaping of American Anthropology, 1883-1911: A Franz Boas Reader* (New York: Basic Books, 1974).

10. Robert Nisbet, *Social Change and History* (London: Oxford University Press, 1969).

11. Nisbet, *Social Change*, 166-88.

12. Melville J. Herskovits, *Cultural Dynamics* (New York: Alfred A. Knopf, 1964 [Original 1947]), 190.

13. Walter Jackson, "Melville Herskovits and the Search for Afro-American Culture," in *Malinowski, Rivers, Benedict and Others: Essays on Culture and Personality. History of Anthropology* Volume 4, George W. Stocking, ed. (Madison: University of Wisconsin Press, 1986), 95-126; Sidney M. Greenfield, "Recasting Syncretism . . . Again: Theories and Concepts in Anthropology and Afro-American Studies in the Light of Changing Social Agendas," in *New Trends and Developments in African Derived Religions*, Peter B. Clarke, ed. (Westport, Conn. and London: Greenwood Press, 1998), 1-15.

14. Jackson, "Melville Herskovits."

15. André Droogers, "Syncretism: The Problem of Definition, the Definition of the Problem," in *Dialogue and Syncretism: An Interdisciplinary Approach*, Jerald D. Gort et al., eds. (Grand Rapids, Mich. and Amsterdam: Eerdmans and Rodopi, 1989), 7-25; Kurt Rudolph, "Synkretismus—vom Theologischen Scheltwort zum religionswissenschaftlichen Begriff," in *Humanitas religiosa. Festschrift H. Biezais* (Stockholm: Almqvist & Wiksell, 1979), 193-212; Charles Stewart and Rosalind Shaw, eds., *Syncretism/ Anti-Syncretism: The Politics of Religious Synthesis* (London and New York: Routledge, 1994).

16. Robert D. Baird, *Category Formation and the History of Religions* (The Hague and Paris: Mouton, 1971), 142-52.

17. With respect to contact between assumedly distinct peoples and its impact on their respective ways of life, the writings of Anthony Wallace are instructive. Wallace tried to bridge and combine the imageries of Boasians and structural-functionalists in terms of what he conceptualized as revitalization. Like Boas, Wallace envisioned a world of small, isolated societies each with its own culture that, after coming in contact with others (in his empirical case Western civilization), were subjected to what he refers to as stress. Employing the organic analogy and its need for equilibrium, he hypothesized that in reaction to the actual or potential disequilibrium (and the dysfunction and potential for disaster it implied) brought about by stress that resulted from contact with another larger, more powerful culture, one or more individuals in the threatened group might reinterpret and revise their traditional cultural beliefs and practices by borrowing and adding to them traits and patterns introduced or imposed on it by the other. The resulting revitalized way of life, as illustrated with data from his research among the Seneca, eliminated the stress and restored the equilibrium of the people and their culture. Although Wallace does not employ the term, syncretism in the Boasian sense played an important role in his thinking and in the way he related empirical events to his theoretical framework. Wallace's thinking, however, had but a minor impact on anthropological research.

18. Göran Aijmer, ed., *Syncretism and the Commerce of Symbols* (Göteborg: IASSA, 1995), 3.
19. Aijmer, *Syncretism*, 6.
20. Greenfield, "Recasting Syncretism . . . Again," 1-15.
21. Droogers, "Syncretism: The Problem," 17.
22. Droogers, "Syncretism: The Problem," 18.
23. Stewart and Shaw, *Syncretism/Antisyncretism*, 7.
24. Stewart and Shaw, *Syncretism/Antisyncretism*, 7.
25. Stewart and Shaw, *Syncretism/Antisyncretism*, 7.
26. Stewart and Shaw, *Syncretism/Antisyncretism*, 7.
27. Stewart and Shaw, *Syncretism/Antisyncretism*, 7.
28. For the example of Brazilian Candomblé see Chapter 7 where Greenfield critically examines this from what we are terming the "objective" perspective.
29. Droogers, "Syncretism: The Problem."
30. There is a parallel with the debate on the definition of religion. Many of the dichotomies that have plagued that debate turn up in the discussion of syncretism: objective versus normative, static versus dynamic, temporary versus permanent, specific versus holistic, erudite versus popular definitions, etc. In the case of religion as a concept, the confusion has not led to widespread abandonment or change in the term. On the contrary, the addition of new theoretical frameworks has only livened debate.
31. Robert Borofsky, ed., *Assessing Cultural Anthropology* (New York: McGraw-Hill, 1994); Sherry B. Ortner, "Theory in Anthropology since the Sixties," *Comparative Studies in Society and History* 26, no. 1 (1984): 126-66.
32. Sally Falk Moore, "Epilogue: Uncertainties in Situations, Indeterminacies in Culture," in *Symbol and Politics in Communal Ideology: Cases and Questions*, Sally Falk Moore and Barbara G. Myerhoff, eds. (Ithaca and London: Cornell University Press, 1977), 210-39.
33. Fernandez, *Persuasions*.
34. Marshall Sahlins, *Islands of History* (London and New York: Tavistock, 1985).
35. Victor Turner, *Dramas, Fields and Metaphors, Symbolic Action in Human Society* (Ithaca and London: Cornell University Press, 1974).
36. Such as Clifford Geertz, *The Interpretation of Cultures* (New York: Basic Books, 1973).
37. Pierre Bourdieu, *Outline of a Theory of Practice* (Cambridge: Cambridge University Press, 1977).
38. Peter Berger and Thomas Luckmann, *The Social Construction of Reality: A Treatise in the Sociology of Knowledge* (Harmondsworth: Penguin, 1972), 79 (italics in the original).
39. Bourdieu, *Outline*.
40. Anthony Giddens, *The Constitution of Society: Outline of a Theory of Structuration* (Cambridge: Polity Press, 1984).
41. Moore, "Epilogue."

42. Ortner, "Theory in Anthropology."

43. Sahlins, *Islands*.

44. Maurice Bloch, "Language, Anthropology and Cognitive Science," *Man* 26, no. 2 (1991): 183-98; D'Andrade, *Development of*; Claudia Strauss and Naomi Quinn, "A Cognitive/Cultural Anthropology," in *Assessing Cultural Anthropology*, Robert Borofsky, ed. (New York: McGraw-Hill, 1994), 284-300; Claudia Strauss and Naomi Quinn, *A Cognitive Theory of Cultural Meaning* (Cambridge: Cambridge University Press, 1997).

45. D'Andrade, *Development of*, 179.

46. Strauss and Quinn, "A Cognitive/Cultural Anthropology," 285; see also the chapter by Zips in this volume.

47. Bloch, "Language, Anthropology and"; D'Andrade, *Development of*, 138ff.; Strauss and Quinn, "A Cognitive/Cultural Anthropology," 285-87.

48. Strauss and Quinn, "A Cognitive/Cultural Anthropology," 286.

49. Bloch, "Language, Anthropology and," 185.

50. D'Andrade, *Development of*, 140.

51. D'Andrade, *Development of*, 140.

52. D'Andrade, *Development of*, 144.

53. D'Andrade, *Development of*, 146.

54. D'Andrade, *Development of*, 149.

55. Pauline Marie Rosenau, *Post-Modernism and the Social Sciences: Insights, Inroads and Intrusions* (Princeton: Princeton University Press, 1992), 6, 10, 148-52.

56. Philippa Berry and Andrew Wernick, eds., *Shadow of Spirit, Postmodernism and Religion* (London: Routledge, 1992); Kieran Flanagan and Peter C. Jupp, eds., *Postmodernity, Sociology and Religion* (London and New York: Macmillan and St. Martin's Press, 1996); Paul Heelas, ed., *Religion, Modernity and Postmodernity* (Oxford: Blackwell, 1998).

57. Peter Beyer, *Religion and Globalization* (London: SAGE, 1994); Mike Featherstone, ed., *Global Culture: Nationalism, Globalization and Modernity* (London: SAGE, 1990); Jonathan Friedman, *Cultural Identity and Global Process* (London: SAGE, 1995); Ulf Hannerz, *Cultural Complexity: Studies in the Social Organization of Meaning* (New York: Columbia University Press, 1992); Roland Robertson, *Globalization: Social Theory and Global Culture* (London: SAGE, 1992).

58. Robertson, *Globalization*, 173.

59. Beyer, *Religion and Globalization*.

60. Joseph Schumpeter, *The Theory of Economic Development* (Cambridge: Harvard University Press, 1959 [Original 1934]).

61. Sidney M. Greenfield and Arnold Strickon, "Entrepreneurship and Social Change: Toward a Populational, Decision-Making Approach," in *Entrepreneurs in Cultural Context*, Sidney M. Greenfield, Arnold Strickon and Robert T. Aubey, eds. (Albuquerque: University of New Mexico Press, 1979), 329-50; and "A New Paradigm for the Study of Entrepreneurship and Social Change," *Economic Development and Cultural Change* 29, no. 3 (1981): 467-99.

62. See for example chapter 7 by Greenfield on "The Reinterpretation of Africa: Convergence and Syncretism in Brazilian Candomblé."

63. Victor Turner, *The Forest of Symbols, Aspects of Ndembu Ritual* (Ithaca and London: Cornell University Press, 1967).

64. Kenneth Pike, *Language in Relation to a Unified Theory of the Structure of Human Behavior*, 2nd ed. (The Hague: Mouton, 1954, 1955, 1960 [1967]); James Lett, "Emic/Etic Distinctions," in *Encyclopedia of Cultural Anthropology*, Vol. 2. David Levinson and Melvin Ember, eds. (New York: Henry Holt and Company, 1996), 282-83.

65. Roger Bastide, *The African Religions of Brazil: Toward a Sociology of the Interpenetration of Civilizations* (Baltimore and London: Johns Hopkins University Press, 1978).

## Chapter 2

# A Yoruba Healer as Syncretic Specialist: Herbalism, Rosicrucianism, and the Babalawo

Frank A. Salamone

### Statement of Problem and Theoretical Framework

This chapter addresses the issue of syncretism in a Yoruba community in Nigeria. Specifically, it builds on the work of Clifford Geertz and Sandra Barnes in focusing on the mixture of indigenous and world religions.[1] The analytical concern is with the lived-in world in which people confront their everyday problems. Precisely, I look at the power of the oppressed from a creolization perspective that builds on the symbolic interactionist's perspective of the definition of the situation. Following Robert Farris Thompson's[2] lead in looking at creolization as a process of "this and that *too*" in the creation of new forms through creative recombination of the old, I apply creolization theory as a means for understanding the work of Prince Doctor, a Yoruba healer in the city of Ife, Nigeria.

## Introduction

Clifford Geertz depicts a society in Java in which religious dogmas and practices intermix even though there is a great deal of hostility among adherents of these religions.[3] Day-to-day life as adherents actually live their "little traditions" is far removed from the ideal typologies of the "great traditions" that Weber[4] and others have put forth. As Barnes has noted:

> Because these categories were grounded in an evolutionary perspective, the tendency when the two types of system were studied in the same frame of reference was—and here is where the legacy persists—to give the great traditions, such as Islam or Christianity, a central position and the little traditions a peripheral one.[5]

Barnes argues persuasively that the very act of forming typologies predetermines the type and direction of change in the analysis. Change, however, is never unidirectional.

In his reworking of Bateson's concept of frames, Goffman proposes adding a processual aspect to them.[6] They are never static but rather metamorphose into other realities in a house-of-mirror fashion that is in keeping with the predominant perspective on African religious and philosophical thought that views reality as ever-changing and unstable, merely presenting the illusion of permanent reality. This skepticism of the presented reality and a subsequent search for underlying structure marks "syncretistic" religion in Nigeria among the Yoruba.

## Yoruba Syncretism

Barnes indicates that Christianity and precontact West African religions so interpenetrate one another that a new religious type has emerged, African Christianity and African Islam. Moreover,

> The blendings range on a continuum that moves from the indigenous precontact religious systems to orthodox European, mission-type systems of Christianity or orthodox Islamic brotherhoods. There are even triple blendings of Christianity, Islam, and indigenous systems.[7]

Syncretization, rather, is best viewed as analogous with those optical illusions in which the image is at one and the same time an old hag and a beautiful young girl and also simultaneously the combination of both of these figures. It is but one more example of the creole quality of being "this" and "that *too*!" as Robert Farris Thompson terms it.[8] The Catholic saint is present as is the Yoruba orisa. At the same time both are seen simultaneously at some other level.

For many years there has been talk in Nigeria of incorporating traditional doctors in the overall modern health care of the country. That traditional healers play a significant, albeit generally unsanctioned, role in Nigeria's health care is beyond dispute. As the Structural Adjustment Program (SAP), imposed on Nigeria's economy in response to World Bank demands, increasingly imposes stringent restrictions on consumer consumption and importation of foreign goods, alternate means of health care appear as a panacea to many in the modern medical profession, not to mention politicians. There is a serious movement within Nigeria, in fact, to integrate traditional healing practitioners within medical training programs at university medical schools. A significant obstacle, however, to the implementation of these suggestions has been the failure to differentiate among both the many different types of healers within any given Nigerian ethnic group and between healers, healing systems, and concepts of health between any of Nigeria's more than two hundred separate ethnic groups. The predominant cause of this failure to make adequate discriminations in this vital area has been the erroneous conception that all traditional African medical systems attribute any illness to the supernatural, and, therefore, all African healers are in some fashion spiritualists. Evans-Pritchard so influenced subsequent work on traditional African healing that his overstatement of the Azande's situation has distorted a significant proportion of the work in the area.[9] Although the supernatural has a significant part in the etiology of many diseases in African traditional thought, it is sheer foolishness to argue that no traditional system has a category of diseases that are *purely* natural in their etiology. We hold that at least some systems have such categories and that some healers are simply that, healers, and do not claim to have spiritual or supernatural power. Their cures, they claim, are strictly natural and as such are open to normal scientific investigation. It is to these healers, who more or less maintain a scientific or natural basis for their cures, that those who seek to incorporate traditional healers into the modern health services would do best to look.

Yoruba believe in the unity of mind and body. In a very real sense no illness is *either* mental or physical. To pose the issue in that manner is nonsensical to a Yoruba. All illness has elements of both. Perhaps, it is better to conceive of illness as an imbalance of relationships, as a more-or-less rather than an either-or situation. It is the primary task of the healer to right wrong relationships.

In order to do so, the healer must be a wise person who understands the nature of harmonious relationships. Therefore, it is generally the case that the healer be a longtime resident of the area in which he, or she, practices. Moreover, the healing power customarily is inherited, and there is specialization among healers. Not all healers, for example, are able to cure all illnesses. Some specialize in madness; others in venereal diseases. Still others choose malaria, measles, women's diseases, or others.

## The Prince Doctor

In this chapter I wish to examine a healer who has managed to take the Yoruba's fine art of reconciling differences to its farthest limits. The man whom I term, following Olu Moloye, "Prince Doctor" claims to be a Christian, Muslim, Rosicrucian, monogamist, polygynist, herbalist, Babalawo-in-training, and anthropologist with no contradiction and as the occasion requires.[10] Examination of his beliefs and behaviors sheds light on Yoruba syncretism and the overarching principle of *iwà* in Yoruba life.

Ogbomosho is a city of about 500,000 and is located in the northern area of Yorubaland. Prince Doctor is a member of a lineage of herbalists within Ogbomosho's royal family. Therefore, he came by his medical training and interests naturally. His father attended the London School of Tropical Medicine and the Prince Doctor still has his father's textbooks and notes for ready reference.

Prince Doctor was working at the University of Ife when Olu Moloye met him. He wished to gain admission to the master's program in anthropology at the University of Ibadan. Moloye agreed to aid him provided that in return he would explain exactly what herbalists do in their curing. Specifically, the Prince Doctor was asked to explain which leaves were used to cure which diseases and how diagnoses were made. The Prince agreed and provided valuable insights into traditional medicine and its practices. Moreover, he provided access to diviners whose skills were generally beyond his own.

The Prince himself is more of a general practitioner and diviner in training. He does specialize in the areas of headache, stomach problems, gynecological difficulties, and fertility. Moreover, he makes sacrifices to invisible spirits to seek their aid in curing his patients. There are a number of shrines to various spirits in his backyard. It is not certain whether he is yet a member of an *Ogboni* society but he does employ certain of their greetings to other Ogboni members, such as greeting people with his left hand. Moreover, he accompanies other members dressed in white to the *Oba* of Ife's palace on special occasions.

Basically, the Prince supports himself through his herbal practice and his travelling pharmacy which supplements his store in Ife. Both feature prepared and packaged remedies for sale. They enable the Prince to support himself as he pursues his academic career, seeking a Ph.D. in anthropology. This mixing of roles as traditional doctor and anthropologist is but one of his many combinations.

The Prince claims to be a monogamist-polygynist, Christian-Muslim, Hindu-Rosicrucian, modern-traditionalist, and various other combinations of seeming opposites. Certainly, this makes it easy for him to feel at home and approach various audiences in Nigeria. Moreover, there is a profound appeal to Prince Doctor and other African herbalists in being able to tap into ancient "secrets." The elite nature of many of these movements and their sense of tapping into hidden wisdom with worldwide distribution, such as Rosicrucians claim, authenticate his own status. This tie proves to the Prince that he is not isolated in a backwater area but part of a global network of healers who possess secret knowledge and power. This is indeed part of what Tunde Lawuyi terms the market mentality of the Yoruba.[11]

However, I believe that more is going on than a mere market mentality raised to a rather high level of development. I suggest that what we have is the Yoruba genius for syncretism and in that syncretism we find a principle of revitalization.

Murphy, for example, notes that the syncretism found in Cuban *Santeria* and other blends of Yoruba religion and Christianity does not really combine the two religions as some sort of hybrid offspring in which the parents' characteristics are merged in Mendelian fashion. Rather the characteristics of each religious system are kept somehow distinct and never confused to the true believer. If, for example, St. Barbara provides a means for appeasing the Roman Catholic hierarchy, so be it. But Shango is nonetheless also present without distortion at the same time.[12] There is here in the Yoruba genius for syncretism an ability to compartmentalize and synthesize that is truly remarkable.

The context determines which principle should be called upon. Thus, if St. Barbara is needed, then it is she whom an image calls to mind. If Shango is required, then he appears. This contextualization of behavior enables Prince Doctor, for example, to become truly all things to all men. I do not believe that he finds any contradiction in his claiming to be "this" and "that too," even when "that too" may be the very antithesis of "this."[13]

It is interesting, for example, to watch Prince Doctor in action in his store and note the manner in which he shifts from modern medicine to traditional. He speaks, for example, of building a two-story combination hospital-store. His consulting room, at the moment, is combined with his store. Much of his raw material is imported and his "traditional" cures come from his father's texts, which came from London. At the same time, there is seen to be no contradiction in his pride at western endorsements from physicians and university professors. In reality, of course, there is no contradiction, for truth is seen to be one, no matter its source.

Therefore, when Prince speaks knowingly of the causes of diseases in western terms and of having his herbs and roots authenticated, it is in this universalistic framework that his words need to be interpreted. He takes pride in differentiating his store and its cleanliness from those of other herbalists. This cleanliness places his work into a different category, appealing to those who take pride in modern things while not forsaking the traditional. Moreover, he keeps his prices within the range of the affordable.

This combination of the modern in which goods are imported from India and roots are often pre-packaged and the traditional in which prices are affordable and packaged in whatever is at hand not only makes the Prince more accessible, it reflects a basic principle of Yoruba life—the harmonization of opposites. To a westerner it may appear incongruous that traditional medicines come in airmail envelopes with expiration dates. A birth control ring, for example, has a ten-year period of use. It may seem either heartwrenchingly sad or hopeless to find sickle cell anemia cures sold for one naira, about a nickel in 1990, smug in our western knowledge that there is as yet no cure for the disease.

The willingness of Prince Doctor, however, to work with western-trained doctors and to have his roots, fruits, and herbs authenticated in modern laboratories reflects the holistic basis of his medicine. The Prince says he sees only good medicine and bad medicine. Moreover, the line between the natural and the supernatural is not quite so clearly drawn there as in the western world.

Those shrines in his backyard play a large role in his work. Faith, clearly, plays a role in his cures. The fact that Prince says he believes that the whole person is involved in a cure and that the separation between the body and soul is not so great as many westerners believe requires that in his framework the spirits have a great part to play in effecting cures. Not surprisingly, he states that those who lack faith in his cure, even Yorubas, often find that his medicines do not work while westerners who do trust him are often cured.

## Some Typical Cases

A few examples of the Prince's cures provide some insight into his practice. On a hot, but pleasant day in March, 1990, for example, in his workshop-store he said to me with a twinkle in his eye while pointing to his impotence medicine: "Prof, take this medicine home with you. You have not seen your wife for some time and it will help provide a good reunion."

Olu nodded positively in response to my glance asking for his confirmation of the medicine's efficacy. The Prince continued saying that many people, even old men with young wives, had come to him for help and had never been disappointed in the medicine's power. Indeed, the Prince had implicit confidence in his stock of medicines. When I asked for examples, he was quick to supply them in abundant detail. "Prof, I just finished treating a patient for a thin blood disease with these herbs here," he stated showing me some leaves as I videotaped his demonstration. "The boy was unable to be aided by doctors. His parents were in despair so they brought him to me. They knew I could help him. And I did. He is a healthy boy today."

I asked Prince Doctor for more examples. He supplied them without pause. "I helped a young child suffering from sickle cell anemia. This bottle here has the cure. You must take it faithfully or it doesn't work. Over here is a cure for dyspepsia. There is the cure for AIDS." The Prince was open with Olu and me. Olu questioned him quite closely as the video makes clear, pushing into areas in which I hesitated to go. He asked the Prince about venereal diseases and raised his eyebrows to demonstrate his skepticism, while speaking to me in asides.

The Prince never lost his good humor and reminded Olu of how he had helped him with his allergies. Olu admitted that he had done so. Olu also offered the Prince advice on arranging his stock in the storage room and on keeping them fresh and clean. Watching the two, in fact, proved an instructive and pleasant cultural lesson in itself.

## The Concept of Ìwà

Trust or its lack is related in Yoruba belief to the concept of *ìwà*. Although sometimes translated as "destiny," it means more than mere destiny before which one is helpless. It includes the notion of character and the working out of one's destiny within the limits of one's character. Thus, a person's future is not entirely determined. Neither is it entirely free. A person must come to know what propensities are to be found within his or her character and then work within those limits. As Adejanu writes:

> *Iwà* plays an important role in the life of a person and hence, it can affect one's destiny adversely. For there is a very strong relationship between one's character and destiny. While it is held that the destiny of man is unaltered, among the Yoruba, the destiny of a person can be subject to change. This then explains the reasons why people guard against all things that can bring calamity or misfortune into their way and they often placate the divinities so that their happy destiny may not become an unhappy one.[14]

Ìwà is a core value of Yoruba morality. Adejanu suggests that life is intrinsic to its meaning "since *ìwà* reveals what life stands for and this is related to destiny."[15] Moreover, *ìwà* is seen to be a protection against evil as the proverb has it, *Ìwà rere l'èsó enia* (It is good character that is a person's guard). Ìwà also contains within itself the idea of live and let live summed up in the proverb *Je, nje ni ayò, fí adu*n (Win-and-let-win is what makes the game of *ayò* interesting).

Inherent within the concept of ìwà, therefore, is a unification of apparent opposites, freedom and predetermination. It is this habit of mind that is at the very root of syncretism and which Prince Doctor so clearly displays. Thus, he believes that his destiny is to be a healer. That entails his learning the best manner of serving the people. It requires him to harmonize disparate elements and to combine medicines into a harmonious mixture to cure patients. His curiosity leads him to seek new knowledge and information, in conformity with his own father's example. Anthropology itself can serve not only as a means for that search but also as a paradigm for what the Prince wishes to achieve: namely, the harmonization of old and new. He states that if all truth is one, then true medicine must also be one and no danger lurks in submitting traditional remedies to modern tests.

In fact, Prince Doctor avers that he is quite proud that his medicine in many cases has been authenticated by modern tests and he eagerly seeks out new areas to display his skills. At the same time, he incorporates techniques, methods, and ideas from modern medicine into his practice. He is aware of criticisms that modern physicians level at traditional herbalists. Therefore, he is careful to learn and practice hygienic methods and to standardize his dosages. He uses modern terminology and seeks to earn his Ph.D. This movement between the old and new is not unique to the Prince but the manner in which he works out his destiny is, in fact, idiosyncratic but in keeping with the concept of ìwà which as Abiodun argues requires each person to acknowledge everyone else's unique identity. It is in this recognition of individual uniqueness, he argues further, that true beauty lies, for *"iwà* is the deity, which, depending on the degree of our devotion to it, blesses us (with its beauty)!!"[16]

## Conclusion

In her insightful and influential study of herbal medicine in Ibadan, Una MacLean notes

> Habits which have once been established and small rituals which have been learnt provide for most people a sense of security and an assurance that all is going smoothly. This feeling of security can rapidly revert to anxiety if the precautions are ignored and the routine is seriously disrupted. Ritual forms a necessary part of everyday life and extends to such minutiae as the manner of purchasing, preparing and sitting down to meals.[17]

She continues to note just how tenacious the hold of tradition is on West Africans, citing the works of Jahoda in support of her contention.[18]

She then concludes in a statement consonant with our own conclusion:

> Nigerian medicine is constantly changing with the times to accommodate and incorporate new methods, may be giving way to commercialism here and metamorphosing into *aladura* cults there, yet it retains the ability to supply meaningful answers to questions which are perceived as relevant by practitioner and patient alike.
>
> Faced with many treatment possibilities Ibadan people may choose one or other or all of them, exercising an empiricism which is entirely appropriate and justifiable. They will even patronize unsuccessfully a series of *babalawo* without ever losing hope of a fortunate outcome to their search. Patients and healers share

their confidence in the divination process and in the supreme power of the appropriate spoken word, uttered with authority to the accompaniment of the correct ritual procedure. . . . The enduring value of African medicine lies not in its materials but in the methods and the concepts which underlay them and its continuing power is a tribute to the practitioners of this ancient art.[19]

Since MacLean's study there have been many others emphasizing the essential importance of the holistic nature of African traditional medicine.[20] These studies emphasize the importance of trust in the delivery of effective health care and of fitting the delivery of modern Western medicine.

At the same time that I acknowledge the tenacity of traditional medicine in Nigeria, I would be remiss if I did not also notice the dangers that accompany the application of traditional medicine in nontraditional settings. There is undeniably danger in removing the healer from the context and control of a governing community. The traditional healer was a functioning part of an ongoing system. To make a healer a specialist who could support himself independently of a particular grounded tradition opens up the distinct possibility of abuse. It decontextualizes the process and ultimately holds it up to exploitation and ridicule, playing on people's nostalgic longing for what is remembered as a golden past. There is the definite danger of a medicine show approach to curing, which in fact has appeared in various markets throughout Nigeria. There is also the hazard of neglecting the holistic, homeopathic, approach to healing common in Nigerian rehabilitation.

Cures occur within a definite spiritual and physical context; specifically, within a particular set of relationships. Taking the healer away from that context threatens to cause him to overlook the context in which African curing takes place. Patently, also, the new prestige of African healers is tied to the cult of Africanization currently sweeping Nigeria. In itself, it is a commendable process, potentially healthy and curative of the slanders of the colonial and neo-colonial period.

Interestingly, however, no one is really seeking to revive the historical context of the traditional healer, for that context is gone beyond retrieval. What is happening is the justification of the old in terms of the new, as Prince Doctor does. Specifically, African medicine is justified in terms of the fact that many of the herbs contain modern medicine—penicillin or reserpine, for example. Such an approach is beside the point. No one doubts that herbs can heal. What is important, however, about *any* traditional medicine is its recognition of the unity of mind and body and its approach to healing that takes the holistic nature of health into account.

There is a danger of losing that very *African* component of healing in the attempt to standardize and "scientize" traditional healing. Such an approach, ironically, seeks to validate African medicine while using a Western model. It is, alas, doomed to failure because it seeks to isolate elements of African medicine that work according to a European-American model of medicine at the very time that such a model is coming under increasing criticism in its own centers of power.

Along with the danger of losing African medical tradition through explaining it in western terms, there is the danger of losing it through a seeming incorporation in Christianity. The Prince Doctor's syncretism also alerts one to the possible dangers in this apparent reconciliation of antithetical traditions.

Through his combination of elements from various domains, Prince Doctor presents a unified picture of life in Nigeria today. He does so, I believe, through consolidating them in a manner consistent with the principle of ìwà which encourages individuals to reconcile disparate ingredients into a harmonious whole. It reflects a basic tolerance in Yoruba thought which searches for underlying unity, basic truth, among apparently contradictory phenomena. This tolerance and willingness to allow people to work out their own destiny within the boundaries of the communal good help explain the Yoruba genius for syncretism and, consequently, for the revitalization that marks Yoruba cultural history.[21]

## Notes

1. Clifford Geertz, *The Interpretation of Cultures* (New York: Basic Books,1973), 142-169; Sandra Barnes, ed., *The Many Faces of Ogun* (Bloomington: Indiana University Press, 1989).

2. Robert Farris Thompson, "Guest Lecture on Creole Culture," in NIH Seminar on African Derived Music, 1989, Yale University.

3. Geertz, "Ritual and Social Change," in *Interpretation of Cultures*.

4. Max Weber, *Basic Concepts in Sociology* (New York: Carol, 1999), 33.

5. Barnes, *The Many Faces of Ogun*, 21.

6. Irving Goffman, *Frame Analysis: Essay on Organization* (New York: Harper and Row, 1974).

7. Barnes, *The Many Faces of Ogun*, 11.

8. Thompson, "Guest Lecture."

9. E. E. Evans-Pritchard, *Witchcraft, Oracles, and Magic among the Azande* (Oxford: Clarendon Press, 1937).

10. Moloye was invaluable to the research I conducted in 1989-90, giving unselfishly of his time in a true spirit of professional cooperation and friendship. Prince Doctor was Moloye's master's student in anthropology at the University of Ibadan.

11. Personal communication.

12. Joseph M. Murphy, *Santeria: An African Religion in America* (Boston: Beacon Press, 1988).

13. Robert Farris Thompson elaborated this point further in his "Guest Lecture."

14. Henry Adejanu, "Iwà." Unpublished manuscript, 1990, 1.

15. Abiodun convincingly argues that it is related to the Yoruba concept of beauty as expressed in the proverb *iwà l'èwà* (Destiny is character). Rowland Abiodun, "Introduction: An African Art History," in *The Yoruba Artist*, Rowland Abiodun, et al., eds. (Washington: Smithsonian, 1994), 11-35. See also Robert Farris Thompson, "Aesthetic of the Cool," *African Arts* 7 (1973): 44-45, 64-67, and "Yoruba Artistic Criticism," in *The Traditional Artist in African Societies*, Warren L. D'Azevedo, ed. (Bloomington: Indiana University Press, 1973); Wande Abimbola, "*Iwapele*: The Concept of Good Character in Ifa Literary Corpus," in *Yoruba Oral Tradition*, Wande Abimbole, ed. (Ife: Department of African Languages and Literature, 1975).

16. Abiodun, "Identity and the Artistic Process," 26-27.

17. Una MacLean, *Magical Medicine: A Nigerian Case Study* (Baltimore: Pelican, 1974 [original 1971]), 151.

18. Gustav Jahoda, "Scientific Training and the Persistence of Traditional Beliefs among West African University Students," *Nature* 220 (1968): 1356, and "Traditional Healers and Other Institutions Concerned with Mental Illness in Ghana," *International Journal of Social Psychiatry* 7 (1968): 245-268.

19. MacLean, *Magical Medicine*, 155-156.

20. See, for example, Charles M. Good, *The Community in African Primary Health Care: Strengthening Participation and a Proposed Strategy* (Lewiston, NY: Edwin Mellen Press, 1968); Nina Etkin, "Ethnopharmacology: Biobehavioral Approaches in the Anthropological Study of Indigenous Medicines," *Annual Review of Anthropology* 17 (1988): 23-42; ASO. Okwu, "Life, Death, Reincarnation, and Traditional Healing in Africa," *Issues* 9 (1979): 19-24; Olugbene Moloye, et al., *A Preliminary Assessment of the Socio-Economic Impact of Onchocerciasis (River Blindness) in Nigeria with Particular Reference to Selected Communities in Kwara State* (Ibadan: Nigerian Institute for Social and Economic Research, 1988); Frank A. Salamone, "The Drug Problem in a Small Emirate," *Human Organization* 32, no. 3 (1973): 322-325, and "Religion as Play: Bori, A Friendly 'Witchdoctor,'" *Journal of Religion in Africa* 8, no. 3 (1976): 201-211; Peter Worsley, "Non-Western Medical Systems," *Annual Review of Anthropology* 11 (1982): 315-348; and Alan Young, "The Anthropologies of Illness and Sickness," *Annual Review of Anthropology* 11 (1982): 257-285.

21. The new religion of "Chrislam," a combination of Islam and Christianity, is a logical outgrowth of this tendency.

# Chapter 3

# Population Growth, Industrialization and the Proliferation of Syncretized Religions in Brazil

Sidney M. Greenfield

### Introduction

At the beginning of the twentieth century, Brazil—presently the fifth largest country in the world, with a land-mass larger than the United States not including Alaska—had a population of some seventeen million people.[1] As the century comes to a close there are an estimated 170 million Brazilians, some ten times the number there were a hundred years before.[2]

Along with this absolute increase in numbers, there has been a dramatic rural to urban redistribution. In 1940, for example, two-thirds of the population of almost 41 million lived in rural areas. By the late 1970s, following two decades of large-scale internal migration, the rural/urban percentages were reversed; and by 1990 almost 80 percent of all Brazilians—more than 125 million people—

lived in urban areas which with but few exceptions are located within one hundred miles of the Atlantic coast.[3]

As the population grew and relocated itself in cities, the national economy was being transformed from reliance on the export of raw materials into a producer of manufactured goods for an expanding domestic market and for sale overseas. Spurred by high rates of growth in recent decades, Brazil has become the world's ninth largest economy.

To conclude from this that Brazil is a modern, or even modernizing national society, it also would follow, at least according to the theoretical perspective that has dominated the social sciences, if not all western thought during most of the century, that it also has secularized. Modernization theory maintained that religion would decline in its importance as a society industrialized, urbanized and modernized. But in Brazil religion has not declined. Instead, the role it plays in the lives of the people has increased at a rate perhaps equal to the very impressive increase in human numbers.

At the close of the nineteenth century Roman Catholicism was the only religion officially sanctioned in Brazil. A century later a broad variety of groups, with their roots in Africa, Europe, Asia, North America and in the native peoples of the continent, actively compete with it for a still growing number of followers.[4]

The purpose of this chapter[5] is to explain how and why this combination of religious growth along with urbanization, industrialization and modernization came about in Brazil. I shall proceed by viewing the increase in the number of religious groups and active participation in them by so many Brazilians against the background of changes in national population and the political economy in the twentieth century.[6]

My approach to the growing variety of religions in Brazil and increased participation in them by the expanding population will be to view them in this chapter as adaptive strategies. I argue that each competing group, in what I characterize as a religious marketplace, offers a combination of material as well as spiritual assistance to its devotees and to potential members. Those in need of help—in both the other world and this—will be shown to choose a religious affiliation according to whether or not it helps them to satisfy their needs and wants.[7] Their behavior will be shown to fit the traditional model of patron-client exchanges, but modified to adapt to the contemporary situation of religious pluralism.

The concept of syncretism is used in the "objective" sense[8] Herskovits envisioned it when he first introduced it into anthropology as a dimension of reinterpretation. As Droogers and I have summarized this usage in chapter 1, his objective was to picture what happened to a once isolated people and their culture when they entered into ... contact with another, usually more powerful, often colonial or imperial culture. The imagery was that when acculturation takes place, each people may take from what it finds in the other certain forms, culture traits and/or their meanings, that they may reformulate in terms of their own understandings, behaviors and practices. The new forms that may result might be composed of elements from the other culture taken over wholesale, or a mixing of aspects of its own traditions and those of the other.[9]

While syncretism has been used most often in the analysis of changes in the beliefs and/or practices of a single group resulting from contact, I use it here to account for similarities across a number of otherwise quite different religious traditions that today are competing with each other for followers. I argue that each has adopted, in mixed form, a model of exchange between an adept and an otherworldly being believed to offer him or her access from the other world to resources needed in this one.

## Brazilian Industrialization, Increasing Inequality and Poverty in the Twentieth Century

Industrialization in Brazil did not begin until after the massive rural to urban shift was well under way. Brazilian industry, moreover, was capital rather than labor intensive. From the outset, jobs were not created in numbers sufficient to employ the constantly growing population.[10] Furthermore, only a tiny fraction of the rural migrants had the skills required to obtain employment in industry.[11] Jobs in other sectors of the economy did not grow in proportion to the number of people added to the labor force each year. As a result, Brazil's fast growing cities, like the rest of the nation, contain large and growing numbers, frequently majorities, of both unemployed and underemployed.[12]

This disastrous situation has been made worse by the restructuring of the world economy. Along with privatization, decisions about production, finance and employment practices are now being made by transnational corporations. National governments and local influences are being bypassed. Downsizing is the order of the day. Jobs located until recently in the industrial sector and protected under hard-fought union contracts and covered by social security, health and other benefits are being outsourced and moved into the informal sector where workers are given short-term contracts without any protection or benefits.[13] Real wages in both industry and agriculture have declined. The minimum wage, earned by so many of the Brazilians who have jobs, has decreased in what it can purchase. At the end of the century a larger, and still growing, percentage of Brazilians than ever before are having difficulty supporting themselves and their families.

One way to conceptualize the extensive poverty is in terms of inequality in the distribution of wealth and the national income. While there have been great disparities in the living standards of the rich and the poor in Brazil since the colonial society and its economy were first organized, inequality has become even more extreme with industrialization and modernization. In 1995, for example, the poorest fifth of the population—32 million people—received only 2.5 percent of the national income. The poorest 40 percent received slightly more than 8 percent of the pie, and the poorest half only one-tenth of it. This contrasted with the richest quintile who received 64.2 percent of the national income. In the United States, which has a much higher national income, the poorest 20 percent received almost twice the share received by their counterparts in Brazil, 4.8 percent, while the richest fifth of the population received almost 20 percent less than the richest Brazilians, or 45.2 percent of the national income.[14] As President Fernando Henrique Cardoso stated in his 1994 election platform, Brazil is one of the most unjust nations in the world. And, according to the president of the Inter-American Development Bank in a statement made before the present economic crisis, it will take as much as a century at best to eliminate poverty and make it just.

Brazil's cities, like most throughout the Third World, were not prepared for the massive influx of rural migrants and the dramatic increase in numbers. They did not provide the infrastructure to accommodate them.[15] There are not enough dwellings, for example, to house the population. Vast and ever-growing numbers of people live in squatter settlements, generally known as *favelas*. Energy sources are inadequate as are means of transportation, telephone lines, water and sewage. One inevitable result is the presence of endemic and chronic diseases such as cholera, dengue fever, meningitis and other viral and bacterial infections.

A consequence of the economic inequities that has received extensive media coverage is the fact that very young children have been forced into the marketplace in search of remunerative employment. As the ability of their parents and other relatives to influence them declines, tens of thousands have moved onto the streets where they are exposed to drugs, gangs and prostitution. Shopkeepers and merchants, claiming fear of the effect these children might have on business, have taken action against them. In many parts of the country off-duty policemen have been hired to "take care of the problem." More than seven thousand street children have been reported assassinated in Brazil over the past four years alone. Children are routinely tortured by law enforcement authorities. Young women and girls are regularly raped by the police and other authorities. Clandestine cemeteries have been established throughout the country for the bodies of street children and others who have been summarily executed.

In spite of at least half a century of national experience with and debate over these conditions, hunger, illness, poverty and other human suffering still tend to be conceptualized and treated as the problem of the sufferer. Consequently, most Brazilians, primarily though not exclusively the poor, see themselves and are seen by others as having "problems" that they need help to resolve. Politicians at first took the lead in presenting themselves as the ones best able to assist a growing electorate, in exchange for their votes. Religious groups, as we shall see, also have come to offer to help those in need, in exchange for their affiliation.

## Popular Catholicism, Patron-Client Exchanges and a Functional Model of Brazilian Religions

Roman Catholicism was the official religion of Brazil from the time of its discovery until it became a republic at the end of the nineteenth century. The Catholicism practiced, however, as Bastide and others have observed, always was turned more toward the saints and the Virgin than to God.[16] Its focus was on the cult of the saints, pilgrimages and processions, practices whose role in the official Church was greatly diminished after the Reformation. In light of this, students of religion in Brazil have contrasted what they refer to as the popular Catholicism practiced by the masses to the formal Catholicism of the Church.[17]

I hypothesize this popular Catholicism to be the paradigmatic cultural form the other religions competing for followers in the marketplace of contemporary Brazil have used—not always intentionally or consciously—as they reinterpreted and syncretized their own beliefs and practices in the twentieth century.

Popular Catholicism, according to Thales de Azevedo,

> consists of a propitiatory and suplicatory ritualism with therapeutic ends, in which the individual and collective religious acts, . . . are expected to have their own efficacy in pleasing the "saints," inclining them to reply favorably to the appeals of their devotees in cases of difficulty and crisis. These replies would depend very little on the merits of the supplicants or the action of Grace. . . . In "hours of agony" or of "need," the "saints" are asked for health, life, tranquillity of spirit, protection, help, good luck—in short, for "aid in time of need." [Worshippers] seek in the "other world" the means to influence "this world."[18]

Of the numerous religions that at the end of the twentieth century have grown so in the number of their followers and in their importance in social life, each, I submit, at present offers a pantheon of supernaturals who in response to appeals offer help from the other world to worshippers with problems in this one. Whereas the African-derived groups, such as the *Candomblés, Xangôs, Batuques* and *Tambor de Mina*, may differ considerably, both among themselves and from

European Kardecist-Spiritism, mixed Afro-Catholic-Spiritist *Umbanda*, Pentecostal Protestantism, and from popular Catholicism as to their specific beliefs and ritual practices, all offer access in the other world to entities or beings they propose will help members and potential members with problems in this world.[19]

The logic that underlies this behavioral pattern, I suggest, rests on the answers most Brazilians would give to questions about the Judeo-Christian version of the story of creation which in its main form is accepted by almost all of the diverse religious groups: (1) Was the creation finished before God rested on the seventh day? and, if not, (2) Who is to be responsible for completing it?

It would be inconceivable for most Brazilians to accept the idea that a being as perfect as God would make a world as imperfect as this one. Certainly more still needs to be done if the world is to be worthy of its maker. But who will do it? Who is responsible for perfecting God's creation?

The post-Reformation answer, so commonplace in the day-to-day understandings of the peoples of Western Europe and North America, is that humankind, the high point of the creation, will complete what God started; and it will be done by means of work. One significant implication of this is that humanity—collectively or in part—is to be held accountable if the task is not accomplished.

Most Brazilians, in contrast, along with other Latin Americans and Mediterranean Europeans, answer this question in pre-Reformation terms. For them God, and God alone, will complete what He started; furthermore, the creator and not humankind is responsible for what happens.[20]

The logical consequence of this for civilization is not the blind fatalism that some might imagine. Although God is assumed to have absolute control over everything, including our individual destinies, we each are able to better our lot by appealing to the divine and omnipotent creator in prayer. But who would have the temerity to approach such a distant, all-knowing and all-powerful being directly? Instead, Brazilians appeal to God indirectly, through intermediaries.

The saints, who once were mortal and now are in heaven close to the creator, are assumed to understand and be sympathetic to humans and their problems. The faithful pray to the saints, asking them for their help—as intercessors—in order to obtain what they need to improve their life.

"The saints," according to Ribeiro de Oliveira,

> represent all of the possible supernatural allies the faithful can count on to gain happiness in this life and the other, and [are] a source of permanent supernatural power that can be invoked to obtain solutions to the problems of this world.[21]

To North Americans and Western Europeans such a supernatural intervention would be considered a miracle. To Brazilians, however, *milagres* (miracles) are everyday occurrences, to be expected. But why should a saint, who has many important tasks to perform and is besieged with countless requests from so many, take action on behalf of any specific petitioner? The answer, as De Kadt and others remind us, is the exchange implicit in the votive offering.[22] The devotee and the saint, as Magnani adds, enter into a contract.[23] A worshipper offers the saint something of value to it in exchange for its intercession. But what do the living, especially the poor and the suffering, have that would motivate a saint to accept their bargain? The answer is worship and reverence. Consider only what becomes of saints who cease to be venerated.

A believer in need may make an offer such as the following: If you, St. John, St. Francis, St. Peter, etc. help me with my problem, I will visit your shrine, light candles there in your honor, have masses, novenas, and other prayers recited in your name, perform acts of penance, or dress in a way that shows that I am paying homage to you as a Saint. "The most common and binding relationship of the faithful to the Saints and God," writes Thales de Azevedo, "is through a *promessa*, consisting of a petition of *proteção*, or help, in a crisis, under the promise of compensation."[24]

The model for the relationship between devotee and saint is one of patron-client exchanges and relationships as described by George Foster[25] and others[26] several decades ago. The petitioner's offer to his other-worldly patron, however, is conditional. He is not expected to fulfill his part of the bargain—pay his *promessa*—until or unless the saint first fulfills its. Should he not recover his health, obtain the job or promotion requested, or receive whatever else he has asked for, he may "punish" the saint, breaking its statue or turning it upside-down in its place in the shrine in his home. He also is not obligated to deliver to the saint what he promised.

But the petitioner has not obtained what he needs. What might he do about it? He could go back to the saint and try again, perhaps augmenting his original prestation. And if St. John does not accept his offer, and provide him with help, he may turn to St. Francis. And he may keep trying until hopefully one member of the pantheon—or a folk or popular saint reported to have performed miracles in his locality who has not been and may never be authenticated and canonized by the Vatican—will hear his plea and assist him.

But what if his best offer is not accepted by any of the saints? He may accept the situation and a life of suffering and deprivation, believing himself to be unworthy, or he may question his belief system and perhaps reject the faith.

## Other Religions Practiced in Brazil

Prior to the twentieth century our hypothetical Brazilian striving to improve his lot in life had no alternative to the Catholic saints.[27] Before the country became a republic, Roman Catholicism was, so to speak the only game in town. This, of course, is not to say that there weren't people within the national territory practicing other religions before the twentieth century. Since they were neither formally recognized nor legal, however, they were practiced most often by those who were marginal to the emerging national society.

Candomblés, for example, had been established in Bahia in the early part of the nineteenth century,[28] as were other what today are called "Afro-Brazilian" groups such as the Xangôs,[29] Tambores de Mina,[30] Macumbas and Batuques. The small numbers of mostly poor and marginal former slaves who were their adherants were located, for the first four decades of the twentieth century, in a few urban centers such as Salvador, Recife, São Luis, Rio de Janeiro and Porto Alegre. Although they had been exposed to the patron-client exchange dynamic of the popular Catholicism practiced by their ex-masters, and probably were influenced by it, it appears not to have been overly important in the African (derived) religious practices at the time, at least according to their historians and present-day leaders.

Kardecist-Spiritism had been introduced into Brazil from France sometime in the last third of the nineteenth century. While at first seen as a kind of entertainment for the upper classes, it soon came to be practiced more as a philosophical system than a religion per se, by small numbers of mostly educated white members of the urban, middle classes. Its emphasis on communication with spirits of the dead, combined with the importance it placed on doing charity, was to enable Spiritism to become the principle catalyst in the later syncretism of the African belief systems and popular Catholicism.

Protestantism, brought to Brazil by free immigrants recruited in Europe who started arriving shortly after independence in 1822 and continued through the first two decades of the twentieth century, also was practiced by small, isolated populations mostly in the rural areas of São Paulo, Paraná, Santa Catarina and Rio Grando do Sul. Their numbers, however, did not begin to grow significantly until well into the twentieth century. As with the other alternative, or non-Catholic religions, the idea of seeking an exchange with a supernatural being to satisfy the needs or wishes of their adherents was foreign, as it was to missionaries (mostly from North America) to arrive later in other parts of Brazil.

Although the Republican constitution did away with the monopoly held by the Roman Catholic Church and made the practice of these other religions legal, all in one way or another were subjected to varying degrees of official, as well as informal repression and harassment until almost the middle of the twentieth century. In the following five decades, however, not only have the number of practitioners of these religions increased greatly, their number and the variety of religious groupings also have grown. More importantly for our purposes, just about all of the religious groups competing for followers today offer now, as central to their beliefs and practices, access to supernatural beings who may be approached, by both members and potential members, with a prestation that usually includes a promise of devotion inviting them to establish a patron-client exchange relationship with the petitioner that will provide resources to resolve their problems and satisfy their needs and wants on the patron-client exchange model of popular Catholicism.

The religious syncretism that took place in these diverse religions, as they each were reinterpreted to include a patron-dependency exchange with a supernatural offering help, came about, I suggest, in response to the demographic and socioeconomic features set out above. As they began to compete for converts with Catholicism and each other, especially those to establish themselves in the urban centers, they found parallels in their respective traditions with the culturally pervasive exchange dynamic of popular Catholicism. Gradually each, it appears, came to offer alternative saints, their own supernaturals to whom prestations could be made by those who had not been successful elsewhere. In the Candomblés, for example, the Yoruba òrìsà (*orixás*) came to offer help with life's problems, in exchange for the devotion of followers. The several other African (derived) traditions likewise offered their respective supernaturals as potential patrons, at first combined (syncretized) with the Catholic saints, as in the Candomblés, and more recently separate and independent of them.

Spiritism, in an elaboration of Kardec's emphasis on doing charity, came to offer access to enlightened spirits (of the dead) in exchange for the needy petitioner learning and participating in its mission of doing charity. One example of this is the return—by incorporating in mediums—of deceased doctors and other healers (independent of their karma cycle) to treat the sick.[31] More important, however, was Spiritism's contribution to the founding and growth of Umbanda in which new entities were created whose exclusive role is to help the living. Combining the African practice of spirit possession with Spiritism's communicating with the dead, Umbanda has added to the number of spirits in the Brazilian universe—from whom help can be obtained—a host of other-worldly beings whose specific function is providing help, as charity, to those in need. These spirits of dead Africans (the *pretos velhos*), Indians (the *caboclos*), *exus* (a category from Brazilian history that includes gypsies, prostitutes, rogues and others) and children (the *crianças*) incorporate in *pais* and *mães-de-santo* (its religious leaders who are mediums) and negotiate exchanges that lead to their resolving the problems of those who turn to them. As with the other religious groups, the predominant prestation is the offer by the petitioner of devotion to the spirit by becoming a member of the religion. Umbanda for a time was the fastest growing of Brazil's alternative religions until replaced by a revival by the Candomblés.

The traditions of diverse Amerindian groups also have been reinterpreted and at times mixed with African and/or (popular) Catholic practice. Today they provide yet additional supernatural beings who may be turned to for the help that once was available only from the Catholic saints. In an interesting turn of events, the most successful Protestant denominations, which now have replaced the Candomblés as the fastest growing religion, are the Pentecostal groups in which the Holy Ghost is viewed as offering (through Jesus) solutions to problems and help in satisfying this-worldly material needs and wants.[32]

The Roman Catholic Church meanwhile added hundreds of new saints as the century progressed.[33] A Brazilian who has not had his petition accepted by the traditional saints and wishes to remain within the faith may turn to them. And if they do not help him, he may try one of the popular saints, such as Padre Cicero,[34] who although proposed, have not yet been canonized by the Church. And if still unsuccessful, he may try one such as the Anestácia, the black popular saint who may never have lived at all.[35] Those not yet accepted and those invented appear to be answering petitions and helping people as evidenced by the large numbers flocking to their shrines to pay their promises and show devotion. In spite of these new "Catholic" options, large and still growing numbers, mostly the urban poor, have not had their petitions acted upon by either the old saints or the new ones. This has led them to move on to see if they could get help from the "saints" of the other religions.

In the twentieth century then, as more people with ever-increasing needs were added to Brazilian society, a substantial number of alternative "saints," each part of a separate and independent religious tradition, were added to those Brazilians may turn to for the help only the Catholic saints were believed to provide in the past. As a result, growing numbers have done what would have been unimaginable a century ago: they have left the Roman Catholic Church to join another religion, most often one whose "saints" already have helped them with their problems.

## The Brazilian Religious Marketplace at the End of the Twentieth Century

Theorizing abstractly about situations of religious pluralism, Peter Berger argued that religious ex-monopolies, because "they can no longer take for granted the allegiance of their client populations," must market themselves. Affiliation, he adds, "must be 'sold' to a clientele that is no longer constrained to 'buy.'" This lead him to conceptualize the situation of religious pluralism as "above all, a *market situation*." He concludes that "a good deal of religious activity in this situation comes to be dominated by the logic of market economics."[36]

In Brazil, however, we have seen that the logic for making decisions and choices for satisfying needs and wants was not, and still is not, that of formal economics. Instead, individuals seek out exchanges with someone (or some being) closer to the assumed other-worldly source of power that can provide them with what they need or want by serving as their intercessor with the all-powerful creator God. The Brazilian social dynamic is one of patron-client and not market exchanges. A more useful model for Brazilian religious pluralism, I submit, is that of a marketplace in the sense that Karl Polanyi[37] proposed the term, in which the logic of patron-client exchange prevails and not that of the market system.

In this religious marketplace people with needs, material or spiritual, are continuously "shopping." They go from one religious ritual to another making prestations to a variety of supernatural beings. Their hope is that one of them will accept their offer and satisfy their needs. Should they find success, they will "pay" their promessa by joining the group, becoming a convert to a new creed. Should their future needs not be met by what are now "their saints," they usually will go back into the market in search of others who, if they help, will be repaid by their converting once more.[38]

## Conclusion

Prevailing social science theory assumed that society would become more secular as it industrialized, urbanized and modernized. In Brazil, however, the number of religious groups and the place of religion in daily life increased in tandem with the forces that theory taught would lead to its decline.

I have argued this was because Brazilians, like members of other Latin Catholic and pre-Reformation societies, made decisions and choices based on assumptions that differed from those made by the theorists and the members of the societies with which they were familiar. Modernization theory appears to have been based on the ethnocentric assumptions that peoples throughout the world would behave as did those of the West who, at least for a time, did become more secular.

Brazilian religion is pre-Reformation. Its Roman Catholicism has always been, and in its popular form still is, based on the assumption that God alone will complete His creation. Consequently there is nothing sacred to Brazilians about either working or maximizing. Instead, what makes sense to them is offering, in the hope of having it accepted, a prestation that leads to an exchange with a being closer to God who can intercede with Him on their behalf. Patron-client relationships follow from these assumptions and not market ones.

The ten-fold increase in the Brazilian population during the twentieth century, combined with its urbanization and the industrialization and modernization of its economy—in a way that intensified the inequities in the distribution of resources—can be assumed to have led to an increased number of offers being made to the (Catholic) saints that were not (in the eyes of those making them) accepted and acted upon. Religious pluralism, legitimized under the Republic, added new (and competing) intermediaries to whom prestations could be made (in the hope of reciprocity) by ever growing numbers of people with ever greater needs. The numerous religious groups in the Brazilian religious marketplace today compete with each other for followers by providing alternative supernaturals "shoppers" may turn to in their search for help. An individual seeking assistance with problems today may go from one religious group to the next making offers. Since paying (one's promise or vow) is conditional on the request being satisfied, it is made, i.e., people "convert," *if* and *when* their "prayers" are answered. Brazilian religion has grown so dramatically in the twentieth century, it appears, because it provides those with needs a means to satisfy them which makes sense within their cultural framework, especially when everything else around them is changing as rapidly as it is.[39]

## Notes

1. This was only seventy-eight years after Portuguese colonial authority had been overthrown—without violence—and national independence obtained with the famous *grito de Ipiranga*, when Dom Pedro, the heir to the Portuguese crown, cried *fico*, I will stay (in Brazil where he had remained after his exiled parents had been returned to their thrown by the Congress of Vienna), rather than return to Europe and become a king. It was just twelve years after the slaves had been emancipated, with Brazil being next to the last country to terminate the evil institution the Portuguese had introduced into the New World to provide labor for the production of commercial export crops. And it was only eleven years after the Imperial order of Dom Pedro's son had been overturned, again without violence, and a republic established.

By the end of World War I, the number of inhabitants in Brazil had almost doubled, and by World War II it surpassed forty million. At mid-century there were fifty-two million Brazilians and seventy million by 1960. In the next three decades the population doubled again, reaching 146 million in 1990.

2. Luis Roniger, *Hierarchy and Trust in Modern Mexico and Brazil* (New York: Praeger, 1990); Milton Santos, *A Urbanização Brasileira* (São Paulo: Editôra HUCITEC, 1993).

3. Santos, A Urbanização; *Anuário Estatístico do Brasil* (Rio de Janeiro: IBGE, 1987), and *Censo Demográfico do Brasil* (Rio de Janeiro, 1991). As of 1990 there were a dozen cities in Brazil whose metropolitan areas contained in excess of a million people and 185 with populations of more than 100,000.

4. See, for example, the chapters in this volume by M. Ferretti, S. Ferretti, Greenfield, Motta and Sjørslev.

5. This is a revised version of a paper presented at the symposium, "Mediating the Boundaries of Belief: Papers in Honor of Morton Klass on Contested Constructions of Modernity in Anthropology," at the 97th Annual Meeting of the American Anthropological Association held in Philadelphia, PA, November 1998.

6. Malthus, I might note, had little to say about the role of religion in society and Marx, like modernization theorists a century later, believed that it would (and for Marxists

should) disappear. I mention these influential theorists because the theme of the 1998 American Anthropological Association conference was "Population and the Anthropological Imagination," with specific reference to the works of Maltus, Marx, etc. I am pleased to note that Peter Berger, one of the more notable modernization theorists to write about religion, recently repeated that he was wrong when earlier in his career he claimed "that modernity necessarily leads to a decline in religion" (NY Times 9/5/98). See also Peter L. Berger, "Epilogue," in *Making Sense of Modern Times: Peter L. Berger and the Vision of Interpretative Sociology*, James Davison Hunter and Stephen C. Ainlay, eds. (London: Routledge & Kegan Paul, 1986), 221-235. Ethnographers, who observed flourishing religious rituals and practices while doing fieldwork, have known this for some time.

7. This is not to say that most practicing members of religious groups intentionally and deliberately seek out affiliations to obtain practical benefits, nor that they are necessarily conscious of those that accrue to them by virtue of their joining a particular religious group. Many, however, are aware of the transactional process I shall describe.

8. See André Droogers, "Syncretism: The problem of Definition, and the Definition of the Problem," in *Dialogue and Syncretism: An Interdisciplinary Approach (Currents of Encounter: Studies on the Contact between Christianity and other Religions, Beliefs, and Cultures)*, J. D. Gort, H. M. Vroom, R. Fernhout and A. Wessels, eds. (Grand Rapids, MI: Wm. B. Erdmans Publishing Co., 1989), 7.

9. Page 26.

10. Even in the cities such as São Paulo, Rio de Janeiro, Belo Horizonte and Porto Alegre where the factories were located.

11. And by the time their descendants obtained them, if indeed they were able to, there were many more applicants than there were positions available.

12. "Popular Religion, Patronage and Resource Distribution in Brazil: A Model of an Hypothesis for the Survival of the Economically Marginal," in *Perspectives on the Informal Economy*, M. Estelle Smith, ed., Monographs in Economic Anthropology No. 8, Society for Economic Anthropology (Lanham, MD: University Press of America, 1990) 123-146; William P. Norris, "Informal Sector Housing: Social Structure and the State in Brazil," in *Perspectives on the Informal Economy*, M. Estelle Smith, ed., Monographs in Economic Anthropology No. 8, Society for Economic Anthropology (Lanham, MD: University Press of America, 1990), 73-96.

13. In São Paulo, Brazil's largest city—the fourth largest in the world—and the center of the nation's industrial plant, for example, eithty-one out of every hundred jobs created between 1990 and 1994 were in the informal sector or in small businesses. Ninety percent of the 803 thousand jobs created between 1988 and 1996 were without a formal labor contract.

14. *New York Times*, 24 July 1999, B1.

15. For lack of resources and/or the political will of their leaders.

16. Roger Bastide, "Religion and the Church in Brazil," in *Brazil: Portrait of Half a Continent*, T. Lynn Smith and Alexander Marchant, eds. (New York: Drydan Press, 1951), 346.

17. Riolando Azzi, "Elementos para a história do Catholicismo popular," *Revista Ecliástica Brasileira* 36, Fasc. 141 (1976); Bastide, "Religion and the Church"; Bernadino Leers, *Catolicismo Popular e Mundo Rural* (Petropolis, RJ: Editora Vozes, 1977); Francisco C. Rolim, "Condicionamentos Sociais o Catolocismo Popular," *Revista Eclisástica Brasiliera* 36, Fasc. 141 (1976).

18. Thales de Azevedo, "Popular Catholicism in Brazil: Typology and Functions," in *Portugal and Brazil in Transition*, Raymond S. Sayers, ed. (Minneapolis: University of Minnesota Press, 1968), 177 and 178.

19. See articles in this volume by M. Ferretti, S. Ferretti, Greenfield, Motta, Sjørslev.

20. It follows from this that work is not the means by which to improve one's life in this world. It also gives full meaning to the "se Deus quiser" (God willing) uttered by most Brazilians after any statement of plan or intent.

21. Quoted in Rolim, "Condicionamentos Sociais," 147.

22. Emanuel De Kadt, "Religion, the Church, and Social Change in Brazil," in *The Politics of Conformity in Latin America*, Claudio Velez, ed. (London: Oxford University Press, 1967), 196; see also José Guilherme Magnani, "Curas e Milagres," in *A Religiosidade do Povo*, Lísias Negrão et al., eds. (São Paulo: Ed. Paulinas, 1984), 123-149.

23. Magnani, "Curas e Milagres," 137.

24. Thales de Azevedo, *Social Change in Brazil* (Gainesville: University of Florida Press, 1963), 76.

25. George Foster, "The Dyadic Contract in Tzintzuntzan, II: Patron-Client Relationship," *American Anthropologist* 65 (1963): 1280-1294.

26. Sidney M. Greenfield, "Charwomen, Cesspools and Road Building: An Examination of Patronage, Clientage and Political Power in Southeastern Minas Gerais," in *Structure and Process in Latin America*, Arnold Strickon and Sidney M. Greenfield, eds. (Albuquerque: University of New Mexico Press, 1972), 71-100, "Patronage, Politics and the Articulation of Local Community and National Society in pre-1968 Brazil," *Journal of Inter-American Studies and World Affairs* 19, no. 2 (1977), 139-172, and "Domestic Crises, Schools and Patron-Clientage in Southeastern Minas Gerais," in *Brazil: Anthropological Perspectives*, Maxine Margolis and William Carter, eds. (New York: Columbia University Press, 1979), 363-378; Daniel Gross, "Ritual Conformity: A Religious Pilgrimage to Northeastern Brazil," *Ethnology* 10, no. 2 (1971): 129-148; Bertram Hutchinson, "The Patron-Dependent Relationship in Brazil: A Preliminary Examination," *Sociologia Ruralis* 6, no. 1 (1966): 3-29; Luis Roniger, "Caciquismo and Coronelismo: Contextual Dimensions in Patron Brokerage in Mexico and Brazil," *Latin American Research Review* 22, no. 2 (1987): 71-99; and Arnold Strickon and Sidney M. Greenfield, eds., *Structure and Process in Latin America* (Albuquerque: University of New Mexico Press, 1972).

27. The descendants of former slaves would be excluded from this generalization since prior to abolition (in 1888) because they were not permitted full participation in

Brazilian society and culture. Instead some are reported to have appealed to their own African derived supernatural beings who, though illegal, continued to be worshipped.

28. See chapter 7 by Greenfield in this volume.

29. See chapter 3 by Motta in this volume.

30. See chapters 5 and 6 by Sergio and Mundicarmo Ferretti in this volume.

31. See Sidney M. Greenfield, "The Return of Dr. Fritz: Spiritist Healing and Patronage Networks in Urban, Industrial Brazil," *Social Science and Medicine* 24, no. 12 (1987), 1095-1108.

32. See John Burdick, *Blessed Anastácia: Women, Race and Popular Christianity in Brazil* (New York: Routledge, 1998), 82-88.

33. John Paul II alone, for example, has canonized 280, more than any one of his predecessors, since becoming pope in 1978. In 1988 alone he canonized 122 and beatified 22 more. The process also has been simplified. The number of miracles has been reduced in half, from four to two, and the devil's advocate, who argued against the prospective saint's cause, had been done away with (Paul Elie, "The Patron Saint of Paradox," *New York Times Magazine*, 8 November 1998, 44; Kenneth L. Woodward, *Making Saints: How the Catholic Church Determines Who Becomes a Saint, Who Doesn't and Why* (New York: Simon and Schuster, 1990). The total number of official saints, however, remains small in comparison with the increased number of petitions made by the many Brazilians, most of whom are poor, added to the population in the twentieth century.

34. See Ralph Della Cava, *Miracle at Joazeiro* (New York: Columbia University Press, 1970). Brazil, it should be noted, is not the only place where the faithful treat special people not recognized by the church as saints, by holding processions for them, praying to them and asking for their intercession. Students of the subject estimate that some 10,000 or more such individuals are treated as popular folk saints by local communities worldwide.

35. Burdick, *Blessed Anastácia*, 65-77.

36. Peter L. Berger, *The Sacred Canopy: Elements of a Sociological Theory of Religion* (New York: Anchor Books, 1969), 138. Italics in the original.

37. Karl Polanyi, Conrad M. Arensberg and Harry W. Pearson, eds., *Trade and Markets in the Early Empires: Economics in History and Theory* (Glencoe, IL: The Free Press, 1957).

38. Berger's interpretation, it should be noted, has been criticized recently by a group of scholars developing what they propose as a New Paradigm for the sociological study of religion. See R. Stephen Warner, "Work in Progress toward a New Paradigm for the Sociological Study of Religion in the United States," *American Journal of Sociology* 98, No. 5 (1993): 1044-1093. First, they maintain that the loss of monopoly status by a once official religion refers more to the situation in Europe and not in the United States where competition among diverse groups has existed since the colonial society was first established. Based on this, they go on to argue that the market model is even more applicable to both the study and understanding of American religion than Berger indicated or imagined.

39. A paradigm for the study of religious pluralism such as the one I am proposing—based on patron-client and not market assumptions—may be viewed as a contribution to what would be a truly cross-culturally applicable framework for the study of religion in which separate models (or paradigms) appropriate to the distinctive cultures and histories of each of the several world areas would be developed as the basis for their analysis and comparison before generalizations are made. This would avoid the unfortunate penchant of western intellectuals to ethnocentrically impose the culture and history of the west—the United States and western Europe—on the rest of the world as the basis for their examination and analysis without adequate regard for their unique features.

## Chapter 4

# Ethnicity, Purity, the Market and Syncretism in Afro-Brazilian Cults

Roberto Motta

### Preliminary Remarks

In this paper I examine the mixed Indo-Afro-European religions I have been studying in Brazil for more than two decades—mainly, but not only, in the northeastern city of Recife. I approach them in terms of what I call the "Brazilian Paradox." While they assert ethnicity and ethnic identity at one level, they seem simultaneously to negate and deny it at another. Whereas faithfulness to authentic Indian or African origins is proclaimed on the one hand, new converts are recruited without distinction as to their color, ethnicity, or national origin, on the other. New members are constantly being sought in what in Brazil has become a national "religious market."

As it is used in this paper, the concept of this market derives from the writings of Peter Berger and refers to the idea that the Brazilian people presently "shop" and choose among alternative rituals and belief systems much the way they select items in the consumer market for material commodities. The "man in the street," writes Berger, "is confronted with a wide variety of religious and other reality-defining agencies that compete for his allegiance or at least attention, and none of which is in a position to coerce him into allegiance." This results in a competition among religious groups for followers.[2] Needless to say, the existence of a religious market in Brazil presupposes the end of the religious monopoly once exercised by the Roman Catholic Church. The existence of a market implies the presence of religious entrepreneurs, who will be dealt with throughout this paper implicitly.[3] A religious entrepreneur is understood as a person, or group of persons, who bring new "products" to the (religious) market by introducing new (religious) goods and services, or by recombining previously existing ones to satisfy changes in demand prevailing among consumers.

Another theoretical strand that pervades practically every paragraph of the paper relates to the concept of "religious fraternization," first proposed by Gilberto Freyre in his classic book, *The Masters and the Slaves*. Since limitations of space do not permit an extensive treatment of this notion here, I will limit myself to a single, if somewhat lengthy quotation.

> What took place in our country was a deep going and fraternal association of values and sentiments. . . . This was a kind of fraternization that could only with difficulty have been realized under any other type of Christianity than that which dominated Brazil during its formative period. . . . It was this domestic, lyric, and festive Christianity, with its humanly friendly male and female saints and its *Our Ladies* as godmothers to the young, that created the first spiritual, moral and aesthetic bonds between the Negroes and the Brazilian family and its culture. . . . It was religion that became the point of contact and of fraternization between the two cultures, that of the Master and that of the Negro, and there was never any stern and insurmountable barrier between them.[4]

In this essay I shall use the concept of *identitophagy*, which may be understood as a latter-day equivalent, indeed as the direct continuation of Freyre's "fraternal association of values and sentiments" and of his "religion [as] the point of contact and fraternization" between the cultures and races of Brazil. My interpretation of Brazilian religion, society and culture, therefore, will be far more optimistic, for example, than that of Ortiz who sees in religious contact and syncretism "the white death of the black sorcerer,"[5] or of Fry, who sees it as the sheer expropriation of symbols, rather than a commingling and sharing of beliefs and values.[6]

Three main varieties of Indo-Afro-European religions may be recognized[7] in Brazil.[8] Each will now be discussed in turn.

## *Catimbó*: A Healing Cult with Indian Roots

Catimbó, the Indian-most of all of the syncretic religions to be discussed, is based on the worship of *Caboclos*, healing spirits supposedly of Indian origin, and *Mestres*, also healing spirits, but of Luso-Brazilian and at times Gypsy and African origin.[9] It is the oldest of the popular cults extant in Brazil. A stream of documents suggests that it has been practiced, in unbroken continuity, since as early as the sixteenth century, mainly in *aldeias* (villages) of Indians who had been converted, at least nominally, to the Roman Catholicism of the Portuguese. Along with at least some of the beliefs and practices of their conquerors, they retained some, but by no means all, of the traits of their original religion.[10] From these aldeias Catimbó spread to cities such as Recife, Salvador, and Rio de Janeiro. *Catimbozeiros* (i.e., practitioners of Catimbó) generally see their rites as Indian or Caboclo.[11] Even if much of what they believe and practice does have undeniably native roots, it is equally clear that Catimbó has been affected significantly by Iberian and also African influences, both in the origin of many of its supernaturals and in its styles of singing and dancing.

The liturgy of Catimbó is rather simple. It consists of an invocation—in song, or singing and dancing combined—by a medium, of a Mestre, or a Caboclo. Then, when the spirit incorporates in the medium, of a request for advice on some pressing matter such as the health of a client, his or her employment, love, etc. The Mestres go by names such as Carlos, Inácio, Castelhano, Malunguinho, Junqueira, Antônio dos Montes, Francisco Rei dos Ciganos, Zé Pilintra, Maria do Acais, Maria Padilha, Laurinda, Luziara, Paulina, while the Caboclos are known as João da Mata, Jurandir, Pena Branca, Jurema, Jacira, Jandira, Rei de Urubá, Rei Canindé, Rei Tamandaré, etc.

The use of tobacco, which usually is shunned by the orthodox forms of Afro-Brazilian worship, is the hallmark of ritual sessions of Catimbó. Catimbó is, in a sense, a cult of tobacco smoked in the form of cigarettes and cigars, or in pipes. Incorporated Mestres and Caboclos blow smoke on needy devotees as the simplest of their healing rites. Catimbozeiros also take a ceremonial drink, called *jurema*, the basic component of which is the root of the *jurema preta* tree (*Mimosa Hostilis, Benth*). Jurema is reputed to be a hallucinogen. Based on my own observations, however, and on my personal experience, I veer to the conclusion that the consequences of the drink are due to another of its ingredients: *cachaça* (raw rum). I have found that only token pieces of jurema preta are actually added to the beverage.

Catimbó groups are on the average smaller and less formal than the more traditional Afro-Brazilian houses (such as those of Bahia and the *Xangôs* of Pernambuco). While *Candomblé* and Xangô centers may be viewed as congregations, in the sense that they are organized around a priest and his or her followers (i.e., are a church) as proposed by Weber[12] and Joachim Wach,[13] Catimbós, in contrast, are organized around what might be thought of as a "magician" and his or her clients.

Catimbó is most prevalent in those areas of northeast Brazil where Amerindian identity has been preserved the longest. Since the aldeias were located primarily on land that was marginal, and of little use to the large-scale plantations of sugar cane and other commercial crops that dominated the area, the Catimbós may be considered a kind of peripheral cult, or in its purest form as cults of the peripheral poor. To a far greater extent than the Candomblés and the Xangôs, the Catimbós were and still are concentrated in areas inhabited by often illiterate, under- and unemployed recent migrants from the interior to the large cities. This seems to be associated, in Recife at least, with the ecologically peripheral distribution of Catimbó centers in the hills that surround the city, or on low ground that is subject to seasonal flooding.

The Mestres, Caboclos and other supernaturals of Catimbó correspond to the spirits Lewis terms "peripheral."[14] They offer people with little or no other means of escape from social and economic deprivation the "prestige" that may derive from entering a trance and being possessed, and from the practice of magical medicine. Like Candomblé and Xangô, Catimbó does not propose a system of abstract ethics to their devotees. It does not meet Max Weber's criteria of asceticism and rationality. Moreover, in Victor Turner's terminology, it is a religion that stresses the *icon* rather than the *logos*.[15] For its adherents, as also is the case for followers of Candomblé and Xangô, everything revolves around contracts and vows that should be kept, without much attention paid to psychological, ethical or metaphysical considerations.

## Candomblé-Xangô: Gods, Contracts and Conformism

Candomblé-Xangô represents what may be considered the "classical" form of Afro-Brazilian religion.[16] It is based on the worship of a number of deities, the orixás, of African, mainly Yoruba, origin. These supernatural beings are syncretized or mixed with the saints of popular Catholicism. At the root of this mixing of the two pantheons is a similarity in the roles attributed to the spirits in West African religions and to the saints in traditional Ibero-American Catholicism.[17] The orixás and saints must somehow be the same, or at least share a similar essence or force, since they are believed to be equally responsible for certain natural phenomena or for the same kind of human activity.[18]

Like the popular Catholicism prevalent throughout Latin America, Candomblé also is not an ethical religion. Its basic tenet is represented in a contract, based on an exchange, that binds the practitioner to his or her personal god or goddess.[19] In exchange for gifts, sacrifices and other offerings made by a petitioner, either under the more or less spiritualized forms of a vow and/or consecrations, or in the full materiality of the blood of slaughtered animals—and of his own body in order to enable the god to manifest itself—the believer receives support and protection in his daily life, especially in periods of crisis.

Candomblé is a religion of the feast. Singing and dancing are accompanied by the effusion of the fluids that express and transmit life. The sight and smell of blood, the heads of sacrificed animals, libations of rum and joy, leading to ecstasy, are at its essence. There is nothing like it in Western religions as they exist today. This helps to explain the attraction of this religion (to both its practitioners and to European and North American researchers whose fascination has led many to be initiated into its highest ranks) and the repulsion it also can arouse.

Candomblé is the antithesis of a rational religion as outlined by Max Weber.[20] In it the sacred is the object of an emotional and immediate intuitive reaction. In contrast with most Western traditions, it also is not a salvation religion. For its devotees it either will help them survive in this world or else it will be of no use to them at all. They assume that society and the world in which they live will continue as it is now without change. Their social class position, their access to power, etc. also will remain unchanged in the future. I have often observed, for example, a deep-seated (and amused) skepticism on the part of ritual leaders of Candomblé with regard to projects of social and political transformation. The more things change, they seem to be saying, the more they will remain the same.

The only changes that really count for them are those that affect single individuals, as may be seen in the following quotation from a *pai-de-santo* who tried to convince me to write the name of one of my enemies on a slip of paper and drop it in a sacrificial bowl where it would be covered with blood, meat, and feathers.

> You don't know the name? Really? No guess at all? Listen, suppose you're on a battlefield. Wouldn't you then kill a hundred of your enemies in order to stay alive? Now, Roberto, life is this battlefield. If you don't kill them, you may be sure that your enemies won't spare you.

The mixed Indo-Afro-Iberian religions of Brazil distinguish themselves in this way both from cults of symbolic protestation, which preach that (on a purely spiritual plane, or by miraculous means in a future world) "the last shall be first, and the first last." They also differ from the religions of effective protestation, such as the branch of Roman Catholicism influenced by the theology of liberation, which urges the faithful to break away from relationships of patronage and clientage which constitute the very fabric of Brazilian society and to work for the advent, in a relatively short period, of a society in which there will no longer be oppressors or oppressed.

The organization of Candomblé is far more formal than that of Catimbó. Its congregations, called *terreiros*, have a strongly hierarchical structure. They are headed by a priest or priestess, called *pai* or *mãe-de-santo*, "father" or "mother in sainthood," with whom the faithful maintain a personal relationship of dependence and subordination. There is, however, no centralized church. Candomblé follows a "congregational" model, despite the affinities and alliances that may be observed among some terreiros. But competition among terreiros is often very keen, giving rise to all kinds of schisms and excommunications.

Each Candomblé group (terreiro) claims to represent the tradition of one African ethnic group, or *nação* (literally nation). There is the *Nagô* (or Yoruba) nation, for example, which is subdivided into the *Ketu, Oyo, Ijexa*, etc. Others are the *Jeje, Mina, Xambá, Congo, Angola, Moçambique*, etc. The correspondence with specific African tribes, peoples, countries or regions, however, is at best usually conjectural. In a general way, the Yoruba tradition has dominated the beliefs and ritual practices of Brazilian Candomblé, no matter the nation claimed by any given terreiro. In Recife, for example, there were no noticeable *Bantu* traits in the cult center of the late Father Apolinário Gomes da Mota, in spite of the Father's claim to represent the Congo tradition. The liturgical language was Nagô and only a few Jeje (a tradition with roots among the Ewe people of today's Benin) practices differed from those of other centers.[21] Father Apolinário, in addition, exhibited in his *pegi* (chapel) a drawing of the old flag of the Dominion of South Africa from the 1940s.

The Afro-Brazilian nations do not form ethnically exclusive groups, nor are they a united political force. They may be thought of as a diacritical mark, a *flatus vocis*, allowing some terreiros to differentiate themselves from other centers implying, as Costa Lima has shown, "an ideological and ritual model," that is, an assertion of ancientness and orthodoxy.[22] This is very clearly the case with some of the more famous Nagô establishments of Salvador, such as *Engenho Velho, Gantois* and *Axé Opô Afonjá*, which claim to be able to define what is true and authentic in matters of ritual, doctrine, and even metaphysics, especially after the publication of books and articles by researchers, both Brazilian and foreign, who have, using the word in its literal meaning, canonized their "Nagô rite" as the norm both of good ethnography and of proper religion.[23]

## *Umbanda* and the Rise of the Project

Filiation with the tradition of an African nation or ethnic group that may be recognized as a sign of orthodoxy offers a religious group an advantage in Brazil's competitive market of religious goods and services. Yet, emphasis on Africanness is but one of the possible strategies that may be followed. While it has the favorable connotation of authenticity to some, it also has been associated by others, and during certain periods, with primitiveness, immorality, and being abhorrent, characteristics that have been attributed to some myths and ritual practices such as the sacrificial slaughtering of animals.

Perhaps in reaction to this, a new religious movement appeared in the early years of the present century whose intent was to purify and civilize the African and Indian-influenced religions of Brazil by subjecting them to a process of reinterpretation based in large part on theological principles drawn from the writings of Allan Kardec, the French codifier of the nineteenth-century reinterpretation of Christianity in terms of both Asian beliefs and scientistic lore that came to be know as Spiritism.

The new movement adopted an Afro-Brazilian name, Umbanda, which used to designate Rio de Janeiro's equivalent of Recife's Catimbó and Bahia's *Candomblé de Caboclo*.[24] Since it was neither monolithic nor uniform in that each group or center was autonomous and able to make its own selections from the range of beliefs and practices being reinterpreted, Umbanda soon came to refer to a wide variety of religious groups. At one level the name also came to be used as a more dignified way of referring to Candomblé, Xangô and indeed practically the whole Afro-Brazilian religious spectrum.[25] The presentation that follows refers to what Brown and Ortiz[26] have conceptualized as *Umbanda Branca*, the more Europeanized form.[27]

Umbanda Branca, in an ideal-typical sense, has adopted the notion of spiritual progress from Kardecist-Spiritism. It postulates that the universe is composed of two planes of reality, the spiritual and the material. The latter is animated by beings from the former who return periodically or reincarnate as part of their transcendental mission. Communication is believed possible between the believers on the material plane and those in the spirit world. Umbanda Branca redefines the ecstasy of Candomblé in mediumistic terms, changing it into a kind of verbal possession in which the ordinary personality of the medium is replaced by that of an entity prone to offer advice and prescriptions useful for what ails people morally and/or materially.

Its groups (called *centros* rather than *terreiros*) would be designated as sects in the terminology of Troeltsch and Weber rather than as churches.[28] They are, at least at the level of their own image of themselves, communities of believers, to the exclusion of practically all criteria of magic or sacramental initiation. Yet, in actual practice, this kind of religious democracy is often subordinated to the charisma of a leader, a healer, or a diviner, who finds it suitable to adopt the discourse of Umbanda in order to legitimize his or her own personal power. I will not dwell here on the conflict between the egalitarian and bureaucratic model and the charismatic practices. Let me only say that a similar opposition between an ideology of rationality and a practice of *personalismo* seems to pervade much of the texture of Brazilian society.

Both Candomblé and Catimbó, as we have seen, are based on reciprocal exchange between gods and men and between men and men. Umbanda, in contrast, although there often is considerable divergence between lofty professions and actual behavior, accepts the Christian based, Kardecist imperative of doing charity: the giving of disinterested aid to one's neighbor. A further opposition between the Afro-Brazilian cults and Umbanda stems from the former's orientation toward the relief of the sorrows and afflictions of daily life, while among *Umbandistas* (who, however, are certainly not opposed to the more tangible and immediate aspects of religious consolation) one can discern the beginnings of a sense of history, entailing a *project* which presides over the evolution of the spirits and the development of individual devotees.

All spirits are welcome in Umbanda if they will conform to its rules of interpretation. Believers have no objections to welcoming orixás, which some would rather term Pretos Velhos (Old Black People), Caboclos, Mestres, Gypsies, and other entities, provided they accept the ethos of spiritual development. They are, however, considered low-level, primitive spirits who, as they recognize their backward state and need for improvement, are turned instantly into saints. Redeemed, they become redeemers themselves. Their subjection to exploitation, deprivation, and even slavery in previous lifetimes is believed to enable them to understand and forgive the foibles of incarnate mankind. Umbanda, in a way, adopts the myth of the noble savage. It may be thought of as a back to nature movement, subject to the qualification that the virtues of savages can acquire full meaning only as their spirits are being developed.

According to Umbanda's theoreticians, the average Brazilian is still too backward spiritually to converse with Saint Louis, Joan of Arc, Pascal, Emmanuel, and other advanced spirits. The masses, however, they maintain, might benefit from interacting with less developed Black or Indian spirits, who themselves—and this is a central tenet of Kardec's version of the theory of progress—some day inevitably will reach the highest level of moral and intellectual development.

According to its founders, Umbanda, given its integrating and harmonious blend of the African, Indian, and European aspects of Brazilian culture, is destined to become a national religion of a dynamic and modernized Brazil, combining into a single system of doctrine and ritual the contributions of the three races that have blended to form the Brazilian people. In this respect it might be considered the prototype of the brave, new world, which some would refer to as postmodern.

Umbanda, as the subtitle of a previously mentioned book by one of its leading students implies, is "the white death of the Black sorcerer."[29] Africa and its traditions are being expropriated and made to serve the cause of the unity and the moral and material progress of the Brazilian nation. Little did Umbanda's founders anticipate, however, that an increasing number of devotees of the Afro-Brazilian groups, spearheaded primarily by Nagô priests and priestesses in Bahia behaving as religious entrepreneurs—with the technical assistance of some anthropologists and sociologists, both Brazilian or foreign—would, in the name of African authenticity, produce a revitalized alternative able to compete with, and perhaps supplant, theirs in the religious marketplace of the large cities of southeastern Brazil. The very name Umbanda, which in large and fashionable circles of Afro-Brazilian devotees in the early 1970s represented a dignified way to refer to traditional Candomblé and Xangô, has come some twenty-five years later to acquire a negative and politically incorrect connotation as a kind of Uncle Tomism. Neither the entrepreneurial leaders of Umbanda and their followers, nor their "well behaved" Pretos Velhos and other entities, not to speak of the more advanced spirits with whom they communicate, seem to have foreseen, and been prepared for, the changes in the religious market that have taken place in the past few decades. Far too many consumers have turned away from the integrationist goals of Umbanda's founders in favor of a return to specifically African traditions. To many of them, the avowed syncretic integration of Umbanda has come to be viewed as a defilement of an idealized pristine purity of African beliefs and rites. To them, to the extent that it was intended as a defense of and spiritualization of Africanhood, Umbanda, although it should by no means be considered as dead, is finding itself outdated and redundant.

## The De-ethnicization of Ethnicity

Let me now return to what I have called the Brazilian paradox. The several religious groupings discussed above, whose followers once were ethnically based, have divested themselves of their original affiliation. Membership in them is now being offered to an anonymous body of consumers of goods and services of a magical and religious kind, independent of the racial and ethnic sources from which they emerged. The result I call the de-ethnicization of ethnicity. Ethnicity no longer is a characteristic of the worshippers, but it remains as the hallmark of the authenticity of the commodity being offered to persons of all racial and national origins. The consumers of these religious commodities should by no means be read as participants in ethnic movements. While Black political movements exist in Brazil, they are limited mostly to groups of artists and intellectuals. And their attitudes towards, and those of adepts towards them, is at best ambivalent. Candomblé, however, without severing its ties to the major priestly families of Bahia (or Recife)—the source of their legitimacy in the religious marketplace—has turned itself into a universalistic religion, appealing, without any discrimination of color or ethnic origins, to all Brazilians, indeed to all people. It is spreading throughout Brazil and beyond its borders as a competitor to other churches and sects, including Roman Catholicism which once also claimed to be the true religion of the Brazilian people.

A second Brazilian paradox is the seeming reafricanization that is taking place along with rapid and intense changes in social and economic structures. The recent economic and political history of the country seems to be replicating, with only the delay of a few decades, the history of western Europe and North America. Yet how do we explain the proliferation of religions, especially those discussed above that are based on the magical manipulation of gods and humans, that were believed doomed to oblivion in the wake of modernization in the rationalist theories of most scholars?[30]

Space limits me to but some brief suggestions. First, we must certainly take into account the social and economic history and present organization of the Brazilian nation. Even in its more industrialized regions, vast numbers of people do not participate in the more modernized sectors of the economy, or do so only marginally. The markedly concrete and direct character of the economic and social behavior of the people who make up the large informal sector of the economy seems to be in substantial agreement with the view of the world of the Afro-Brazilian religions, which, even in their most intellectualized versions, depend on immediate contact with supernatural powers through trance and through the personalized alliances established between the faithful and their deities.

Traditional Catholicism, in its popular form, which in contrast with the official church position is based primarily on the worship of the saints, also has a markedly concrete character. The survival of African-influenced or -derived religious practices seems to have been possible in Brazil primarily because of "supporting structures"[31] and the niches found that were not totally dominated by the Catholic Church. Personal devotion to the saints, who were syncretized with the African orixás in the formation of Candomblé so typical of Ibero-American popular religious practice, seems to show the Afro-Brazilian religions as replicating popular Catholicism. At the risk of oversimplifying a very complex issue, we may hypothesize that both Candomblé and Umbanda, like other religions nowadays competing in the Brazilian religious market, have attempted to fill the void caused by official Catholicism distancing itself from its traditional Ibero-American religious roots.

This may be considered as a process of identitophagy. Africanness advances in Brazilian society to the degree to which it separates itself from Blackness. We should not forget that the accelerated growth of the Afro-Brazilian cults, and the recognition of Africanness as a source of personal identification and of communal life, is associated with no project for social and political change and proposes no program to alter the standards or styles of living of the Black or Mulatto population in any concrete way. We are faced once again with the Brazilian racial paradox, compounded by another paradox of a cultural and historical kind. Afro-Brazilian religion, which rightly or wrongly is seen as primitive, becomes a religion of modernity and, some might say, postmodernity.[32]

## The Three Races and Their Identitophagic Relationship

In this examination of Brazilian syncretic religions I have summarized the contributions of the three major races to Brazilian national culture. Catimbó, as we have seen, with its Caboclos, to whom Mestres, Gypsies, and other spirits were later added, represents the contributions of the Indians who were incorporated and integrated, albeit forcibly, into colonial Luso-Brazilian society. Candomblé is the worship of the gods of Africa, who have been mixed and often confused in popular devotion, with the saints of the Roman Catholic Church. Umbanda incorporated and added to the Afro-Indo-Iberian components the evolution of the spirit taken from the spiritualist writings of Kardec. It then made a deliberate effort at doctrinal and ritual rationalization by trying to encompass and even replace the other cult groups who were considered by its theoreticians to be too primitive for a modernized Brazil. Africanness, however, is staging a vigorous return to popularity, rejecting all claims of cultural and religious subordination.

Yet, and this is perhaps the supreme religious and social paradox of Brazil, this movement of ethnic fundamentalism is not directed toward the Black and Mulatto masses. It is offered instead anonymously and impersonally on a market whose consumers are primarily Whites of European descent living in the large cities in the southeast. Ethnicity, in this context, refers above all to the authentic quality of the religious article being offered to the consuming public. The Brazilian paradox stems from this kind of identitophagy in which the search for ethnic authenticity leads to its concomitant de-ethnicization.

I have attempted in this paper no comparisons with religious developments in other countries and on other continents. I might propose the process of identitophagy, however, as an hypothesis to be tested elsewhere in the postmodern, posthistorical world—although it might be too closely tied to the specifics of Luso-Brazilian culture history with its fraternal association of values and sentiments. Or it may be that in the long run identitophagy will prove too weak to withstand, even in Brazil, the resurgence of a politically militant ethnic nationalism. Perhaps it is again a case of *après nous, le déluge*. For the moment, however, let us not think of the flood elsewhere and dance while we can.

## Notes

1. Peter L. Berger, *The Sacred Canopy: Elements for a Sociological Theory of Religion* (Garden City, NY: Doubleday, 1967), 127.

2. As Berger puts it "the religious tradition, which previously could be authoritatively imposed, now has to be *marketed*. It must be 'sold' to a clientele that is no longer constrained to buy. The pluralistic situation is above all, a *market situation*. In it, the religious

traditions become marketing agencies and the traditions become consumer commodities." Berger, *The Sacred Canopy*, 138.

3. Since the early stages of the fieldwork I conducted in Recife, I have been convinced that *terreiros*, among other things, are small capitalistic ventures directed by entrepreneurs (Cf. Roberto Motta, "Meat and Feast: The Xango Cult of Recife, Brazil." Unpublished Ph.D. dissertation, Department of Anthropology, Columbia University, 1988); see also Sidney M. Greenfield and Arnold Strickon, "A New Paradigm for the Study of Entrepreneurship and Social Change," *Economic Development and Social Change* 29, no. 3 (1981), 467-499.

4. Gilberto Freyre, *The Masters and the Slaves: A Study on the Development of Brazilian Civilization* (Berkeley: University of California Press, 1986 [Original 1933]), 372-373.

5. Renato Ortiz, *A Morte Branca do Feiticeiro Negro* (Petrópolis, Brazil: Editora Vozes, 1978).

6. Peter Fry, *Para Inglês Ver* (Rio de Janeiro: Zahar, 1982).

7. The names for religious groupings employed are derived from my own research experience conducted primarily in Recife. They differ somewhat from those used in earlier typologies of Afro-Brazilian religions by Roger Bastide in *The African Religions of Brazil: Toward a Sociology of the Interpenetration of Civilizations* (Baltimore: Johns Hopkins University Press, 1978) and Edson Carneiro, *Ladinos e Crioulos* (Rio de Janeiro: Civilização Brasileira, 1964) which were based almost exclusively on data from Bahia. Yet there are close parallels. The Xangô of Recife (and Maceió), for example, corresponds to the Candomblé of Salvador, while Catimbó, with some minor variation, is the equivalent of the Candomblé de Caboclo of Bahia. The two latter cults would roughly correspond to what used to be termed Umbanda in Rio de Janeiro, but is now known as Macumba. My typology, as tends to be the case with typologies in general, in spite of precautions and qualifications, is articulated around some ideal types. These certainly are based on real phenomena, but necessarily fail to take into account aberrant and intermediate cases. From Catimbó to Xangô and from either to Umbanda there are continuities rather than sharply demarcated boundaries. Thus my typology and those of others may be criticized as reification.

8. Bastide's *The African Religions* and his earlier *Le Candomblé de Bahia (Rite Nagô)* (La Haye: Mouton, 1958) are still the standard references on the Afro-Brazilian cults. For an extensive bibliography of what has been written after 1958, see Roberto Motta, "Indo-Afro-European Syncretic Cults in Brazil: Their Economic and Social Roots," *Cahiers du Brésil Contemporain* 5 (1988), 27-48. For those cults specifically in the area of Recife, see René Ribeiro, *Cultos Afro-Brasileiros do Recife: Um Estudo de Ajustamento Social* (Recife: Massangana, 1978) and Roberto Motta, "As Variedades do Espiritismo Popular na Area do Recife: Ensaio de Classificação," *Boletim da Cidade do Recife* 2 (1977), 97-114.

9. This description applies above all to the traditional Catimbó of Recife. But following a trend that started with Rio's Macumba, Catimbozeiros have been attributing an

increasing ritual and mythological importance to Exu, or rather to the Exus who often are associated with the demons of popular Catholicism.

10. René Vandezande, "Catimbó: Forma Nordestina de Religião Mediúnica." Unpublished master's thesis, Departamento de Ciencias Sociais, Universidade Federal de Pernambuco, 1975.

11. In Brazilian parlance the term caboclo (beside designating a certain kind of spirits) may mean a full-blooded Indian who adheres to his or her native culture and society, or an Indian integrated into Luso-Brazilian society, or a person of partly Indian origin or, still, a peasant, irrespective of ethnic background.

12. Max Weber, *Economy and Society: An Outline of Interpretive Sociology* (Berkeley: University of California Press, 1978).

13. Joachim Wach, *Sociology of Religion* (Chicago: University of Chicago Press, 1944).

14. Ioan Lewis, *Ecstatic Religion* (London: Penguin Books, 1971).

15. Victor Turner, "Symbolic Studies," *Annual Review of Anthropology* 4 (1975), 145-152.

16. Candomblé is the typical Afro-Brazilian religion of the large cities such as Salvador, Maceió, and Recife of the Brazilian northeast that were associated with the economic system based on large plantations of sugar cane. Yet, it is essentially an urban phenomenon and as such different from originally rural Catimbó. In the past Candomblé was used to refer specifically to the Bahian religious groups. In Maceió and Recife they were known by the name Xangô. An equivalent of Candomblé-Xangô called *Tambor de Mina* is found in Sao Luis, where *Jeje* (Fon) influence is as strong as, or stronger than, the *Nagô* (Yoruba) influence that dominates elsewhere in Brazil.

17. This idea is made very clearly in Azevedo (1968); see also Sidney M. Greenfield, "The Reinterpretation of Africa: Convergence and Syncretism in Brazilian Candomblé," in this volume.

18. The religions of Africa, like most so-called primitive religions, are not exclusionistic. (See Donald Warren Jr., "Notes on the Historical Origins of Umbanda," *Universitas* [Salvador], no. 6-7 [1970], 15-16). They are quite receptive to alien deities, above all when their faithful are transported to other lands. This was known to the author of 2 Kings 17:24-41 (Origin of Samaritans).

19. For details on the content of this contract see Thales de Azevedo, *O Catolicismo no Brasil* (Rio de Janeiro: Ministerio da Educação e Cultura, 1955) and "Popular Catholicism in Brazil: Typology and Functions," in Raymond Sayers, ed., *Portugal and Brazil in Transition* (Minneapolis: University of Minneapolis Press, 1968), 176-178; George Foster, *Tzintzunzan: Mexican Peasants in a Changing World* (Boston: Little, Brown, 1967); Sidney M. Greenfield and Russell Prust, "Popular Religion, Patronage, and Resource Distribution in Brazil," in M. Estelle Smith, ed., *Perspectives on the Informal Economy* (Washington, D.C.: University Press of America, 1990); and Daniel Gross, "Ritual and Conformity," *Ethnology* 10, no. 2 (1971), 129-148.

20. Weber, *Economy and Society*, chapter VI, "The Sociology of Religion," 399-634.

21. As noted by Berger, who had in mind a North American setting, "If group A decides not to merge with group B, despite the fact that their products have become highly standardized, something must be done to enable consumers to distinguish between the two products and to be able to make a choice between them. Emphasizing the "confessional heritage" of each group is one obvious way of doing this. . . . It may also happen (probably more frequently) that the differentiation is one of "packaging" only—inside the package there may still be the same old standardized product" (Berger, *The Sacred Canopy*, 149).

22. The concept of nação (nações), which I have argued is now used by cult members in their struggle for an increasing share of the religious market, was first presented by Costa Lima (1971) in a thesis that was published in a limited edition by a small university press in Bahia (Vivaldo da Costa Lima, *A Familia de Santo nos Candombles Jeje-Nagô da Bahia* [Salvador: Universidade Federal da Bahia, 1977], 21). I develop this idea in my critique (Roberto Motta, "Carneiro, Ruth Landes e os Candomblés Bantus," *Revista do Arquivo Público* [Recife] 30, no. 32 (1976), 58-68) of the Nagô model proposed by Edson Carneiro, *Negros Bantus* (Rio de Janeiro: Civilização Brasileira, 1937) and *Candomblés da Bahia* (Salvador: Museu do Estado, 1948); Ruth Landes, *The City of Women* (New York: Macmillan, 1947); Bastide, *Le Candomblé de Bahia*.

23. On the often extravagant claims of terreiros pretending to represent the nações of olden times and the process of "ecclesification" of Candomblé, see Roberto Motta, "A Eclesificação dos Cultos Afro-Brasileiros," *Comunicações do ISER* 7, no. 3 (1988), 31-43. The canonization of the Nagô rite is largely due to Carneiro (Negros Bantus and Candombles de Bahia); Landes, City of Women; Bastide, Le Candomblé de Bahia; and, more recently, Juana Elbein dos Santos, *Os Nàgô e a Morte* (Petrópolis: Vozes, 1976).

24. For the early meaning of the word Umbanda, see Arthur Ramos, *O Negro Brasileiro* (São Paulo: Companhia Editora Nacional, 1940).

25. In one of my early papers on the Afro-Brazilian religions of Recife, I distinguished three different meanings of the word Umbanda. According to the context it could mean: 1) *Umbanda Branca*; 2) the whole Afro-Brazilian religious domain; 3) all Afro-Brazilian cults other than traditional Candomblé-Xangô. In the course of my research I have found that the same individual was able to shift his meaning of the term as the context changed. When we first met, for example, he said, "Oh, I see you are a sympathizer of Umbanda!" Later that evening, however, after we had become more familiar, he said, "Let me warn you that our religion has nothing to do with Umbanda." See Roberto Motta, "As Variedades do Espiritismo Popular na Area do Recife: Ensaio de Classificação," *Boletim da Cidade do Recife*, no. 2 (1977), 97-114.

26. Diana Brown, *Umbanda: Religion and Politics in Brazil* (Ann Arbor: UMI Research Press, 1986); Ortiz, *A Morte Branca*.

27. A detailed history of the Umbanda movement still is to be written. For descriptions see Brown, *Umbanda*, and Ortiz, *A Morte Branca*, who although writing from different theoretical perspectives both emphasize what I am referring to as Umbanda Branca. See also Maria Helena Villas Boas Cancone, *Umbanda: Uma Religião Brasileira* (São

Paulo: Faculdade de Filosofia, Letras e Ciencias Humanas da Universidade de São Paulo, 1987); Valdeli Carvalho da Costa, *Umbanda* (São Paulo: Loyola, 1983); Greenfield and Prust, "Popular Religion"; and Lindolfo Weingaertner, *Umbanda* (Erlangen: Verlag der Ev.-Luth. Mission, 1969).

28. Ernst Troeltsch, *The Social Teaching of the Christian Churches* (London: Allen and Unwin, 1931), and Weber, *Economy and Society*.

29. Ortiz, *A Morte Branca*.

30. It seems that in Brazil we encounter the antithesis of the correspondence between the "real world" of "homogeneous labor" and the religions of "abstract man" in its "bourgeois developments: Protestantism, Deism, etc." as conceived by Marx in the first chapter of *Capital*. See also Sidney M. Greenfield, "Population Growth, Industrialization and the Proliferation of Syncretized Religions in Brazil" in this volume.

31. Bastide, *Le Candomblé de Bahia*; Ribeiro, *Cultos Afro-Brasileiros*.

32. A subtle affinity might be recognized between modernity, at least in its Brazilian version, and the Afro-Brazilian religions. The former rejects the Christian notions of sin (whether original or actual), while the latter, in all of their varieties, make little or no use of these concepts.

# Chapter 5

# Religious Syncretism in an Afro-Brazilian Cult House

Sergio F. Ferretti

### Introduction

This paper describes and analyzes the relationship between the African and Catholic aspects of the beliefs and rituals of the *Tambor de Mina*, a syncretic religious group originally established by slaves in the Brazilian state of Maranhão. After this brief introduction, in which the central problem is presented, I turn to the Afro-Brazilian traditions of the region. The varying uses and meanings of the concept of syncretism are problematized and summarized in terms of four hypothetical categories (situations) that are used to examine the mixing that has taken place in the beliefs and practices of the *Casa das Minas*, the oldest temple of the Tambor de Mina religion in Maranhão. I then turn to the relationship between the work of the anthropologist and the people studied, concluding that the syncretism of the African and the Catholic, plus elements from other traditions, does not discount from the traditionalism of one of the oldest and best known Afro-Brazilian religious groups.

Religious mixture, and the resulting syncretism, it should be noted, is viewed negatively by some researchers, and has been rejected both by the leaders of some of the groups and their followers. The idea of syncretism is considered by many today to "pollute" an assumed African "purity." Although the idea has been rejected, we shall see that syncretism is to be found *de facto*, however, in the everyday rituals, beliefs and practices of the majority of Afro-Brazilian cults, including those of the most traditional groups.

This essay is based on the author's doctoral thesis about the Casa das Minas of Maranhão[1] which was grounded theoretically in the affirmation of Roberto Da Matta that *relacionar*, to link together, is a basic Brazilian characteristic that tends to construct bridges, uniting separate trends by distinct traditions. For Da Matta, this "synthesizing," or remaining in the middle of things, appears to be the central element of the dominant Brazilian ideology.[2] The works of Mikhail Bakhtin[3] and Carlo Ginzburg,[4] which are fruitful in understanding the reciprocal influence between the culture of the subaltern classes and that of the dominant ones, also are used, both here and in the thesis. Furthermore, I adopt the perspective of R. Panikkar[5] and his understanding that encounters of religions are not always a dialogue between two traditions of the same level, as for example Christianity with Buddhism. Panikkar searches for an inclusive model, concerned with the meeting of different traditions, encircling external values that have similar forms.

I adopt also Melville Herskovits' view of syncretism as a reinterpretation of cultural traits.[6] This position, put forth in the 1930s and 1940s, was taken up in Brazil by Arthur Ramos,[7] who in his final works was concerned with the linking of the problems of acculturation with imperialism and cultural domination. Herskovits' students conducted important studies of acculturation in Brazil. Since the end of the 1950s, however, writings focussing on acculturation have been considered out of date and replaced by other theoretical interests, such as social class and structuralism. Studies of syncretism, meanwhile, have become stagnant and repetitive.

Recently, however, syncretism in Brazil has been reconsidered in the context of the symbolic studies inspired by Victor Turner, Clifford Geertz and others. As noted by Droogers and Greenfield in chapter 1, we are not discussing syncretism here for the purpose of defending the religious "truth" of the facts we investigate. Instead, we aim to understand and analyze these "truths" as social facts.

## Afro-Brazilian Traditions in Maranhão

Maranhão is the second largest state in northeast Brazil, with an area of about 200,000 square miles and a population of five million. The large Afro-Brazilian population in the state is concentrated along the northern coast, in the large river valleys where there are sugar and cotton plantations, and in the island capital city of São Luís. During the colonial period and until independence in 1822, Maranhão and the Amazonian region were subject to an administration separate from that governing the rest of Brazil. Maranhão remained relatively isolated for an extended period of time, preserving its distinct traditions. The Brazilian state has much in common with the Caribbean, and Maranhão may be considered one more "island" in the region. With the development of mining and the occupation of the Amazon, the state of Maranhão has recently entered a phase of relatively rapid economic and population growth.

The several Afro-Brazilian religious groups in Maranhão, whose rituals and practices differ in detail, all have been influenced by African, European and indigenous religious elements. Collectively they are referred to, as they are throughout northern Brazil, as Tambor de Minas. Two main groupings, whose leaders and participants are predominantly women, developed in São Luis. One is the *Mina-Jeje*, originating from the African Kingdom of Dahomey. About sixty spiritual deities called *voduns* in the *Fon* language, grouped in five families, are worshipped. The second is *Mina Nagô*, as practiced in the Casa de Nagô, in which voduns, *orishas*, and *caboclos* are venerated. These are of Fon, Yoruba and Brazilian origins respectively. The main model of Tambor de Minas, which is found throughout São Luis, comes from the Nagô tradition. Other traditions existing around São Luis include the *linha de mata* in the city of Codó, located in the valley of the Itapecurú River, and the healing rituals or *pajelança* on the northern coast of Guimarães and Cururupú. The cosmologies of these religious groups include mainly Brazilian spiritual entities who are not necessarily indigenous, as well as African beings whose precise origin has not yet been identified.[8]

Most recent researchers of Afro-Brazilian religion have regarded syncretism with disdain. Many leaders of religious groups, influenced by these researchers, continue to place greater value on other traditions of African origin, such as *Candomblés* found in Bahia. The classic imagery put forth by Nina Rodrigues in 1895, and adopted by Arthur Ramos, Edson Carneiro and Roger Bastide, places special value on Yoruba religious traditions. Although challenged by later researchers, these assumptions have prevailed for more than eighty years and contemporary Afro-Brazilian studies remain imprisoned by a nostalgia for a "purity" represented by the *Nagô-Ketu* (Yoruba) tradition of Candomblé. Based in this imagery spiritual leaders of the most traditional religious houses of Bahia recently have condemned syncretism as an outmoded strategy since a "Catholic mask" is no longer necessary. In Maranhão, a similar view is shared by members of the black movement, composed mostly of youth who have achieved a secondary or higher education but who are not actively involved in Afro-Brazilian religious traditions.

Syncretism is therefore regarded as a decadent fusion that pollutes the purest African traditions. This perspective does not acknowledge that, as in other regions of the Americas, the first Afro-Brazilian religious groups adapted African traditions within the context of Brazilian culture, or that Africans had already been exposed to different religious orientations before they were brought to Brazil. In this regard, recent historians show an extended penetration of European Christian practices in the African continent since the time of the arrival of Portuguese missionaries in the middle of the fifteenth century, particularly in the Congo, Angola, Gambia, Sierra Leone, Guine, Nigeria (*Warri*), Benin (*Allada*), Cape Verde, São Tomé and Príncipe.[9] According to Thornton, Christian and African religious practices were being fused since as far back as the seventeenth century. In various regions, African gods were given Christian names. For example, in the language of Allada, *Lisa* corresponds to Jesus Christ, and Vodun to God, as is *Nzambi* in *Kikongo*. Many slaves brought from the Congo and Angola regions were already baptized as a result of Portuguese imposition and the presence of Spanish and Italian missionaries. The missionaries were assisted by converted Africans who knew various languages. By 1624, Portuguese missionaries had already published catechisms in *Kinbundo* and Kikongo in Europe and in the Americas. In 1708, a Portuguese Jesuit translated a catechism in Allada which was to be used in Brazil to aid in the religious conversion of slaves.

The importance of Catholic saints in Brazil is well known. St. Anthony and St. George are particularly popular among the black population of different regions of the country. In Maranhão, St. Benedict is believed to protect Afro-Brazilians as well as rich and poor devotees. People also believe that St. Benedict was black and enjoyed the dancing of the *Tambor de Crioula*, performed in homage to him by many blacks.[10] In Pará, as well as in Maranhão, St. Benedict corresponds to Verekete or Averekete, who is considered to be the head of the *linha da mata* ceremony of the Tambor de Mina.

## Uses and Meanings of the Concept of Syncretism

One of the main criticisms that has been made of syncretism as a concept referring to social processes is that every religion may be regarded as an integrated whole. By referring to a religion as syncretic we may be led to think of it as a patchwork quilt, a bricolage, a strange agglomeration. It also may lead us to make oppositions such as fusion versus purity, fusion versus separation, or in the case of Afro-Brazilian religions, of whitening versus blackening, Brazilianness versus Africanness, or homogeneity versus heterogeneity. In addition, it may be regarded as fertility, a new synthesis, convergence, an amalgam, analogy, juxtaposition, parallelism, or even as religious bilingualism, or as equivalence, a mask or coalescence. Moreover, besides the religious sphere, syncretism also occurs in the realms of philosophy, art and science.

For the purpose of analysis the main meanings of syncretism may be grouped in terms of the following four hypothetical situations:

1. *Separation*—no syncretism
2. *Interpenetration*—linkage
3. *Parallelism*—juxtaposition
4. *Convergence*—adaptation

We may say that all of these types of syncretism correspond to situations that can be found in Afro-Brazilian religions. *Convergence*, for example, exists between African concepts and those of other religions with regard to notions of God and reincarnation. *Parallelism*, juxtaposition and in some cases bilingualism exist in the relations between the orishas and the Catholic saints, and in the integration of popular Catholic festivals. *Interpenetration* is to be found in many *terreiros* (religious centers) in the observance by members of Afro-Brazilian religions of Christian rituals such as baptism and the litany. *Separation* exists in specific rituals, including initiation rites, animal sacrifices, funeral ceremonies and dances of the divinities.[11] Therefore, in each religious house and in different ritual moments, it is possible to encounter separations, interpenetrations, parallelisms and convergences. Each must be identified in specific circumstances. Parallelism and convergence, we might note, should not be thought of as referring only to concepts of gods, voduns, saints or orishas, nor do separation and interpenetration refer to rituals, as a first reading of the examples given may lead the reader to believe.

In the majority of the religious festivals of the Tambor de Mina, religion syncretism is manifest in the convergence of time as seen in the adoption of the Catholic calender, even though the objectives of each festival may be distinct from those of the Catholic Church. In funeral rituals convergence may be seen in the acceptance of the concept of reincarnation. Interpenetration was noted in the participation in the seventh-day mass, which together with the Catholic baptism marks the entrance of the devotees into and their exit from the human world. In the same way there is separation in the celebration of diverse funeral rites with specific chants of the *tambor de choro*, which is quite distinct in form as well as in meaning from the rituals of other religions.

In my view these situations are not the product of a singular historical process, but rather should be understood as variables that can be arranged in a number of diverse conceptualizations of syncretism, as I have shown elsewhere.[12] Here I present some examples of the application of these concepts. I can state that the word "syncretism" may take on various meanings, which many times interpenetrate. In the literature on Afro-Brazilian religion and culture some of these diverse meanings easily can be seen. I shall arrange them in terms of the four situations.

In the beliefs and rituals of the Casa das Minas, as already suggested, we may identify instances of: 1) no syncretism; 2) interpenetration; 3) parallelism; and 4) convergence with other beliefs. The situations may be thought of in terms of a continuum. The purpose of the scheme is to conceptualize the existence of different types of situations and not to design a system of rigid classifcation. The next section provides some examples that demonstrate the range of syncretisms in diverse situations.

## Syncretism in the Casa das Minas

Tambor de Mina has integrated many elements from Catholicism, Kardecist-Spiritism and Amerindian religious practices. Correspondence of forces can be found in Tambor de Mina between voduns and Catholic saints, although many of the voduns do not have a corresponding saint. Practitioners claim that Tambor de Mina at times has everything that other religions have, while also having mysteries not present in the others. Confrontations and radical divisions are avoided by believers who also seek to bring together African religious elements with those from other religions.

The *Casa das Minas-Jeje* (the Big House of Minas) is considered to be the oldest Tambor de Mina religious house. Other Tambor de Mina groups are believed to have branched out from it to other parts of Maranhão and Amazonia. Although the number of participants has diminished considerably in recent years, the Casa retains its prestige in Maranhão and among followers of Afro-Brazilian religions. Researchers working in Maranhão consider it to be the most orthodox or pure of the Tambor de Mina centers, comparable to some of the Nagô-Ketu Candomblé centers of Salvador. According to Verger, the Tambor de Mina was brought to Maranhão by the widow of king *Agonglo*, queen *Na Agontime* who was sold as a slave along with other members of the royal family of the kingdom of *Adondozan* (1797-1818).[13] The house was most likely established in the first half of the nineteenth century. All the lyrics of the songs are still sung in Jeje or in Fon (from Dahomey). Initiates are possessed only by voduns and not by non-African caboclos.

Religion in the Casa das Minas is imbued with great mystery and secrecy. The divinities are given nicknames and never referred to in public by their proper names. This extreme discretion and secrecy most likely has contributed to the loss of many myths, rituals and considerable knowledge. Although the rituals in Tambor de Mina are generally quite elaborate, with an attention given to ritual detail that is almost baroque, few myths and legends have been recorded. Moreover, since the Yoruba tradition has been privileged by students of Afro-Brazilian religions, any Tambor de Mina myths that might have been collected were not adequately examined.

Although there are examples of myths without rituals and rituals without myths in many Afro-Brazilian religions, I suggest, in agreement with many other anthropologists writing on the subject, that there is an intimate relationship between the two. In observing a dance in a terreiro of the Tambor de Mina, it is quite easy to make the claim that the presence of gestures, details of clothing, words of chants, passes or movements in the dances are clearly related to specific myths. Yet in contrast with Candomblé, these myths most often are not part of the conscious understandings of the participants. The excessive rigor in the preservation of secrets that surrounded these cults, I suggest, caused many myths to disappear or become known by only a small number of initiates. These adepts prefer not to divulge them, fearing punishment or other penalties. For these and other reasons, many myths have not been reported by students and were not, in Hobsbawm and Ranger's terms, perpetuated by the reinvention of traditions.[14] Older practitioners of the Tambor de Mina say that the meanings of the gestures and of the rites are contained in the chants. Yet many no longer understand the texts they are singing. In spite of this, however, they debate interpretations at times acrimoniously. Many *mineiras* (practitioners of the Tambor de Mina) say that they cannot reveal all of the little they know, especially with respect to the meanings of the chants, the herbal leaves, the colors of the beads and other elements of the rituals.

In Maranhão, it is said that the voduns are devotees of the Catholic saints, as are human beings. The vodum *Toi Averequete*, for example, is said to pay homage to St. Benedict, *Toi Bade* to Saint Peter and the twins, *Toçá* and *Tocé*, to St. Cosmos and St. Damion. Although this suggests that the vodum is subordinate to the saint, there are voduns that are not devotees of any specific Catholic saint. On St. Benedict's day, many people of different social classes from the Afro-Brazilian religious houses attend the large procession that is held in the city. The initiate from the Casa das Minas who becomes possessed by Toi Averequete usually watches the procession, waiting for its arrival in the church. The moment at which the bearers lower the image of the saint to enter the church, Averequete enters the body of the initiate (known as his daughter), and is greeted by everyone in the vicinity. After the church ceremony, Averequete, still incorporated in his daughter, proceeds to the Casa das Minas for a festival prepared in his honor. The festival opens with a Catholic liturgy sung in Latin, followed by songs in Jeje and a ceremony that includes drumming.

In many respects, Catholic elements in the Casa das Minas seem to be superimposed on African elements, as if they were stuck together. The Catholic and African elements, however, remain distinct, as if they were parallel compartments that approach each other but do not interpenetrate and become one. Although Catholicism and the Tambor are equally respected, they are practiced in different areas in the house. Catholicism is practiced in a public space in the front room, which has a Catholic altar. African practices are held in the secret spaces, such as the chamber in the center called the comé where sacrifices and offerings are privately made, and semi-private spaces in the kitchen at the back of the house. Catholicism thus occurs in the front of the house while African practices are held at the back. Dances, for example, start at the altar and proceed to the interior and back, or to the verandah. This verandah, where chromolithographs and pictures of the saints hang on the walls, is the place where Afro-Brazilian music and dance usually is performed. The separation between the Catholic and African religions is thus most evident in the secret chambers of the house, while convergence is most evident in the front room where the altar is kept, and where a Catholic litany sung in Latin is followed by one sung for the voduns in Jeje. Parallelism is evident in the verandah where the voduns dance in the presence of pictures of saints hanging on the walls. Clearly, separation is not that rigid, and mixture is not that profound. Syncretism in Tambor de Mina has thus emerged from specific historical circumstances and has not inhibited the traditional African religion, such that Catholicism exists alongside the African religion without restraining the traditional cult.

During the year, specific Catholic festivals are celebrated in the Casa das Minas, which occur at the same time as important festivals for the voduns. The banquet for dogs, held in honor of the animals associated with St. Lazarus, is held on one of the most important dates of the house, the festival for *Acossi-Sakpata*, the vodum of the earth who cures smallpox and the plague. Another important festival, held in almost all Tambor de Mina centers in São Luis, is that in honor of the Holy Ghost. It is held at the same time as the anniversary of the founding of the house, or during celebrations for a noble spirit who is head of the house. In the Casa das Minas the festival honoring the Holy Ghost is held at the same time as that in which *Nochê Sepazim*, the princess daughter of King *Dadaro*, is celebrated. This is a great ceremony that continues for many days. Children play an important role. Some sit, dressed in regal clothes, at a throne constructed at the altar and are greeted with special dances by women who play drums and by other children who carry banners. The house is carefully decorated, and a banquet of sweets is offered to the participants. A flagpole is put up in the garden, which, among other things, indicates that the house is having a festival. Many people are attracted for the occasion.

These popular Catholic festivals may be viewed as parallelism or juxtaposition. In both the banquet of the dogs and the festival of the Holy Ghost, African practices that occur during the festival remain practically unseen by the general public. For example, many of the people who attend the festival and who do not know the rituals do not notice when some of the initiates become possessed with spiritual entities and receive special praise.

In some public rituals at the Casa das Minas, Catholic and African practices are kept completely separate. These include the banquet (*arrambam*) held at the beginning of Lent, a festival for payment of the musicians, and the funeral mourning rituals.[15] In other public ceremonies additional syncretic elements from such diverse origins as Spiritism, Judaism and Masonic practices may be identified occurring alongside the more private ceremonies of African origin, such as the sacrifice of animals and initiation rites.

## Relations Between the Work of the Anthropologist and the People Studied

Before concluding, I should explain the role my wife, Mundicarmo, and I are playing in what may be considered the canonization of the Tambor de Mina religion. We live and do research in São Luis, the relatively small city where the religion started and is strongest. By publishing the results of our studies of this unwritten belief system, we find ourselves put in the position of being authorities on it, not only by our fellow scholars but by practitioners and those who report on them in the media as well. We are regularly called upon to participate in debates about the Tambor de Mina and Afro-Brazilian religions in general. Acquaintances of ours when considering becoming clients of an Afro religious group usually ask us for help in choosing a trustworthy cult leader (called a *pai* or *mãe-de-santo*) or a respectable temple. Among both the *povo-de-santo* (persons initiated in the Mina community) and academics, we at times have been assumed to be planning to open a *casa-de-santo* (religious house) in the near future. Outside of São Luis, especially in the south of Brazil where the tradition of Tambor de Mina is spreading, our writings circulate among devotees. Much of what is becoming considered orthodoxy found in texts being written by *gente-do-santo* (practitioners) is based on ideas data, and information taken from our work.

As several scholars have remarked, many of those who read books by anthropologists about Afro-Brazilian religions are the participants themselves.[16] Some of them at times think of the anthropologist as a theologian of their religion because he or she puts on paper beliefs and ritual practices that previously had been transmitted orally. It is even believed that some pais and mães-de-santo, the ritual leaders of the religion, learn aspects of their practice from anthropological texts. In the Afro-religious environment of Maranhão, we find ourselves treated with more than the respect that would be given to us as university professors and scholars. I attribute this to our role as codifying authors.

I have trouble determining the extent of my own influence on the beliefs and practices of the specific Casa das Minas group in which I conduct most of my studies. What I say when the group reflects on problems seems to be received with special attention. Unofficially I do what the *ogan* in Candomblé does, although Tambor de Mina has no comparable position. I donate small amounts of money for festivals and defend the group against outsiders. In addition to being recognized as professors, my wife and I are considered collaborators. We are invited to participate in semi-private rituals, and are treated as friends who are protected by the voduns. For this reason we were given our own protective rosary. Although we exchange ideas with everyone in the group, we have not read or discussed what we have written with the *vodunsis*, the fully initiated members of the Casa.

## Conclusions

In examining the different situations with which the term "syncretism" is associated—separation, interpenetration, parallelism and convergence—I have shown that the Casa das Minas may be considered both traditional and syncretic. This suggests that although syncretism may be present in the practices of a religious group, its maintenance of tradition need not be compromised. Syncretism therefore may be said to occur even in the more traditional Afro-Brazilian groups that incorporate Catholic, Kardecist-Spiritist and other religious practices. The initiates and the voduns encourage people to attend mass, even though the vodunsis may not always go. It is said that one should go to church and then proceed to Afro-Brazilian religious centers, since although the church has much to offer, Tambor de Mina is more powerful.

Overall, syncretism may be viewed as a strategy for marginalized groups to continue religious practices, in this case of African origin, along with other forms of religious worship. It can be interpreted as a strategy of adaptation and conflict avoidance in a society characterized by prejudice which privileges those who are white and their religious and other cultural practices. African elements have remained central to Tambor de Mina, affirming its African origins. Although the Casa das Minas shares traits with Catholicism and other religions, it remains primarily an African religion.

The Casa das Minas then, although syncretic, but in which African elements predominate, also may be seen as a dynamic nucleus of cultural resistance that contributes to the preservation of an Afro-Brazilian identity. Even in this most traditional Afro-Brazilian religious group in Maranhão, therefore, the boundaries between syncretized beliefs and practices and those from any one tradition are ambiguous.

## Notes

1. Sergio Figueiredo Ferretti, *Repensando o Sincretismo. Estudo sobre a Casa das Minas* (São Paulo: EDUSP/FAPEMA, 1995).
2. Roberto da Matta, *A Casa e a Rua, Espaço, cidadania, mulher e morte no Brasil* (Rio de Janeiro: Ed. Guanabara, 1987), 117.
3. Mikhail Bakhtin, *A Cultura Popular na Idade Média e no Renascimento. O contexto de François Rabelais* (São Paulo: Hucitec-UNB, 1987).
4. Carlo Ginzburg, *O queijo e os vermes. O cotidiano e as idéias de um moleiro perseguido pela Inquisição* (São Paulo, Companhia das Letras, 1987).
5. R. Panikkar, *The Intrareligious Dialogue* (New York: Paulist Press, 1978).
6. Melville J. Herskovits, *Antropologia Cultural* (São Paulo: Ed. Mestre Jou, 1969).
7. Artur Ramos, *Introdução à Antropologia Brasileira* (Rio de Janeiro: Casa do Estudante do Brasil, 1947), 475-483.
8. Mundicarmo Ferretti, "Non-African Spiritual Entities in Afro-Brazilian Religion and Afro-Amerindian Syncretism," in *New Trends and Developments in African Religions*, Peter B. Clarke, ed. (Westport, CT: Greenwood Press, 1998), 37-44.
9. John K. Thornton, "On the Trail of Voodoo: African Christianity in Africa and the Americas," *Américas*, XLIV, no. 3 (Jan. 1988): 261-278.
10. Sergio F. Ferretti et al., *Tambor de Crioula, Ritual e Espetáculo* (São Luís: SIOGE, 1979).
11. Ferretti, *Repensando o Sincretismo*, 78.
12. Ferretti, *Repensando o Sincretismo*, 91.
13. Pierre Verger, "Le Culte des voduns d'Abomey aurait-il eté apporté à Saint-Louis de Maranhon par la mère du roi Ghèzo?," in *Les Afro-Américains*, Pierre Verger, ed. (Dakar: IFAN, 1952), 157-160.
14. Eric Hobsbawm and Terence Ranger, *A Invenção das Tradições* (São Paulo: Paz e terra, 1984).
15. Sergio Figueiredo Ferretti, *Querebentan de Zomadon, Etnografia da Casa das Minas* (São Luís: EDUFMA, 1985); and Ferretti, *Repensando o Sincretismo*.
16. See for example, Artur Ramos, *Aculturação Negra no Brasil* (São Paulo: Companhia Editora Nacional, 1942), 44; Roberto Motta, "A Cura no Xangô de Pernambuco: O Rito do Amansi como Terapia," in *Sistemas de Curas: As Alternativas do Povo*, R. Parry Scott, ed. (Recife: Universiade Federal de Pernambuco, Mestrado em Antropologia, 1986), 79-80.

## Chapter 6

## The Presence of Non-African Spirits in an Afro-Brazilian Religion: A Case of Afro-Amerindian Syncretism?

Mundicarmo M. R. Ferretti

### Introduction

One of the best known characteristics of Afro-Brazilian religion is the ritualistic trance, or possession of mediums by African spiritual entities such as *orixás, voduns,* or *inkissis.* In several branches of this religion, however, such as the *Tambor de Mina* and *Umbanda,* the majority of mediums are possessed by entities that are not from Africa, but which instead emerged gradually from within Brazilian ritual centers. A great proportion of these spirit entities are generically referred to as *Caboclos.*

Although opinion is not unanimous concerning the etymology of the word Caboclo, most students of Brazilian religion believe that it derives from the indigenous (*Tupi*) word *kari'boka,* which means descended from the white (man).[1] It is not known if the term already was in use in Brazil in 1739 when a charter issued by the King of Portugal reaffirmed hierarchical differences then existent in the mother country (and reproduced in Brazil), providing specific titles for each social category, or class.[2]

According to Cascudo, until the end of the eighteenth century the term "Caboclo" was used officially as a synonym for Amerindian.[3] It had a pejorative connotation which is why, on April 4, 1755, its usage was limited by decree of the Portuguese king, Dom José: "I hereby prohibit that my subjects married to Indian women or their descendants be addressed by the name caboucolos (sic.), or other similarly injurious."

Nowadays in Brazil Caboclo is used to refer to a mestizo from mixed white and Indian parentage; a copper-colored person with straight hair; or a "hick" with little education and rustic ways. In Afro-Brazilian religions, however, its referent generally is a specific category of spirit beings.

In one Afro-Brazilian religion known as the *Tambor de Mina*, which originated in São Luis, the capital of the state of Maranhão, and is predominant in the north of Brazil, Caboclo, while associated with the Indian, does not necessarily have indigenous roots. Caboclo spirits can be, for example, Turkish or French, or of some other non-Amerindian nationality. Nevertheless, all Caboclos are considered to be Brazilian, in the sense that they came into being (were born as spiritual entities) in Brazil. That is, they first were received by mediums in Brazilian ritual centers.[4]

Caboclos today are time-honored spirits who are venerated in the Afro-Brazilian ritual centers influenced by both *nagô* (Yoruba) and *bantu* (Congo, Angola and Cabinda) traditions. While their numbers have remained relatively small in the Nagô centers, they have grown prolifically in the Bantu ones, to the extent that some of these centers are known as Caboclo Houses, or were the precursors of the *Candomblés-de-Caboclo*—centers in which the most important spirit received is a Caboclo—in which the African identity (Angola, Nagô) is increasingly supplanted by a Brazilian one.[5]

The high incidence of Caboclo spirits in Bantu centers has been interpreted as the result of the earlier arrival of peoples from Angola and Cabinda as slaves in Brazil than *Jejes* (Dahomeans) and Nagôs.[6] It is claimed that having arrived first, they deviated further from their cultural heritage than those who arrived later. Finding the Brazilian territory still largely inhabited by Amerindians, these Bantu slaves are believed to have had extensive contact with native peoples, absorbing many elements from their culture. There has been no attempt, however, to examine to what extent Caboclo spirits should be regarded as indigenous deities or as ancestors. In other words, no one has investigated the degree to which the presence of these entities in ritual centers today can be attributed to the influence of indigenous religions, such as the ancestor cults of many indigenous peoples reported in the literature. The fact that some Caboclos received in Afro-Brazilian religious centers have indigenous names, such as *Tabajara* and *Tupã*, should not be viewed as proof that these centers worship indigenous ancestors and deities. In the cosmology of the Tambor de Mina, for example, the Turkish spirit Tabajara is said to have been born in Damascus and to have received his name in Brazil upon entering the village of *Caboclo Velho* (Old Caboclo—the Indian *Sapequara*).

The preponderance of Caboclo spirits in Bantu centers also is interpreted prejudicially in Afro-Brazilian studies when it is viewed as a consequence of the "religious impoverishment" and the tendency towards syncretism of these centers. Compared to the Nagôs, the Bantus are presented as having a weak mythology, with little consistency,[7] and as a religion largely centered around the cult of the ancestors.[8]

Although the Caboclo is considered to be the Owner of the Land, and it is maintained that Africans were accustomed to adopting the divinities of other peoples whom they ruled politically or in whose territories they settled, the presence of Caboclos in Afro-Brazilian religion has been regarded both by researchers and orthodox practitioners as a corruption and loss of authenticity of the original African religion. For this reason, their presence in traditional (*de nação*) centers—regarded as the preservers of African religious practices—was denied by Roger Bastide until the end of his life,[9] even though much earlier Edison Carneiro affirmed that he had seen dancing and singing for the Caboclos in the traditional centers of Bahia, such as Engenho Velho and Gantois.[10] One of the difficulties with accepting the Caboclo in centers based on African *fundamento* (sacred principles) is that, aside from being Brazilian, these entities are considered to be spirits of the dead (*eguns*) and not deities associated with the forces of nature (like the orixás). In most Afro-Brazilian religious traditions the cult of the orixás is separate from that of the eguns. To justify this separation many *pais-de-santo* (fathers in sainthood, or sect leaders) claim that "Orixás don't like the dead."

The popular notion that the presence of non-African spiritual entities in Afro-Brazilian religion is a result of the early contact between African slaves and/or their descendants with the indigenous peoples (the original "owners of the land" of Brazil), found in the discourses of many researchers and practitioners, is reinforced by the observation of trance rituals involving possession by these entities. In many manifestations of Afro-Brazilian religion, such as Candomblé-de-Caboclo and Umbanda, mediums possessed by Caboclo spirits typically wear articles of Amerindian clothing, actual or inspired (such as loincloths and headdresses of feathers) while many of the spirits have Amerindian names. Certainly it cannot be claimed that, like the orixás, voduns and inkissis, the Caboclos originated in Africa, nor should one discount the impact of the absorption of indigenous culture by the Africans or the valorization of Indians as Brazilian heroes and post-Independence national symbols. Nonetheless, our research on the Tambor de Mina leads us to question the idea that the best way to comprehend the

Caboclo entities is in terms of Afro-Amerindian syncretism (that they are the product of the mixture of African and indigenous cultures). Moreover, our studies lead us to conclude that it is necessary to reconceptualize the Caboclos in a way that is less biased by models of an assumed African purity, which has led many researchers to regard the non-African elements of such religions as a "contamination" by the indigenous culture.

Our intent here is not to present an in-depth examination of the term "syncretism," or an analysis of the influence of indigenous culture on Afro-Brazilian religion.[11] Rather, we propose to examine whether the existence of Caboclo spiritual entities in Afro-Brazilian religion should always be viewed as the product of Afro-Amerindian syncretism—as prima facie evidence of indigenous influence on African-based religions. We will take as an example the case of the Turkish spirits found in the Tambor de Mina, supporting our analysis with ethnographic data, interviews with leading figures and followers of Afro-Brazilian religion in Maranhão, such as Pai Euclides, leader of the Turkish Center since 1972, and the work of other scholars in the field.[12]

In the period of 1984-1992 my husband, Sergio, and I conducted research on Caboclo spirits in the Fanti-Ashanti House, a center opened by the same Pai Euclides in 1958. The center claims to be a preserver of one of the roots of Mina (as the Tambor de Mina is colloquially known), as well as the introducer of Candomblé into Maranhão and perpetuator of indigenous cultural traditions. In that study we endeavored to compensate for the dearth of information on mythology about Caboclos with an analysis of the lyrics of ceremonial incantations. Since the principle Caboclos of that center are Turkish, we concentrated on the family of the King of Turkey. In 1992, we embarked on a second study of non-African spirits in the Tambor de Mina, this time inquiring into other categories and families of spirits from religious centers in the capital, as well as from centers in two other cities in the state where the black population is also substantial: Curupuru (on the coast) and Codó (in the interior).

## The Caboclo in Afro-Brazilian Religions

The non-African spirit entities venerated in Afro-Brazilian ritual centers (*Candomblé, Xangô, Mina, Batuque* and *Umbanda*) have been classified, consistent with the myth of the three formative races of Brazilian society, in the following categories: 1) Caboclos, representatives of the native/indigenous populations or the popular classes of Brazilian society living in rural areas; 2) *Pretos-Velhos*, old blacks, representatives of African slaves; and 3) *Senhores*, white gentlemen or noble folk, representatives of the European colonizers.[13]

The Caboclos appear to be the oldest of these groups, emerging in the northeastern states of Bahia and Maranhão in the Nagô (Yoruban) and Bantu (Angolan, Congo and Cambinda) derived centers. Since the end of the nineteenth century, however, new ritual centers have come into existence in both Maranhão and Bahia which are devoted exclusively to Caboclos. An example is the Turkish Center in São Luis, the capital of Maranhão.

Pretos Velhos are more closely associated with Umbanda and are better known in Rio de Janeiro and São Paulo than in the northeast. In Maranhão they are celebrated on May 13th, the anniversary of the day slavery was abolished in Brazil.

The white or gentlemen spirits, who also are received in Umbanda, are very old entities in the Tambor de Mina religion where they were syncretized with African divinities, as in the case of King Sebastian who is associated with *Xapanã* (*Omolú*).

There is yet another category of spirits that may be considered either as a subtype of Caboclo, or perhaps as an entirely distinct class of Brazilian spirits. They are the *boiadeiros*, or cowboys. These entities, which are extremely popular in the more Africanized Umbanda centers (those influenced by Candomblé), are sometimes referred to as *capangueiros* (pouch carriers) to distinguish them from the *flecheiros* (arrowbearers, of indigenous origin, also known as the feather Caboclos). These particular appellations are derived from the different characterizations presented in the rituals. The mediums embodying the former wear cowhide pouches strapped across their shoulders while the latter carry arrows and/or wear feather loincloths.[14]

In spite of their association with rural activities, the cowboy spirits, as also is the case in Brazil with the descendants of many Indians, are not of indigenous origin. In fact, they are occasionally presented in the lyrics of ritual songs as being from Angola or even Hungary. Their depiction as Angolans certainly reinforces the notion that the appearance of non-African spiritual entities in Afro-Brazilian centers is strongly related to Bantu culture or to the Bantu-based Candomblés. On the other hand, presenting them as coming from Hungary suggests an association with gypsies, nomadic people who most likely originated in Egypt, India and Chaldea and were enslaved or persecuted in Hungary and various other European countries. They were very numerous in Hungary where, in 1761, there was a frustrated attempt to settle them.[15] Tales of gypsies circulated in Brazil as early as the sixteenth century.[16] In São Luis, they appear in the Christmas pageants at ritual centers (represented as coming from Egypt, or in rituals dedicated to female entities (as being from Spain).[17]

Good-night for who's for good-night,
Good-day for who's for the day
Bless me, my father, bless me.
I'm a cowboy, son of Hungary. (Samba Angola, Fanti-Ashanti House)

In the Afro-Brazilian religions in Maranhão the term Caboclo does not apply exclusively to indigenous entities, such as *Cabocla Jurema* (female Amerindian spirit) and Caboclo Velho, nor only to those involved in the raising of cattle, such as the members of the important Maranhão spirit family of *Légua-Boji-Buá*, an entity who commands the Codó forest (an Afro-Brazilian religious celebration held throughout the countryside of Maranhão, which has greatly influenced ritual centers in the capital and elsewhere in Northern Brazil). Nor is it limited to the cowboy spirits received since the 1980s in the Fanti-Ashanti house, when this center introduced Candomblé into the region.

In Maranhão, the category Caboclo also is used to designate Turkish spirits, such as *Cabocla Mariana*, Europeans of noble origin, such as *Caboclo Antonio Luiz* (commonly called *Corre-Beirada,* son of Dom Luis, as the seventeenth-century French king is known) and the entities from the enchanted forest (*mata*), such as the wild *surrupira* spirits who have no connection to cattle-raising and are of debatable Amerindian origin. The name "Surrupira" is reminiscent of *Curupira*, the Tupi mythological figure who protects the forests and frightens hunters. In fact, in some centers the Surrupira spirits are actually called Curupiro, or even Curupira. In centers in São Luis, however, these spirits are regarded as belonging to the *Gangá* forest and are classified (by center leader Mãe Elzita) as *Fulupa*, a term alluding to Africa: the *Felupe* are people from Guiné Bissau.[18] *Gangá* refers to an African "nation" well known in Cuba.[19]

> I am a Caboclo Warrior
> Warrior of Alexandria
> A Warrior is a noble man
> The son of the King of Turkey. (Iemanjá Center, Pai Jorge)

## The Turkish Spirits in the Tambor de Mina: A Case of Afro-Amerindian Syncretism?

In the Tambor de Mina Turkish spirits are numerous and well known. They are believed to belong to the family of the King of Turkey, Ferrabrás of Alexandria, as written about in the *História do Imperador Carlos Magno e os Doze Pares de França* (*Stories of the Emperor Charlemagne and the Twelve Peers of France*).[20] This popular narrative was widely diffused in the Iberian Peninsula and carried to Brazil by the Portuguese where it found creative expression in folkloric dances like the *Cheganças*, which depict battles between the Moors and Christians.[21] In spite of the fact that the Turkish spirits have frequently adopted indigenous names, they are not of indigenous origin.

According to Pai Euclides, the Turkish Center was founded in 1889 by Anastácia Lúcia dos Santos, a black woman of Maranhão from the city of Codó.

Anastácia's principle orixás, or spirit guides, were *Xangô* and *Vó Missā* (Grandma Missa, *Nanā*). She was initiated into the Mina religion by an African (or the descendant of an African) known as Manoel Teus Santos, who headed a center in São Luis. Although she worshipped the West African orixás, Anastácia founded her center in the name of the Caboclo entity, King of Turkey, who took command of a large family of Caboclo spirits. Nevertheless, the Turkish Center became known as being of the (African) *Taipa* (tapa?) nation with vodum spirit *Averequete* serving as spiritual godfather to the Turks.

Prior to the opening of the Turkish Center, Turks already were well known spirits in Maranhão centers. Historically, they were recognizable figures from the well known *História do Imperador Carlos Magno e os Doze Pares de França* popularized in folkloric traditions like the Cheganças.[22] In 1969, we discovered a copy of this literary work at the Turkish Center. It had been presented to Dona Zeca, the founder's daughter, by her godmother in 1934. According to Dona Zeca, her godmother, who also organized Cheganças, used to receive the spirit of Dom João, the Portuguese King believed by followers of the Mina religion to have been a cousin of the Turkish King. The story of the Turks told in Mina centers is a contemporary version of that narrative.[23]

According to Mina mythology, after a battle against the Christians, the King of Turkey fled to Brazil aboard a ship belonging to his cousin Dom João. When they arrived, the King, wishing to avoid his cousin, entered into a village led by Caboclo Velho, the Indian *Sapequara* (the first Caboclo to shout in the Mina centers) where he was well received and remained. There the King's family mixed with their host's (each one adopted the children of the other) and thereafter the King would "arrive" (i.e., incarnate) in Mina rituals together with his entourage as a Caboclo, not as a nobleman. For this reason, in spite of being nobles with no indigenous origin, the Turks are received in Mina as Caboclos.[24]

While it is true that legends of battles between Moors and Christians were re-enacted by Amerindians in the catechisms of Jesuit priests and it is probable that descendants of Amerindians opened ritual centers in São Luis, we do not believe that this is sufficient to explain the origin of Turkish spirits in Maranhão. The Turkish King and his family of spirits spread into the Mina religion from a center considered to be of the (African) *Taipa* Nation. This center, as mentioned earlier, was founded at the turn of the century by a black woman, who was initiated into Afro-Brazilian religion by an African or the descendant of an African and was linked, through ties of ritual kinship, to the vodum deity, Averequete.

The Turks of the Tambor de Mina are Caboclo spirits, but they are not acculturated (i.e., "civilized"), or descendants of Indians, much less indigenous ancestors or mythological beings, as Caboclos were all believed to be.[25] The Turkish Center was not founded by a healer or *pajé* (leader of an Afro-Amerindian cult without the sacred principles contained in Afro-Brazilian religions). It was established by a descendant of an African, initiated in Afro-Brazilian religion who, as a personal friend of the renowned center leader, Mãe Andreza, came to live in the esteemed Dahomean-derived center, Casa das Minas-Jeje.

The widely held notion of an indigenous origin for the non-African (Caboclo) spirit entities, a view prevalent both in the literature and in the discourses of Afro-Brazilian religious leaders, has been reinforced by the hasty interpretation of rituals involving spirits with names and, occasionally, vestments of Amerindian type. A more thorough examination of the characteristics of these Caboclo entities, including an analysis of the lyrics of ceremonial incantations sung by them or for them, as well as a careful reading of the accounts of myths collected in the ritual centers may lead the researcher to consider the non-African spirits in a quite different light.

In the Mina religion of Maranhão, the names of the spiritual entities and their use of indigenous clothing during rituals is not sufficient to confirm their Amerindian origin, although these features attest to the valorization of the Indian in the Tambor de Mina and suggest an association between indigenous cultures and this particular Afro-Brazilian religion. Accordingly, an explanation for the adoption of indigenous names by the Turkish spirits in Tambor de Mina should not be sought either in their ethnic origin or through possible borrowing from indigenous peoples. Rather, it must be located in the historical and social context in which these spirits emerged as religious entities within the Tambor de Mina. The use of indigenous names by several of the King of Turkey's offspring (his consanguineal children) may be interpreted alternatively as: 1) a strategy utilized by the descendants of African slaves to divert the attention of the dominant Roman Catholics away from the pagan origin of the Turks, an origin evidently responsible for their association in Brazilian folklore with the devil (especially the deity Ferrabrás); or 2) a reflection of the necessity to affirm their Brazilian identity, as spirit beings who first appeared in Brazil, which would facilitate acceptance of the opening of yet another ritual center in São Luis (the Turkish Center), since even today establishing a new center is prohibited by the Casa das Minas and discouraged by the Casa de Nagô, Maranhão's oldest and most venerated ritual centers.[26]

The adoption by the Turks of names of Brazilian-Indians (many of whom were pagans like themselves) must certainly be related to the idealization of the native population which occurred after Brazil's independence from Portugal in 1822.[27] It may also be explained when we remember that the Turkish Center was opened in 1890, one year after the abolition of slavery in Brazil, when the former slaves were likely to have been more motivated to affirm their identity as Brazilians than as Africans. The Brazilian identity of the family of the King of Turkey also is evident in the colors chosen to symbolize them in the Tambor de Mina: red, which long ago represented the Turks in Moorish dances, is related to their warlike character, and also is associated with the American Indian ("redskins"), and green and yellow, colors that have symbolized Brazil since it ceased to be a Portuguese colony.

The association of the Turks with the Brazilian nation and the Brazilian Indian also is evident in the discourse of Pai Euclides when he recounts the myth of *Tabajara*, hero of the war against Paraguay (1865-1870) in which many blacks participated in the hope of gaining their freedom. Tabajara, a Turk, was rescued by an Indian woman, *Bartira*, who had found him in a battlefield and nursed his wounds. He married her and became the leader of many Amerindian villages, contributing to their "pacification" and "civilization."[28]

By their portrayal in Mina as spirit beings of the (African) Taipa Nation associated with the (Amerindian) Caboclo Velho, the Turkish spirits were linked to both Africa and Brazil. Diverting attention away from their pagan origins, the Turkish Center was able to secure a place in the Afro-Maranhão religious milieu dominated by the Casa das Minas-Jeje (consecrated to the Dahomean vodum Zomadonu) and the Casa de Nagô (consecrated to the Yoruban orixá Xangô). Since the Turks could not be Owners of the House, or even Owners of the Land (natives of Brazil) in those centers, which were established by Africans, they could only proliferate in the Mina religion after the establishment of a center of their own.

In the Tambor de Mina, other Caboclo spirits, such as the Surrupiras do Gangá, exist who may be more closely related to the indigenous culture than the Turks. They are less accepted than the Turks, however, in the older, more traditional centers of the capital, but equally well known in Mina centers. The name Surrupira do Gangá bespeaks its relation to Africa (Gangá) as well as to the indigenous culture. This spirit is, or is related to, Curupira of Amerindian folklore, portrayed as a small dark-skinned inhabitant of the forest, of non-human origin, whose feet are turned backwards and who is responsible for protecting the wilderness and the hunt—an entity widely feared by forest-dwelling peoples of Brazil.[29] The Surrupira of the Tambor de Mina, like the Curupira of Brazilian folklore, exhibits many characteristics of the indigenous forest entity of the same name. He is similarly dreaded by the Indians, described in the sixteenth century letters of Father José de Anchieta as being dangerous, feared and responsible for unexplained rumors, sudden frights, deaths, disappearances and hunters losing their way in the forest.[30]

## Conclusion

The case of the Turkish entities in the Tambor de Mina illustrates the difficulty with making gross generalizations regarding Afro-Brazilian religions and the risks of interpreting the existence of all Caboclo entities in terms of Afro-Amerindian syncretism. Taking into account the data presented here, to consider these entities as indigenous mythological beings or ancestors would be highly problematic. The primary source of the mythology of the Turks is to be found in the *gestes* of Charlemagne and not in Amerindian myths, as is the case of Curupira, who is clearly related to the Surrupira of the Tambor de Mina. Nor can the Turks be characterized as spirits introduced into the Tambor de Mina by a pajé (Amerindian healer), since the founder of the Turkish Center, besides being Afro-Brazilian, was initiated in a house of African sacred principles (*Taipa*).

However, it is vital to recall that the myth of the Turks in Mina is not a mere reproduction of the *História do Imperador Carlos Magno e os Doze Pares de França*, which continues to be narrated via popular story booklets sold in São Luis, in marketplaces elsewhere in the northeast and in folkloric representations (such as the Cheganças). In the Tambor de Mina of Maranhão, Admiral Balão, Ferrabrás of Alexandria and Princess Floripes are not mere literary figures or folkloric characters; they are spirit beings who entered the Indian village of Sapequara and fought in the Paraguayan war. (Such episodes are alien to the literary text, having been appended in Brazil, most likely in the Turkish Center.) In Mina this narrative also may be augmented by events that occur while mediums engaged in ritual practices are possessed by their spirits. The relationship between the Turks and the vodum deity, *Averequete*, considered in the Turkish Center to be their godfather, is one instance.

The presence of indigenous culture is most salient in the healing or Pajelança ceremonies held in various centers in São Luis. Even there, however, the presence of Turkish spirits should not be considered an example of Afro-Amerindian syncretism unless the ritual exhibited elements drawn from Tambor de Mina as well. Only then could it be viewed as a mixture of Mina and Pajelança and, hence, Afro-Amerindian syncretism.

## Notes

Translated from the Portuguese by Naomi Katz and Daniel Halperin.

1. Aurélio Buarque de Holanda Ferreira, *Novo Dicionário da Lingua Portuguesa* (Rio de Janeiro: Nova Fronteira, 1975).

2. Roberto da Matta, *Relativizando: Uma Introdução à Antropologia* (Petrópolis: Editora Vozes, 1981), 65.

3. Luis da Câmara Cascudo, *Dicionário do Folclore Brasileiro* (Rio de Janeiro: INL/MEC, 1962), 156.

4. Mundicarmo Ferretti, *Desceu na guma: o caboclo do Tambor de Mina no processo de mudança de um terreiro de São Luis—a Casa Fanti-Ashanti* (São Luis: SIOGE, 1993).

5. Ruth Landes, *A cidade das mulheres* (Rio de Janeiro: Ed. Civilizações Brasileiras, 1967 [Original: *The City of Women* (New York: Macmillan, 1947)].

6. Yêda Pessoa de Castro, "Africa descoberta: uma história recontada," *Revista de Antropologia*, 23 (1980): 138.

7. Edison Carneiro, *Negros Bantus* (Rio de Janeiro: Civilizações Brasileiras, 1937), 28.

8. Landes, *A cidade*, 289.

9. Roger Bastide, "La rencontre des dieux africains et des esprits indiens," in Roger Bastide: *Ultima Scripta*, H. Desroche, ed. (Paris: Arquives de Sciences Sociales des Religions, 1974), 19-28. Published also in Roger Bastide, *Le sacré sauvage* (Paris: Payot, 1957), 186-200.

10. Edson Carneiro, *Candomblés da Bahia* (Rio de Janeiro: Ed. de Ouro, 1969), 62. [Original 1948. Museu do Estado da Bahia.]

11. This question is addressed in Mundicarmo Ferretti, "A Representação do Indio em Terreiros de São Luis, Ma.," *Pesquisa em Foco* 5, no. 5 (Jan./June1997): 47-57.

12. Although not as well known in the literature as Umbanda and Candomblé, Tambor de Mina is dealt with extensively in: Manoel Nunes Pereira, *A Casa das Minas: contribução ao estudo das sobrevivências do culto dos voduns, do panteão daomeano, no estado do Maranhão-Brasil*, 2nd ed. (Petrópolis, RJ: Editora Vozes, 1979); Octávio da Costa Eduardo, *The Negro in Northern Brazil: A Study in Acculturation* (New York: J.J. Augustin Publisher, 1948); Seth and Ruth Leacock, *Spirits of the Deep: a Study of an Afro-Brazilian Cult* (New York: Anchor, 1975); Maria Amália Pereira Barreto, *Os Voduns do Maranhão* (São Luis: Fundação Cultural do Maranhão, 1977); Sergio Ferretti, *Querebentan de Zomadonu: Etnografia da Casa das Minas* (São Luis: UFMA, 1985); Sergio Ferretti, *Repensando o Sincretismo* (São Paulo: EDUSP; São Luis: FAPEMA, 1995); Mundicarmo Ferretti, *Desceu na guma*; and others.

13. See da Matta, *Relativizando*, 59, 63.

14. Raul Giovanni Lody, *Samba de Caboclo* (Rio de Janeiro: FUNARTE/INF Caderno de Folclore No.17, 1977).

15. Maria de Lourdes B. Sant'Ana, "Os Ciganos: aspectos da organização social de um grupo cigano em Campinas," *Revista de Antropologia* 4 (1983): 30.

16. Sant'Ana, "Os Ciganos," 33.

17. Gypsy women who tell fortunes with playing cards or read palms in Brazilian city streets are represented in Afro-Brazilian religions. The gypsies, although better known in Umbanda, are found in Maranhão centers, in healing rituals (Amerindian Pajelança practices) such as Baião, as well as in Tambor de Mina. See Mundicarmo Ferretti, *Tambor de Mina, Cura e Baião na Casa Fanti-Ashanti* (MA). LP accompanied by twelve-page enclosure (São Luis: SECMA, 1991). In the Turkish Center they were led by Princess Floripes, sister of the King of Turkey, Ferrabrás of Alexandria, from the well-known *História do Imperador Carlos Magno e os Doze Pares de França* (*Stories of the Emperor Charlemagne and the Twelve Peers of Franca*) [Translated from the Spanish *Bernard del Carpio que Venceu em Batalha aos Doze Pares de França* by Jerônimo Moreira de Carvalho, after Flaviense, Alexandre Gomes] (Rio de Janeiro: Livraria Império, n.d.).

18. Arthur Augusto da Silva, *Direitos civis e penal dos mandingas e dos felupes da Guiné Bissau*, 4th ed. (Bissau: Ed. Dedild, 1983).

19. Jesus Guanche, *Processos Etnoculturales en Cuba* (Habana: Editorial Letras Cubanas, 1983).

20. See Mundicarmo Ferretti, "Rei da Turquia, o Ferrabrás de Alexandria? A Importância de um Livro na Mitologia do Tambor de Mina," in *Meu Sinal Esta no Teu Corpo*, Carlos Eugenio Marcondes de Moura, ed. (São Paulo: EDICON/EDUSP, 1989), 202-218; "Repensando o Turco no Tambor de Mina," *Afro-Asia* 15 (1992): 56-70; and *Desceu na guma*, 188-202.

21. Cascudo, *Dicionário*, 184-185.

22. We first learned of *Charlemagne and the Twelve Peers of France* in the Fanti-Ashanti House. Pai Euclides, in trance and possessed by a Caboclo spirit, told us, "I'm not here to tell you my story. I don't want to, nor can I . . . . If you want to know the story of the Turks, see the *Stories of Charlemagne and the Twelve Peers of France*." We consulted history books in vain, until, one day, while reading the text of a folklorist, we happened upon the Chegança characters of Ferrabrás, Floripes and her father, Admiral Balão, all of whom we had heard about in the ritual center. Afterwards, we found the book cited by Beatriz Góis Dantas in *Chegança* (Rio de Janeiro: FUNARTE/INF Cadernos de Folclore No. 14, 1976). We are indebted to her for providing us with a photocopy of it. This enabled us to compare the literary narrative with that presented orally at the center (see Mundicarmo Ferretti, "Repensando o turco," 56-70). We could only confirm, however, the existence of the book in the Turkish Center in 1969. Our research aroused great interest among the more educated members of the Mina centers. In November of 1996, while viewing an exhibition of early photographs in the Fanti-Ashanti House, we discovered that the story of the Turks had been re-constructed as a result of our work, due, evidently, to the reading of the book. The copy at the center disappeared before the death of Dona Zeca.

23. This book so impressed the Brazilian population that many parents named their children after several of the characters, such as Roldão (a Christian caballero) and Floripes (a Turkish princess who converted to Christianity, like her brother, Ferrabrás of Alexandria). Roldão Lima, late technician for the State's Secretary of Culture, explained to us the origin of his name. In the coastal city of Turiaçu (Maranhão) where he was born, the names of commercial establishments also were taken from the book. Mr. Lima further informed us that he knew a man there who would stand beneath a street lamp each day and read passages from the book to passersby. Apparently, one of his faithful listeners learned several passages by heart.

24. Center leader Pai Jorge, initiated into Mina, like Pai Euclides, in the no-longer existent Egyptian Center, recounts that the Turks, under the command of Luiz IX, crossed the Atlantic Ocean to Brazil after the last Christian crusade against the Moors. Dom Luiz fled to the Nagô House and the King of Turkey fled to the House of Manoel Teus Santos. Afterwards, he went with the Turks to the Turkish Center where some, but not all, of them converted to Christianity.

25. Bastide, "La rencontre," 19-28.

26. According to Pai Euclides, the Turks were received in the Casa de Nagô as spirit entities belonging to the Taipa nation. They were permitted to manifest as did the African entities and shout, spin around in circles, be happy and noisy and drink alcoholic beverages (outside the building).

27. Bastide, "La rencontre," 25, adds that this idealization of the Indian also occurred in other countries in Latin America after independence.

28. This is similar to legends of personages from colonial Brazil, such as João Ramalho, who married a Brazilian-Indian woman of the same name (Bartira), and like Diogo Alvares, the renowned Caramuru, became the leader of many Native-Brazilian villages of "pacified Indians." See Mundicarmo Ferretti, *Desceu na Guma*, 415.

29. Cascudo, *Dicionário*, 262.

30. Serafim Leite S.I., *Cartas dos primeiros jesuitas do Brasil-III: 1558-1563* (São Paulo: Comissão do IV Centenário, 1954).

## Chapter 7

# The Reinterpretation of Africa: Convergence and Syncretism in Brazilian Candomblé

Sidney M. Greenfield

### Introduction

*Minha seita nagô é pura* (My nagô house is pure).

In an effort to have their rituals and practices recognized as an official religion, with a status on par with that of the Catholic Church, leaders of Brazil's Candomblés, breaking with conventional understanding of their history, are disavowing syncretism. They no longer accept their religion as a mixture of African and Roman Catholic beliefs and behaviors. Aided by anthropologists and other sympathetic intellectuals, they instead maintain that Candomblé is purely African, a direct and authentic continuation of traditional Nagô, or Yoruba,[1] practices.[2]

One of the more extreme examples of this attempt at re-Africanization was that by Mãe Aninha, the late spiritual leader of the famous *terreiro* (religious center), *Ilé Axé Apô Afonjá* (the Beneficent Society of St. George), who "stressed that her Nagô sect, or house, was pure,"[3] that it was uninfluenced by either Christianity or other non-African religions. Her successor, Mãe Stella Azevedo, explained that in the nineteenth century "freed slaves, through a desire to 'whiten' themselves, adopted practices that syncretized Catholicism and 'traces of Africanisms.' . . . But, in the present times of total liberation, it is worth remembering that these maneuvers ought to be abandoned."[4]

Mãe Stella proposed the elimination of Roman Catholic practices such as attending mass at the conclusion of a ritual cycle and the use of images of the saints syncretized with the *orixás*.[5] Then, she maintained, Candomblés again will be direct and authentic continuations of the rituals and practices of Yoruba worship.

What is meant by religious purity and authenticity, as we have seen in chapter 1, depends on the theory and its model of reality assumed by the person making the claim.[6] Mães Aninha and Stella, in making their case, use a model first proposed by anthropologists and other students of religion. In the following pages I examine that model. Even if one accepts it, which I do not, I argue that recent evidence indicates that Brazilian Candomblé still cannot be accepted as an uninterrupted, authentic continuation of pure Yoruba forms. I contend instead that there was a convergence of significant aspects of Yoruba beliefs and practices and the Roman Catholicism of the Luso-Brazilians and that as a result the practitioners of each found the religion of the other to be not only meaningful, but also made the adoption and/or incorporation of some of the salient practices of the other acceptable.

## Some Theories and Their Models

Beatriz Dantas reports that the purity and authenticity of Brazilian Candomblé finds support in the writings of most researchers of Afro-Brazilian religion.[7] This search for Africanisms within the cultures of contemporary peoples of color has been a goal of scholars beginning with Nina Rodrigues in the nineteenth century and continuing through the studies of Artur Ramos, Melville Herskovits and Roger Bastide to the present day.[8] The objective of the study of African survivals was to demonstrate the persistence of African cultural practices by the peoples of African descent in the New World. Bastide and Elbein dos Santos, Dantas adds, further assert that "true African thought" is to be found in Brazilian Candomblé.[9]

Based on what often were superficial similarities in the present between aspects of culture observed both in West Africa and in the Americas, at times taken out of context, a typology of terreiros was established for New World societies. Those centers that evidenced the greatest number of similarities were referred to as having the most Africanisms. They were defined as pure in contrast with those with fewer African traits that were interpreted as having been influenced by Christianity and other religions.[10] In the intervening years attention has focused on the small number of centers classified as pure or authentic. The much larger number of mixed practices were of little interest to scholars who subscribed to this theoretical framework. The pure terreiros, most of which were located in the northeast, were derived from and traceable to West Africa, specifically to the Yoruba-speaking region of Nigeria. When in the second half of the twentieth century the Candomblés were reproduced in other parts of Brazil, the leaders of the houses in Salvador and Recife further claimed that their beliefs, rituals, initiation ceremonies and other practices not only were pure, but were the only authentic representations of this African tradition in the country, if not the world.[11] Acceptance of this claim resulted in what Dantas and others[12] refer to as the Yoruba-centricity of most of the literature on Afro-Brazilian religion.

I shall argue here that, even though the Yoruba (or Nagô) houses were in fact organized by peoples from Yorubaland, they incorporated only a part of Yoruba religious culture, a part that was secondary in the worship of the òrìsà (the Yoruba deities—*orixás* in Portuguese), but which corresponded in meaning and practice to the beliefs and behaviors of the Luso-Brazilians to which it was adapted. Therefore, the Candomblés, *Xangôs, Batuques*, etc. of Brazil were not complete representations of Yoruba religion. They are better understood as a selection from Yoruba culture reinterpreted in terms of a parallelism or convergence between Yoruba and Brazilian Catholic assumptions about the universe and specifically the relationship between humanity and the supernatural as constrained by the social and political conditions that prevailed in Brazil at the time. The convergence between the role of the Yoruba òrìsà and the Catholic saints as intermediaries between humans and an all-powerful supreme being, I contend, made it possible for the founders of the Candomblés to seemingly adopt and practice Brazilian religious culture while still following their own beliefs and traditions.

## Yoruba Origins of Bahian Candomblé Nagô

While African religious features no doubt had been kept alive by the slaves for several centuries, mostly on the sugar plantations of the northeast, it was in the late eighteenth or early nineteenth centuries that the organization and establishment of religious groups occurred. This was a time when the city of Salvador was beginning to urbanize, but long before the end of the slave trade and more than half a century before the slaves in Brazil were emancipated.[13] At the time the vast majority of the Africans had come from the Mina coast[14] and spoke mostly Nagô, the French term for what in English is the language of the people who would come to be known as the Yoruba.[15]

Prior to the late eighteenth century few Yoruba had been brought to Brazil as slaves. Attacks by their neighbors against the kingdom of Old Oyo, which for some time had been the predominant Yoruba military and political power, resulted in the capture and eventual sale as slaves of people who previously had been under Oyo's protection.[16]

Continuous trade between Bahia and the Mina coast lasted until after emancipation. This made it possible for the urban Yoruba, unlike earlier generations of slaves on the plantations, to maintain contacts with the land of their birth.[17]

According to Elbein dos Santos, they brought with them an association, called the *egbé*, in which devotion to the òrìsà, their deities, was practiced.[18] The gatherings of the egbé in Brazil were held on unused pieces of land (*roças*) that were called terreiros, a word that has come to mean the place where traditional African religion is practiced. Each terreiro developed into an autonomous community of worshippers of the òrìsà, under the direction of an *Iyálôrìsà*, literally a mother possessed by the òrìsà, in a hierarchically administered community.[19]

Two women who had been priestesses of the *Shangô* cult before their capture and forced relocation to Brazil established what many believe to have been the first Candomblé.[20] Elsewhere Bastide writes, confirmed and elaborated on by Omari, that in about 1830 a woman named *Iyá Nassô*, born to a freed slave mother who returned to Africa, went to Bahia (as a free woman) and founded a Candomblé that was called the *Ilê Ayé Nassô* (the house of mother Nassô) which later came to be known as the *Casa Branca* (White House).[21] "Quarrels over succession resulted in the formation of two additional houses, *Ganitois* in Engenho Velho and *Axé Apô Afonjá*."[22] Most of what are called the Nagô houses—to emphasize their Yoruba roots—in Salvador can trace their origins to one of these three nineteenth-century Candomblé centers.[23] Moreover, the vast majority of the twentieth-century Candomblé houses established in São Paulo, Rio de Janeiro and elsewhere can also be traced—by means of who initiated their ritual leader—to the Nagô houses founded in Bahia over a century and a half previously.[24]

## Religion and Society in Yorubaland

In his provocative and insightful *Black Critics and Kings*, Andrew Apter places Yoruba religion in its larger sociopolitical context.[25] In the centuries before their absorption into the British colonial orbit, the Yoruba had no sense of themselves as a people, other than as being different from their neighbors, though among themselves they spoke a common language and shared other culture features including a myth as to their collective origin. Sociologically they were organized into *ilus*, a term inadequately glossed as towns, that were inhabited by a mostly agricultural population who tilled the land surrounding the urban center.[26] The farmland and uncultivated bush were owned and worked by the several lineages residing in the separate sectors of the urban center. An ilu with its hinterland formed a self-subsistent community.

Each ilu was ruled by an *oba*, a king, together with his *iwarefa* council of civil chiefs. Over the years the more powerful ilus came to dominate the weaker ones creating complex kingdoms with what might be thought of as metropolitan capitals and their subordinate ilu communities. Former kings of vanquished towns dropped in status from oba to baale, denoting their subjection to a metropolitan capital and its oba.[27] Although not unified politically, Yorubaland was organized in a series of kingdoms that vied with each other for supremacy.

Internally, each urban center of an ilu was subdivided into a number of sectors, called quarters, that were dominated by specific lineages and functioned as ritual communities.[28] Within each sector the freeborn men were organized by age into corporate sections which performed military, civic and religious duties.[29] Apter makes explicit the relationship between religion and the organization of the Yoruba people into a series of competing towns and kingdoms. He begins with a discussion of myth—used as the basis for legitimacy by the competing kingdoms—by summarizing the two contending approaches to its understanding: functionalism and historicism.

> The functionalist extreme defines myth as a charter of political and ceremonial relations and interprets variant traditions as rival political claims. Myth is by this definition a false reflection of the past because it is continually revised to fit the present. The historicist extreme regards myth as testimony of the past in oral societies, incorporating history into a narrative which resists revision and remains historically valid through fixed chains of oral transmission. Variant traditions, according to this view, are dismissed as aberrations of more authentic texts.[30]

Historicism, Apter tells us citing Beier,[31] is predominant, as it is in Afro-Brazilian studies. To show "how Yoruba ritual and cosmology transform dominant discourses and the authority structures they uphold,"[32] he develops what he calls a "hermeneutical approach to transcend the "function" vs. "meaning" antimony."[33] By this he means "examining how indigenous forms of knowledge and power constitute the critical conditions of social reproduction and change."[34] His thesis is that "the Yoruba *ritual system* illuminates the politics and history of Yoruba myths and their variant traditions."[35] This leads him to interpret Yoruba ritual as a *critical practice*[36] that is based on the hermeneutics of power. His persuasive argument challenges not only the conventional interpretation of religion and politics in Yoruba studies, but also the understanding of the relationship between Yoruba religion and Brazilian Candomblé.

Given the importance of the origin myth, of which there are many variants, each of which contests the hegemony of rival readings and claims, Apter summarizes the most general form.

> ... at the beginning, Olodumare, the Yoruba High God, had a son, Oduduwa, who climbed down a chain from heaven (*orun*, or sky) to an uninhabited world. Since the world was covered with water, Oduduwa placed a handful of earth on it and a rooster on top of the earth. As the rooster began to scratch the earth about, land spread out over the water. According to this myth, Ile-Ife is the sacred locus of Oduduwa's original descent, where he became the first Yoruba king and fathered future generations of Yoruba kings through sixteen sons.[37]

Apter then argues that the myth is preserved through ritual. He offers as the "most clearly visible" example royal installation ceremonies. These ceremonies

> not only validate the right of a king (*oba*) to a beaded crown by tracing his descent back to Ife, but also emphasize the unique identity and corporate unity of his kingdom. This is accomplished partly by the reenactment of its founding, in which coveted details acquire the authority of political charters.[38]

"Yoruba *orisa* worship," he continues, then

> represents, in its sacred and symbolic idioms, not just the unity of the kingdom but also the diversity of its parts; its cult organization and performance cycle articulate with the structure of Yoruba government ... the king "owns" an orisa for the town (*ilu*) as a whole, chiefs for their quarters (*adugbo*), and subchiefs (often elders) for their lineages (*idile*) clustered within (but sometimes crosscutting) quarters. In Old Oyo, for example, the Shango cult was "owned" by the *Alaafin* and associated with his sacred status; the central shrine within the royal quarter had secondary associations in nonroyal quarters, while cults of chiefs included Sopono and Jabata in Laguna quarter, Oranuan in Agbakin, Oya in Agunpopo.[39]

> The unity of these complex kingdoms was thus subject to a double tension. Within the capital, a powerful chief could break away with his quarter (and clients from other quarters) to establish his own kingdom; ... Beyond the capital, subordinate towns could grow powerful enough to assert their independence. These jurisdictions were contested in idioms of dynastic descent. If the *baale* of a subordinate town traced his descent from Oduduwa and migration from Ife, he could challenge the oba's claim to a beaded crown and legitimize political competition for independent or dominant status.[40]

After presenting several examples to illustrate the point, Apter turns to the cults themselves, each of which is assumed to have originated in Ife and to exist in perpetuity. Following M. G. Smith, he sees them as hierarchically organized corporations whose recruited and initiated members each served a dominant òrìsà.[41] Every Yoruba community contained a number of cults, each located in a different quarter of the *Ilu* and aligned with the group that dominated it. The groups were in competition with each other for political control of the sector and for larger political jurisdictions. As the fortunes of the various groups changed, with new alliances, victories and defeats, each cult group, Apter argues, reinterpreted the basic myth to legitimize its supporters to the detriment of their enemies.[42]

Apter's hermeneutics of power provides a convincing way of understanding what appear to be a variety of conflicting interpretations of the meaning of myth and ritual in Yoruba culture in terms of changes in relations of power. The conclusion to be reached is that the òrìsà cults have been, at least since the seventeenth century, aligned with political factions engaged in competition for hegemony and domination. This interpretation of Yoruba history, I submit, enables us to comprehend the transference of Yoruba culture to Brazil in a new way.

## Another View of the Transfer of Yoruba Religion to Brazil

Most scholars to examine African culture history with an eye to ascertaining their influence on New World cultural patterns have taken specific rights and behaviors out of their social and political contexts when looking for correspondences across the Atlantic. Apter is the first to examine religion and ritual in their larger sociopolitical matrix.

When the Candomblés were first established in Bahia and elsewhere in northeastern Brazil, their founders encountered no ilus of Yorubas (or anyone else), no obas and no councils of chiefs. There were no quarters or sectors of towns with their baales and no corporations organized by age performing military, civil and religious duties. In brief, the competing political groupings the òrìsà cults served in Africa and to which they were aligned were not present. Instead, the founders of the Candomblés encountered a Luso-Brazilian society with a very different social and political structure that rested on an extremely new set of meanings. Moreover, the Yorubas and other Africans in Brazil were mostly slaves whose daily actions, although less constrained than those of their counterparts on the plantations, were still restricted to a point at which considerable limitations were placed on their freedom of movement and other behaviors. The Luso-Brazilians held power. There was no way that the Africans could organize themselves into lineages and sectors of towns to engage in the political and other intrigues that were the context in which the òrìsà cults functioned in Yorubaland. Put simply, if Apter is right, and I find his argument very convincing, it would have been virtually impossible for the newly reconstituted Yoruba cults in Brazil to have been pure and authentic continuations of what had existed in West Africa. At best, the traditions of Africa would have had to have been reconceptualized, reinterpreted, reformulated, reconstituted and reorganized in new ways so as even to be able to survive in this setting.

## The Convergence of Yoruba and Brazilian Catholic Worldviews

Slaves in Catholic Brazil, including the Yoruba, were baptized and exposed in varying degrees to the catechism and teachings of the Church. Moreover, most also observed and often experienced first hand the religious practices of their masters.

Brazilian Catholicism, as Bastide observed, is turned more towards the saints and the Virgin than to God.[43] Its students contrast this veneration of the saints, which they refer to as popular Catholicism, with the rites and rituals of the official church.[44] The religion of the Luso-Brazilians to which the slaves were exposed was this popular, as opposed to official, Catholicism.

No clear separation is made, as it is in post-Reformation, post-Counter Reformation and post-Enlightenment thinking, between the world of living worshippers and the world of the saints and the dead.[45] Instead, there is a continuum between two opposite ends of a single hierarchically ordered universe.

God, the creator, who controls the fate and destiny of all life is at the top, in heaven. Living humans are on earth at the bottom. In between are the saints who, although now with God, were once humans on earth. For this reason they are believed to care about and be sympathetic to the living.

Human suffering is thought to be the result of God's punishment inflicted for disobedience to His will.[46] The supreme being, however, also can remove the punishment, bring healing and provide for the well-being of the living. Because He is distant and aloof, and busy perfecting His universe, God is assumed to be too preoccupied with other matters to attend to petitions from lowly humans. This is the role of the saints.

In traditional Catholic theology the saints are intercessors who mediate between man and God on behalf of the humans. Brazilian popular Catholicism focuses on this relationship of intermediacy in which the saints are the protectors of humans who intercede with God on their behalf.[47]

Popular Catholicism, as Thales de Azevedo summarizes it,

> consists of a propitiatory and supplicatory ritualism with therapeutic ends, in which the individual and collective acts . . . are expected to have their own efficacy in pleasing the "saints," inclining them to reply favorably to the appeals of

their devotees in cases of difficulty and crises. These replies would depend very little on the merits of the supplicants or the action of Grace.[48]

The saints are assumed to be regularly beseeched with requests for their help; but they are few in number in comparison with the petitioners and the amount of requests made to them. They cannot attend to all appeals. How are they to choose the ones on which to take action?

DeKadt provides the answer:

> When the occasion warrants it, man assures himself of their . . . benevolence by an appropriate gift or promise. He pursues his immediate interests by endless bargaining with his celestial protector.[49]

The variant of Christianity to which the African slaves in Brazil were exposed was a highly individualistic and personal religion that focused on a negotiated relationship of exchange between a living human being and a supernatural protector who was an intermediary capable of interceding on behalf of a petitioner with an all-powerful supreme being. Moreover, the requests made by the living were not for salvation in another world after life on earth, but for help with problems in this life, such as finances, health or family problems.

## Aspects of Yoruba Beliefs Congruent with Brazilian Folk Catholicism

The Yoruba creation myth mentioned above goes on to tell that after an hospitable place on earth was made, it was peopled "with a new race of beings,"[50] each one of which Olodumare shapes and to which He gives their fate, or destiny, and individual characteristics.

Like the Catholic God, Olodumare "is often regarded as austere, remote, and difficult to approach. While He is prayed to, no shrines are erected in His honor, no rituals are directed toward Him, and no sacrifices are made to placate Him."[51] He is never approached directly; instead, He created a number of lesser deities to assist Him in running the world and managing His human creations who communicate with Him through them. These lesser deities include the òrìsà who are assigned to specific individuals as their guardian and protector.

The living, however, are believed to forget the fate Olodumare has given them. They recover it by means of divination through Ifá and Esu, two òrìsà known as mediators.[52]

Yoruba also communicate with the supernatural in another way. Through the practice of spirit possession the òrìsà (and occasionally deceased ancestors) come to earth temporarily and occupy the bodies of specially trained individuals through whom they communicate and interact with the living. In Yorubaland those who incorporated òrìsà were priests and priestesses at the shrines that served the oba of a kingdom or a baale of a section, participating in the struggle for hegemony.

Yoruba cosmology then, like the Catholicism practiced in Brazil, included the belief in a remote and powerful creator approached only indirectly through lesser deities. "The divinities," as Awolalu summarizes it, "act as intermediaries between man and the Supreme Being."[53] His words are echoed for the practitioners of Candomblé by Magalhães when he writes that they "are intermediaries between the supreme god Olorum and humans."[54]

This convergence in worldview, I believe, made possible the mixing or syncretism in Candomblé between the òrìsà and the Catholic saints with what often was a one-to-one correspondence between specific saints and one of the Yoruba supernaturals.[55] The same icons, originally statues of the saints, were used to represent both sets of supernatural intermediaries. Whether the former slaves and their descendants kept them separate, relating each to its own pantheon and cosmological scheme, or merged them would be something that only could be determined empirically for each participant at a given time and place.

Mediation in Yoruba culture occurred in many contexts and involved many agents and implicated many sources of power.[56] While all paralleled the relationship between the followers of folk Catholicism and their God through their saints, it was the aspect of Yoruba tradition that emphasized the relationship between the individual and the powerful but remote Olodumare through the òrìsà, I submit, that the founders of the Candomblés selected as they adapted the beliefs and practices of their ancestors to the social and political circumstances in which they found themselves in Brazil. Unable to recreate kingdoms and ilus, and instead of establishing cult centers or shrines at which each deity would be worshipped separately by its own priests or priestesses, the Yorubas in Brazil gathered, as we have seen, as a single autonomous association on unused pieces of land where a hierarchically organized community under the direction of a ritual leader communicated with all of the òrìsà.[57] And in what was to mark them and their ritual practices as distinct from the Brazilian Catholics, the practice of spirit possession was made central to their worship. Instead of the òrìsà coming to and incorporating only in the bodies of initiated priests and priestesses of a shrine, as was the case in Africa, however, each member of the reconstituted religious community became, through the process of initiation, a potential priest or priestess able to receive and serve the deities.

In adapting and reorganizing their religious beliefs and rituals so they might practice them in Brazil, the founders of the Candomblés built on yet another aspect of African culture that was to further accommodate their revision (reinterpretation) of Yoruba tradition with the structure of Brazilian society. They organized themselves into houses, which in Brazil are domestic units in a society that opposed the public and the private domains.

Kinship is very important in Africa.[58] Slaves in Brazil usually were separated from their kinsmen because plantation owners tried to keep apart those with previous ties and who spoke the same language to prevent their possibly organizing in rebellion. The Candomblés, as we have seen, were organized as groups of fictive kin under a ritual leader who was called a father or mother (of the saints). Their disciples (the initiates) were sons and daughters in sainthood. A Candomblé is a house whose members are fictive kinsmen who receive and care for the orixás under the hierarchical leadership of a fictive parent or senior kinsperson.[59] By organizing as families in houses, however, the Candomblés gave up any potential for political participation in their new homeland.

Glen C. Dealy argues that Brazil—and the rest of Catholic Latin America—is characterized by a system of dual morality. In contrast with the United States and other primarily post-Reformation national societies where a single set of normative rules expressed in law are enforced in both the public and private arenas, in these pre-Reformation Latin Catholic countries there are two systems of morality, one applicable in the private or domestic arena and another that prevails in the public sector. Moreover, whereas the one that operates in the private domain is rooted in Catholic religious beliefs, its standards are not applied in the public sector where the rules of Caesar, power, domination and exploitation are given free expression.[60]

## Conclusion

My intent in this paper has not been to diminish what the founders of Brazil's Candomblés accomplished. Nor do I wish to appear to oppose the not unreasonable wish of their leaders to have their beliefs and ritual practices acknowledged as an official religion with a status on par with that of the Catholic Church. Like Wafer

> I am not unsympathetic to the political motivation behind these [wishes]. I recognize that the re-Africanization of Candomblé, based on the idea of throwing off white domination, has considerable symbolic significance. . . . However, the re-Africanization movement in Candomblé has a number of consequences that in some ways undermine the aspirations that inspired it.[61]

Òrìsà worship in Yorubaland, as we have seen, was inseparable from the contest between political segments for hegemony and dominance. This is not so in Brazil where Candomblé is instead an alternative way in which individuals relate to other-worldly intermediaries believed to be able to intercede between them and an all-powerful God. This syncretism, which resulted from the parallelism and convergence of one aspect of Yoruba belief with that of Brazilian Catholicism, made it possible for Yoruba, slave and free, to find meaning in the world in which they had no choice but to live.

"Afro-Brazilian syncretism," as Sergio Ferretti writes,

> was . . . a form of adaptation by the Negro to a colonial society dominated by Catholicism. It provided the means that enabled him to survive and gave him the strength to overcome the difficulties of existence, to surmount practical problems without having to be preoccupied with the logical coherence of syncretism.[62]

To deny this and rewrite history in the name of the politics of the present, no matter how justifiable the goal, will diminish the remarkable accomplishments of the founders of the Candomblés who created something of value that continues to provide meaning to the lives not only of their descendants, but to new generations of Brazilians of all racial groups and social classes.

## Notes

1. The term "Yoruba" as an ethnic designation "could not have been long in vogue prior to 1856." The Yoruba peoples of Dahome, present-day Benin, who were brought to Brazil in large numbers in the late eighteenth and early nineteenth centuries, were known then as *Nàgô, Nagónu,* or *Anàgónu—Anàgó* plus the *Fon* suffix *nu* meaning people. (N. A. Fadipe, *The Sociology of the Yoruba* [Ibadan: Ibadan University Press, 1970], 30, quoted in Juana Elbein dos Santos, *Os Nàgô e a Morte* [Petrópolis, Brazil: Editora Vozes, 1977], 29-30.) In Brazil, especially in Bahia, anything related to Yoruba culture is referred to by the term Nagô.

2. See chapter 4 by Motta in this volume.

3. Vivaldo da Costa Lima, *Encontro de Nações de Candomblé* (Salvador, Bahia: Ianama and Universidade Federal da Bahia, 1984).

4. Quoted in Jim Wafer, *The Taste of Blood: Spirit Possession in Brazilian Candomblé* (Philadelphia: University of Pennsylvania Press, 1991), 56.

5. See Ana Maria Guerreiro, Carlota Gottschall, and Nelito Barreto, "Mãe Stella: Sacerdotista e Guardião do Candomblé na Bahia. Entrevista," *Bahia Análise & Dados* 3 (1994): 4.

6. In chapter 1 the reader was reminded that all attempts to explain empirical events (such as religious beliefs and practices) are social constructions that rest on an assumed model or image of what the world must be like so that we may know it. (Thomas S. Kuhn, *The Structure of Scientific Revolutions*, 2nd ed. [Chicago: University of Chicago Press, 1970]). It was further noted that in the social sciences generally and in anthropology in particular there are multiple competing theories each of which rests on a different image

of what the world is assumed to be like. To further complicate matters, the religious practitioners studied often have their own explanatory model or models based on yet other views that may differ at times significantly from those of the scholars studying them. Finally, the religious leaders may at times employ the arguments of scholars who in turn, for their own reasons, may become involved in the debates of those they study and incorporate them into their theoretical debates.

7. Beatriz Góis Dantas, *Vovó Nagô e Papai Branco: Usos e Abusos da Africa no Brasil* (Rio de Janeiro: Editora Graal, 1988). Like Dantas, I recognize the inadequacies of the term Afro-Brazilian and also find nothing better (Dantas, *Vovó Nagô*, 19, footnote 1).

8. Dantas, *Vovó Nagô*, 19.

9. Dantas, *Vovó Nagô*, 20.

10. The more African houses also were assumed to be centers of resistance to European domination.

11. Sidney M. Greenfield, "Descendants of European Immigrants in Southern Brazil as Participants and Heads of Afro-Brazilian Religious Centers," *Ethnic and Racial Studies* 17, no. 4 (1994): 684-700; Reginaldo Prandi, *Os Candomblés de São Paulo: A velha magia na metropole nova* (São Paulo: Editora HUTICEC, 1991).

12. Roberto Motta, "The Churchifying of Candomblé: Priests, Anthropologists and the Canonization of the African Religious Memory in Brazil," in *New Developments in African Religions*, Peter B. Clarke, ed. (Westport, CT: Greenwood Press, 1998), 45-57.

13. Roger Bastide, *African Civilizations in the New World*, Peter Green trans. (New York: Harper and Row, 1978), 47-48.

14. Donald Pierson, *Negroes In Brazil: A Study of Race Contact in Bahia* (Chicago: University of Chicago Press, 1942), 34-35.

15. As Pierson, following Nina Rodrigues in *Os Africanos no Brasil* (São Paulo: Cia. Edit. Nacional, 1932), observes, Nagô was at the time the língua geral, or general language for the urban black community in Salvador. See also footnote 1.

16. Elbein dos Santos, *Os Nàgô*, 28. She adds on the following page that "These diverse groups from . . . Dahomey and the southwest of Nigeria, who come from a vast region called Yorubaland, are known in Brazil by the generic term Nagô. . . . The Ketu, Sabe, Oyo, Egba, Egbado, Ijesa, Ibeja, brought to Brazil their customs, their hierarchical structures, their philosophical and esthetic concepts, their music, their oral literature and mythology. And above all, they brought to Brazil their religion" (My translation).

17. P. Verger, *Trade Relations between the Bight of Benin and Bahia From the Seventeenth to the Nineteenth Century* (Ibadan: Ibadan University Press, 1976).

18. Elbein dos Santos, *Os Nàgô*, 32.

19. Elbein dos Santos, *Os Nàgô*, 36 and 37.

20. Bastide, *African Civilizations*, 48; see also Edson Carneiro, *Candomblés de Bahia* (Salvador: Secretaria de Educação e Saúde, 1948), 31.

21. Roger Bastide, *Estudos Afro-Brasileiros* (São Paulo: Editora Perspectiva, 1983).

22. Mikelle Smith Omari, *From the Inside to the Outside: The Art and Ritual of Bahian Candomblés* (Los Angeles: UCLA Museum of Cultural History, Monograph No. 24, 1984), 17.

23. In making her case about the relationship between scholars and the claims of the leaders of the traditional Candomblés, Dantas (*Vovó Nagô*, 21) reminds us that every major figure to study Candomblé, from Nina Rodrigues to Edson Carneiro, Artur Ramos, Roger Bastide, Melville Herskovits, Ruth Landes, Peirre Verger and Juana Elbein dos Santos, did their research in one of these three centers.

24. Prandi, *Os Candomblés*.

25. Andrew Apter, *Black Critics and Kings: The Hermeneutics of Power in Yoruba Society* (Chicago: University of Chicago Press, 1992).

26. John D. Y. Peel, *Ijeshas and Nigerians: The Incorporation of a Yoruba Kingdom 1890s-1970s* (Cambridge: Cambridge University Press, 1983), 31.

27. Apter, *Black Critics*, 21 and 22.

28. Peel, *Ijeshas and Nigerians*, Chs. 3 and 4.

29. Apter, *Black Critics*, 40ff.

30. Apter, *Black Critics*, 13.

31. Ulli Beier, "Festival of Images," *Nigeria Magazine*, 45 (1953): 14-20; "The Historical and Psychological Significance of Yoruba Myths," *Odu*, 1 (1955): 17-25; "The Oba's Festival, Ondo," *Nigeria Magazine*, 50 (1956): 238-59; "Obatala Festival," *Nigeria Magazine*, 52 (1956): 10-28; *A Year of Sacred Festivals in One Yoruba Town* (Lagos: Nigeria Magazine Special Publication, 1959); and "Before Odudua," *Odu*, 3 (n.d.): 25-31.

32. Apter, *Black Critics*, 4.

33. Apter, *Black Critics*, 5.

34. Apter, *Black Critics*, 7.

35. Apter, *Black Critics*, 14 (italics in the original).

36. See Anthony Giddens, *The Constitution of Society* (Berkeley: University of California Press, 1984).

37. Apter, *Black Critics*, 15.

38. Apter, *Black Critics*, 19.

39. Apter, *Black Critics*, 21.

40. Apter, *Black Critics*, 21-22.

41. M. G. Smith, *Corporations and Society: The Social Anthropology of Collective Action* (Chicago: Aldine, 1975 [original 1974]), 94.

42. An example is provided in his examination of the development of the òrìsà cults of the kingdom of Ayede.

As external observers with historical hindsight we see Ayede's orisa cults as closed corporations allied to competing and shifting power blocs. The history of the cults can thus be plotted and traced within different Yoruba regions and towns. But seen within Ayede itself, cult histories (*itàn*) remain largely hidden within shrines which house secrets that are infinitely subversive and "deep." (Apter, *Black Critics*, 69).

43. Roger Bastide, "Religion and the Church in Brazil," in *Brazil: Portrait of Half a Continent*, T. Lynn Smith and Alexander Marchant, eds. (New York: Drydan Press, 1951), 346.

44. See, for example, Rolando Azzi, "Elementos para a história do Catolicismo popular," *Revista Eclesiastica Brasileira*, 36, Fasc. 141 (1976); Daniel Gross, "Ritual Conformity: A Religious Pilgrimage to Northeastern Brazil," *Ethnology* 10, no. 2 (1971): 129-148; Bernadino Leer, *Catolocismo Popular e Mundo Rural* (Petropolis, RJ: Editora Vozes, Ltda, 1977); Carlos A. de Medina, *Mudança Social e Atividades Religiosas* (Rio de Janeiro: CERIS/ CNBB, 1972); Carlos A. de Medina and Pedro A. Ribeiro de Oliveira, *Autoridade e Participação: Estudo Sociológico da Igreja Católica* (Petropolis, RJ: Editora Vozes, Ltda, 1973); and Alba Zaluar, *Os Homens de Deus* (Rio de Janeiro: Editora Zahar, 1983).

45. Azzi, "Elementos," 30.

46. Zaluar, *Os Homens*, 84.

47. They also at times are attributed a degree of independence that enables them to respond directly to the appeals of petitioners. Leer (*Catolocismo Popular*, 85) suggests that this may be interpreted as God delegating them the ability to redress grievances.

48. Thales de Azevedo, "Popular Catholicism in Brazil: Typology and Functions," in *Portugal and Brazil in Transition*, Raymond Sayers, ed. (Minneapolis: University of Minnesota Press, 1968), 177.

49. Emanuel de Kadt, "Religion, the Church, and Social Change in Brazil," in *The Politics of Conformity in Latin America*, Claudio Veliz, ed. (London: Oxford University Press, 1967), 196. A petitioner has no guarantee that the saint to whom her or his petition is addressed will accept the offer and act on it. She or he also has no assurance that the intercession will be successful. Therefore, prestations are offered conditionally. She or he will make the pilgrimage, light the candles, walk the stations of the cross with a weight on her head in the noonday sun, etc., if and only if the request is satisfied. "The most common and binding relationship of the faithful to the Saints and God," writes Azevedo, "is through a *promessa*, consisting of a petition of *proteção*, or help, in a crisis, under the promise of compensation" (Thales de Azevedo, *Social Change in Brazil* [Gainesville, FL: University of Florida Press, 1963], 76).

50. E. M. McClelland, *The Cult of Ifá Among the Yoruba*. Volume I: Folk Practice and Art (London: Ethnographica, 1982), 27.

51. E. Thomas Lawson, *Religions of Africa: Traditions in Transformation* (San Francisco: Harper, 1985), 60.

52. Yoruba engage in divinitory consultations at every stage of life: when they marry, when a child is born, when one intends to build a house, to move from one, when a journey is planned, a project with chances of profit or loss is undertaken, when calamity befalls, in sickness and even at the approach of death. (McClelland, *Cult of Ifá*, 10.) They

also consult when things seemingly go wrong. Evil forces, such as spirits and witches, are believed to have the power to frustrate the efforts of individuals to fulfill their destinies. Through Ifá they can learn what might be done to make things right. Invariably this involves the performance of rituals and/or the making of sacrifices.

53. J. Omosade Awolalu, *Yoruba Beliefs and Sacrificial Rituals* (London: Longman, 1979), 5-6.

54. Elyette Guimaraes de Magalhães, *Orixas da Bahia* (Salvador, Brazil, 1973), 17.

55. Only a small number of the hundreds of Yoruba deities are still worshipped in Brazil. As McCarthy Brown also observed for Haiti, "The spirits they brought with them from Africa shifted and realigned in response to their needs. Some were forgotten; others were given a centrality they never had in the homeland" (Karen McCarthy Brown, *Mama Lola: A Vodou Priestess in Brooklyn* [Berkeley: University of California Press, 1991], 100).

56. Lawson, *Religions of Africa*, 64ff. The first of these was at the level of the family where the living head was the channel for communication with the ancestors who after death resided in orun where some came to be recognized as lesser deities. The second was the shrine where a priest mediated through incorporation between those he represented and a specific orisa. The third was a dominant ilu, or one of its satellites, or sectors, where the oba, or a baale represented the political unit. "The fourth context for mediation [was] every act of worship in which one orisa is required to mediate between the ritual practitioner and another orisa" (Lawson, *Religions of Africa*, 64).

57. Elbein dos Santos, *Os Nàgô*, 36-37.

58. Extended kin groups include both the living and their deceased forebears who were believed to be able to influence the lives of their descendants from orun where they resided after death.

59. Vivaldo da Costa Lima, *A Família de Santo dos Candomblés Jeje-Nagô da Bahia* (Salvador: Universidade Federal da Bahia, 1977).

60. In his public behavior, Dealy maintains, the Latin American is an essentially political animal, in contrast with his economically driven North American counterpart. He characterizes this pattern of public, political behavior by the Spanish term *caudillaje*, from the noun *caudillo*. He defines a caudillo, following the *Diccionario enciclopédico ilustrado de la lengua española*, as "one who, as head (chief) and superior, guides and commands people" (Glen C. Dealy, *The Latin Americans: Spirit & Ethos* [Boulder, CO: Westview Press, 1992], 58.) Caudillaje, he adds, "has been defined as the 'domination (*mando*) or government of a caudillo,' an individual 'who doesn't try to get along (*convivir*),' but rather strives 'to dominate'" (Dealy, *Latin Americans*, 58).

While the prototypical North American actor in the public sector, the entrepreneur, is driven by the desire to accumulate material wealth, the Latin American caudillo—who invariably is male (see Dealy, *Latin Americans*, xiv-xv)—is driven to dominate others politically, using a range of behaviors so aptly described centuries ago by Machiavelli in which the ends, political power, justify the means (Dealy, *Latin Americans*, 52-153).

61. Wafer, *Taste of Blood*, 56.
62. Sérgio F. Ferretti, *Repensando o Sincretismo* (São Paulo: Editora da Universidade de São Paulo, 1995), 18 (my translation).

## Chapter 8

# Possession and Syncretism: Spirits as Mediators in Modernity

Inger Sjørslev

### Introduction

In Brazilian cities and towns, spirit possession is a frequent and intense occurrence, often taking place in the darkness of night and always framed by ritual. The possessed are office boys, nurses, maids, teachers, musicians, lawyers, and bus drivers, in addition to professionals, *mães* and *pais-de-santo* (mothers and fathers in sainthood). The possessing spirits are the African Gods (*Orixas*), tricksters, old slaves, Indian spirits (*Caboclos*), sailors and prostitutes, child spirits, Gypsies, and *Bahianos*. Possession takes place in the countless *terreiros*, the ritual houses of *Umbanda* and *Candomblé*.[1]

In these reflections on the syncretism of the Afro-Brazilian religions, I have chosen to look at the role of syncretism in identity politics within the context of modernity. Here, I deal with both Candomblé and Umbanda, and for the present purpose have not gone into the differences between them, although these are important in other contexts. Possession and the role of the body in the ritual praxis are the central elements; and the issue is what syncretism does for the manifestation of identity in possession ritual. My contention will be that syncretism provides the instrument and the opportunity for constant creativity and adaptation to new challenges and interpretations of history, as well as the cultural and social context, and that it lends flexibility to the individual positioning within these. Possession is a form of ritual praxis, and the question of syncretism in these religions also touches upon questions of the relationship between praxis and articulation of the symbolic universe in the form of written rules and interpretations. This again leads to some reflections on the question of ethnographic authority and the reflexive practice of religion.

Within the last twenty years Candomblé has spread to São Paulo from its birth place in Bahia and today, together with Umbanda, presents itself as a complex intermixture of cultural practices, religious beliefs, and philosophical ideas derived from many different sources. As such, the Afro-Brazilian religions are the epitome of syncretism. The religions have been regarded as syncretistic in the classical sense of combining a traditional religion with a new layer of religious belief originating in Christianity,[2] and indeed the African Orixas are all associated with Catholic saints. It seems more fruitful, however, to see the religions as syncretic in the broader sense of the term, implying a bricolage, and recognizing that the religious can not be strictly separated from the non-religious. In fact the traditional view of the religions as syncretistic in the sense of having concealed the cultivation of the African Orixas behind the worship of Catholic saints is not as true to life as the idea of the religions being religiously and culturally bricolaged.

Although in current anthropological discourse, syncretism has not acquired the same popularity as the concepts of creolization, collage, interculture, hybridity, etc.,[3] it does seem reasonable to assign the term a wider scope, encompassing intercultural aspects of the modern, globalized world. In my application of the concept of syncretism to the Afro-Brazilian religions, I thus go beyond the idea of syncretism in the classical sense and follow Stewart and Shaw in their emphasis on power and agency and the politics implied in the competing discourses concerning syncretism, as well as syncretism's capacity to contain paradox, contradiction and polyphony.[4] In relation to the modern condition, this implies "from the viewpoint of agency [. . .] a time/space of choice, of aesthetic-expressive reflexivity, in which agents previously structured by tradition are now free to choose from 'symbolic repertoires,' free to try on masks, to try on identities."[5] In this sense the religions and their growth in popularity can be regarded as a phenomenon closely attached to modernity.

The bricolage of the Afro-Brazilian religions is thus one that reaches beyond religion and implies history and cultural identity in a broader sense. The body is a key factor in the practice of this, with spirit possession as the ritual core. Ritual embodies a complexity of religious ideas, just as possession shapes individual and collective experience. Social experience is condensed into (spiritual) entities with reference to history and culture.

These spiritual entities are thus mediators in more than one sense. In the traditional religious sense they mediate between the human and the spiritual world, the worldly and the transcendent. In a contemporary social and cultural sense they mediate between the individual and the collective, between the past and the present, and between cultural tradition and the demands of modern life.

The religions combine both the promotion of a type of individuality associated with modern society, and the particular kind of belief in destiny and the control of exterior forces that is mostly related to traditional societies. Candomblé and Umbanda are both traditional and modern, and they may be viewed in relation to a postmodern situation associated with a society of extreme risks, and a high degree of freedom, individuality and reflexivity—a reflexivity that is here reflected in the sphere of the religious. The success of these religions is based upon their adaptability to the modern condition, while relying on a rich fundament of traditional ritual practice and cosmology—a fundament that has been cut off from its original social context. The explanation of their popularity and growth must be sought for in this ability to combine different elements, in a relation between identity and modernity, i.e., the need to manifest, and in the providing of means to define a personal and collective identity in a world of rapid and radical change. Like the people of Bali, as described by Frederik Barth, Brazilian city people "participate in multiple, more or less discrepant universes of discourse; they construct different, partial and simultaneous worlds in which they move; their cultural construction of reality springs not from one source and is not of one piece."[6]

The interpretation of these religions also involves ethical and political questions, among other things in terms of "the practice of identity and the production of historical schemes,"[7] or in terms of the power and control implied in the discourses about syncretism and anti-syncretism.[8] This all implies the crucial element of reflexivity, both in the sense of externalization of culture by practitioners and a conscious manipulation of culture in the discourses about African tradition and orthodoxy. On another and more implicit level, reflexivity is found in the practice of possession, where the individual finds his or her way of interpreting the role of mediator, as well as his or her relationship with the gods and spirits, and with great skill exercises a "commentary" to the cultural and social world by way of the religious symbols.

## Identity

Living in a modern, complex society implies both confusion and insecurity, with respect to identity and otherwise, but it also provides a flexibility of definitions, a selection of types of explanations from which to choose, and a myriad of cultural elements from which to build up identity, both cultural and personal. The adherents to the Afro-Brazilian religions choose "tradition," in a symbolic sense, as a solution in a complex world. They are not modernists in the sense that they ward off superstition in the name of rationalization and development, but the religions as such may be regarded as a phenomenon of "low modernism" or "modernism in the streets."[9]

On the collective level, the praxis of identity is closely related to conceptions of the past, and discourses about the present seen in relation to the past. Syncretism has entered into native discourse as a consequence of the reflexive attitude to one's own past and the discourse on power, both explicit—as exemplified in the discussions on the location of the magical, cosmological force *axé*—and implicit, as the discourse on personal, ritual and, to some extent, economic power of the practitioners of the religions. This is a type of discourse that must be seen in relation to the implications of modernity for economic survival, but more importantly here, for the need and possibility to define cultural identity, among other things by way of interpretations and re-interpretations of the past.

The concept of identity has many dimensions, and I will refrain from a deeper discussion of these. For the present purpose, it suffices to say, with Stuart Hall, that "identity is always in part a narrative, always in part a kind of representation. It is always within representation. Identity is not something which is formed outside and then we tell stories about it. It is that which is narrated in one's own self."[10] This is a conception of identity that applies to both individuals and groups, and the issue of the relation between the two is fundamental in anthropological dealings with identity. A systematic interrelationship between the individual and the group is considered vital to personal identity; and a certain correspondence between private and cultural maps is presumed to be a condition for the experience of fit between subjective understanding and the cultural means available for the interpretation of present and past.

Experiences with the religions at hand point to the need for a clearer understanding of the interrelationship between subjective experience, whether referring to individuals or groups, and the cultural symbols and collective representations used in the construction of identity. At the core of Afro-Brazilian cosmology, we find a symbol that can be interpreted as being related to a specific sense of identity in modernity, namely the trickster god Exu. In Brazil this figure has been syncretized with the Devil, and is popularly referred to as the slave or "the man of the street." The symbolism of Exu is related to both personal identity and individualism;[11] to ritual, fate, coincidence, the complexities and ambivalence of modern life; and most of all to the fundamental paradox of being and becoming, of stability and dynamics, continuity and change. In my interpretation, this master of paradoxes provides a key to an understanding of the whole phenomenon of

Afro-Brazilian religions and its continuous presence and renewal in modern Brazilian society.[12]

The postmodern contention has been the one of identity as choice.[13] Obviously, however, identity as choice is an abstract idea, which in no way applies directly to the subjective experience of being who one is. Furthermore, there are obvious limits to this choice. To define oneself as a socially acceptable heterosexual may be the most attractive choice, even in supposedly tolerant modern societies, but still a difficult one for whoever lives with the subjective experience of him- or herself as homosexual. In theory, one may claim to be a reincarnation of Jesus Christ and have a strong subjective experience conforming to this, but society will still define whoever does so as mentally ill. Identity as a choice must be understood in the abstract sense, but in this sense, the investigation of the potentials and possibilities for self-identification must be viewed within the limits that are established and defined by the cultural institutions. The rupture of signs from their original referents, which is an often-mentioned characteristic of (post)modern society, provides space and flexibility for choosing cultural signs in the formation of identity adapted to a changing world. Cultural symbols and collective representations provide a framework for understanding the particular positioning in the world, for the shaping of experience, both individually and socially; but in modernity this framework is neither stable nor fixed. The looseness of it, and the flexibility of the signs, may be regarded as the opening up of a space for the creation of one's own conceptual universe and the ensuing externalization of culture, accompanied by the self-conscious application of cultural elements and the reflexive attitude towards ideas of past, present and future.

The possession ritual, in which the symbol of Exu is a key dynamic factor, provides the ideal framework for this activity. In possession, person and spirit are mutual instruments. The spirit is a vehicle for personal expression, and the person is a vehicle for a collective representation. But an expression of individuality is understood and accepted, i.e., socially valid, only when articulated within the collectively accepted, ritualized language. The statement that a person has, or belongs to this or that spirit, or that this or that god is the owner of his or her head (*sou de Ogum*, or *a dona da minha cabeça é Oxum*—I am Ogum's, the owner of my head is Oxum), is at the same time a statement about the Orixa whose medium the person is, and too, about the identity, i.e., the self-conception, of that person. The possessed person is at the same time an instrument for the god, the spirit's vehicle, and her- or himself, both medium and Orixa, simultaneously person and representation. Thus, in a quite literal sense, the body becomes a symbol of the social, a mediator between the individual and the collective. The possessed body is a mediator between the intimacy of the personal and the cultural symbols, between the past and the present; it is the instrument for the mirroring of self through the spirits, spirits that are at the same time collective and individual. A delicate balance is preserved between the "invention"—or arrival—of spirits that express personal identity and the conforming of those spirits with the cultural types that fit into the collectively accepted cosmological system. Thus, there is an obvious limit to the invention of spiritual types. New types must be within the range of accepted spiritual stereotypes, and while there is room for individual creation, there is also a definite limit to such creations. Thus, when the increasing dominance of gays, especially in Candomblé houses in São Paulo, has brought forward a formerly rare Orixa like the androgynous *LogunEde*, this is an "invention," a new creation, but no more so than LogunEde was already present within the cosmological system.

## Strategies and the Discourse on Ritual Praxis

In possession, the body becomes a social sign. When a medium is possessed by an Orixa, a Gypsy, an old slave, a child spirit or an Exu, he or she, with his or her individual performance, is an element in a collective narrative, a common history that has to do with understanding oneself in the world. A ritual performance, in which the spirits are present, is thus at the same time for the individual medium a confirmation of personal identity, through the presentation of self, *and* a manifestation and reflection of the historical and social context within which the individual is placed. Personal and collective identity come together in ritual possession, and in contrast to the common sense belief that trance is some sort of stepping out of oneself, possession can be regarded as rather a controlled incorporation of something outside the self in the self, namely the collective story of identity. In the possession ritual, it is possible to be intimate and public at the same time; to cultivate individuality within the same process that creates and manifests conceptions of historical and cultural coherence, through the use of elements from the culturally syncretized universe. The role of ritual in the process of definition, re-definition and interpretation of history and in the shaping of historical and cultural experience and the striving for a hegemonic definition of history, authenticity and purity—all of this is revealed in the discourses on ritual practice and in the constant discussions carried out among the adepts of the religions. Discourses center around the concrete ritual performances, as well as on the overall rules and correct practices of ritual. Different strategies are employed in the discourses on purity and orthodoxy within the religions. They all contain conceptions about religious dogmatism and ritual practice, and the whole endeavor to reflect upon and define true religion is closely attached to the competition for power.

One strategy is the attempt to purify Umbanda, which implies a de-Africanization and a detachment from what are considered barbaric and primitive elements of the African tradition, like the animal sacrifices. The "purification" is conducted by self-authorized experts on dogmatism and the esoteric knowledge behind Umbanda, and reveals itself in many of the writings on the Umbanda religion. Ironically, however, the "purification" of Umbanda maintains the syncretistic elements in the religion, and among other things strives to align and consolidate the relationship between Orixas and saints.

Another strategy is represented by the de-syncretizing attempts, mainly within Candomblé, where the new Africanists, most of them located in São Paulo, strive to achieve a "cleansing" of the religious practice, ridding it of the elements that have entered through Catholicism. In that there is in fact very little Catholicism in the ritual practice, these efforts mainly aim at "tearing down the saints from the altars," as the adepts say, referring to Umbanda and a number of Umbanda-Candomblé mixed altars with the colorful figures of the saints of the Catholic church. A third strategy is attached to the creation and invention of ancestors from among the most orthodox representatives of the Bahian Candomblé. In São Paulo, a number of younger mães and pais-de-santo either go to Bahia for initiation (or supervision) by well-known and respected heads of Candomblé centers, or they trace their spiritual ancestry through other mães and pais-de-santo in the city who in turn can present links back to spiritual grandparents (*avôs*) in Bahia. This strategy regards the syncretism as part of the true and original Brazilian Candomblé. It also respects the practices of the older ritual leaders who for example often claim to be Catholic and start their ceremonies with a mass in the church.

In addition to these more or less articulated strategies, there is still a great majority whose definitions and constant negotiations about the true practice of the religions lie mainly in the doing, i.e., in the ritual performances. The discussions and negotiations are articulated mainly in the *fofóca*, that constant gossiping about etiquette, which is an inescapable part of every public ritual performance. All in all, both Candomblé and Umbanda are very pragmatic in their attitude toward practice, and moreover quite adaptive, using for instance the concept of the spiritual force axé as closely related to the non-religious realm of career, economics, social power, etc. Although the discourse about the differences between Candomblé and Umbanda is serious and intense, as is the constant attempt to separate them, in reality many of the adepts, to a smaller or greater extent, mix the elements of the two. Going from Candomblé to Umbanda, or the other way, from Umbanda to Candomblé, and defining oneself as a practitioner of one or the other, has in many cases just as much to do with practical and economic matters as with dogmatic attitudes. Nonetheless, the discourses that do go on are significant.

When the adepts move from Candomblé to Umbanda or from Umbanda to Candomblé, it usually happens by way of the possessing gods and spirits. Choices are made by these, and the mediums have to follow. Thus it is praxis that again carries the dynamics and the changes, and particularly that core of ritual praxis that is possession. There seems to be some contradiction in this, and one of the roles of syncretism is to make life possible, in spite of this contradiction. Ironically, it is also a contradiction that, in a sense, makes it possible for the religions to sustain themselves. This contradiction can be attributed to the fact that praxis and pragmatism are the real forces of survival, while the articulated discourses on purity and orthodoxy are based on the argument that a consensus on these subjects is needed in order for the religions to survive. The articulation of the roots and rules of the religions, whether in discourses or in the numerous publications on Umbanda in particular, is viewed by some adepts as a necessity for the religions to survive, while in reality it seems to be the more or less pragmatic and disordered practice, along with the constant dynamics and inventions, that together provide the route and supply the energy for the survival and renewal of these religions.

The writings on Candomblé, and especially Umbanda, are numerous, and many of the published books and pamphlets are written by adepts of the religions, some of whom are also leaders and organizers within one of the federations of Umbanda and Candomblé. So far, the number of Umbanda federations have by far exceeded the ones that deal with Candomblé, but these are increasing in numbers. A good part of the writings comprise eclectic samplings of bits and pieces of myths, into which are bricolaged phrases from the social sciences, references to anthropological authorities on the religions, statements regarding government politics towards the Umbanda, and moralistic imperatives directed towards the adherents to the religions. Regardless of the actual content of these writings, the fact that such texts exist, and in such great numbers, can be regarded as an expression of some sort of ritualization of textuality. Writing and publishing on the religions reveal that something else is going on besides the business of putting experienced *content* down into textual *form*. Many of the texts have adopted and formalized the style of science to such an extent that some of it seems more scientific than science itself, while still preserving a theological tone. At the same time, the Umbanda texts also reveal in their style of writing their legacy to rationality, and some passages can be seen as almost pastiche on modern social scientific writing.

In the ritual practice, the adherents to the Afro-Brazilian religions employ spirits in their construction of identity. Religious writings are employed as one element in the attempt to affirm the religions—and this goes mainly for Umbanda—as a socially accepted phenomenon. The existence of a text is not only proof that some lived experience has been transformed into writing; it has a symbolic value that reaches beyond its immediate content. At the same time, breaking the barrier into writing is breaking the barrier into mainstream society and majority culture, and it can also be viewed as an attempt to gain access to the power represented by the majority society.

There is no doubt that the attempts to control and regulate the practice of the religions are ways of trying to achieve dominance and establish hegemony. They establish a type of hierarchy and power relations that have as much to do with the surrounding society as with the internal nature of Umbanda. The religious writing is a significant element in this process of control and dominance, and in this sense, the theologians who write might be regarded as exercising a sort of rigorous schoolmaster function, in opposition to the creative activity in the terreiros themselves. In my own experiences with the Candomblé and Umbanda houses in São Paulo, I have rarely seen these writings being used. Although the adepts may own a few books, it has never been my impression that their content was directly referred to in the orally conducted discourses on ritual practice and symbolic meaning. This supports the interpretation that an understanding of the meaning and significance of the written dogmas lies in their existence as such, more than in their concrete content. Both the continuity and the necessary flexibility of the religions are provided by practice, whether this be the actual ritual practice or the practice of talking and gossiping about the correctness and power of the agency in religion.

In the same vein, anthropological writing may be said to exercise a kind of schoolmaster function, if not deliberately, at least in the way some classical anthropological literature is being employed by those who dominate the religions. In the revival of the Candomblé in São Paulo, the works of the highly estimated French anthropologists Pierre Verger and Roger Bastide are seen as the authoritative sources of correct praxis, and anthropological writings are employed in the efforts in support of orthodoxy and the attempt to reclaim what is considered practice in the true African sense.

The paradox is that the existence of the discourse on orthodoxy and its lack of success in arriving at any consensus conclusion are probably equally important for the continuous vitality of the religions. The success of a rigid dogmatism, of any anti-syncretistic idea, would mean the death of the religions, or at least their turning into meaningless empty ritual in the common sense of that term. And the protection against this is provided by the gods and spirits, in that the arrival of spiritual entities in the rituals is precisely what carries the renewal and creativity of the religions; thus the human, social efforts to streamline practice always will be up against the power of spiritual agency, and so far, it seems that the latter wins.[14]

## Authority and Authenticity

The question of what syncretism means in relation to the praxis of possession also points to the current anthropological criticism of concepts like purity, wholeness and authenticity, and the ensuing enthusiasm, within the anthropological hegemony, for the postmodernist paradigms that "take apart practices and identities which are phenomenological realities for those who use them ('your tradition is invented'). In our enthusiasm for deconstructing syncretic traditions we may have invented another kind of intellectual imperialism."[15] This again has a lot to do with ethics and the question of ethnographic authority. It also has to do with the question of identity in another sense.

The practice of anthropology requires both the acceptance of the legitimacy of the voice or text of the other and a claim to an ethnographic authority in order to analyze and discuss the assumptions comprised in voices and texts of the others. It must also maintain the right to call these by their right name, and state the fact that sometimes they must be regarded as symbolic truths rather than historical or social truths.[16]

An anthropological interpreter would perceive much of what is going on in the Brazilian religions as the creation of new concepts in the building and definition of tradition and the past. Most protagonists of the religions would, however, see it as a gradual revealing of, and return to, the true and original foundation of the religion. The practitioners of the Brazilian religions employ ethnic concepts as well as certain notions of history in their self-definition and self-understanding, although these definitions are not always explicitly stated. In Candomblé, they manifest themselves more in the practice of ritual than in voice or text, whereas in Umbanda, the production of religious texts, containing visions of a historic past and to some extent a utopian future, does play a certain role in the participants' confirmation of self and their right to a definition of reality. Ethnicity has been claimed as "the necessary place or space from which people speak."[17] Umbandistas and Candombleiros do not, automatically, so to speak, have a platform from which to expound a clear and unambiguous ethnic identity. Brazil is ethnically mixed, and ethnicity is not a clear marker. Indian spirits, Africans, Gypsies, etc. are created "ethnics," and the place to speak from is found in symbolic creations, both in the sense of another world and in the sense of the creation of a mythological ethnic past. The past thus becomes not only a position from which to speak, it also becomes a necessary resource in what people have to say.

Participants in Candomblé and Umbanda have learned to tell themselves a story of the past, a story of their own construction. A number of modern adherents are in their own view researchers tracing their historical roots, and in this process, they base their knowledge upon ethnographic sources. This state of affairs is not just one exotic case of life imitating art, or science; rather it is one that is becoming the normal situation in many parts of the world. It has further accentuated the question of who has the right to define the past, which is also the question of Western scientific hegemony versus native conceptions.[18] This problem becomes all the more clear when dealing with a religion that bases itself to a large extent upon doctrines written (and rewritten) by contemporary protagonists: when the subjects of study become theorists of themselves. Umbanda writers are to a great extent ethnographers within their own field. The question is whether this should lead to placing their interpretations on the same footing as an anthropological interpretation. A relativist answer might be yes, but as long as these interpreters of their religion operate within a set of uncontested and to them unquestionable truths, the answer, I would contend, must still be no.[19]

## Syncretism, Reflexivity and Modernity

To be one's "real self" in the religions based on possession, one must be firmly integrated within one's culture, i.e., one must be well acquainted with the cultural symbols applied in the religions. The participation of individuals with a firm belief in their own identity is a precondition for the continuation and creativity of the symbolic content of the religions. Contrariwise, the flexibility and variety of the cultural system may be regarded as a precondition for the stability of personal identity. The experience of unity in personal self is based on a possibility within the cultural system of expressing different aspects of the social self.

The spirits and their mediums live in modernity, where nothing is given, where order and human self are a matter of thought, of concern, of awareness and reflexivity, both individually and collectively. In the Afro-Brazilian religions traditionalism is to a great extent practiced reflexively, as an element in the search for identity through the definition of tradition. Doomed to recreate their own universe, people choose the symbols of tradition, of unity, of wholeness. "'*Sou de Ogum*,' I am Ogum's," not only expresses self, it also means, "I am part of something bigger." As signs, the spirits are anchored to new meanings, and the purpose of this is exactly to create a new sense of wholeness.[20] As mediators, they unify individual and collective identity in the rituals, which are at the same time repetitive and open to a certain creativeness. Syncretism is what provides the openness of the symbolic universe and the flexibility of the signs, while at the same time being an element in the ongoing discourse about identity, about history and authenticity, and ultimately about power.

Modern or not, the real question is perhaps whether such categories as modern, traditional and postmodern are at all applicable to the Afro-Brazilian religions, and whether the use of such categories illuminates the subject in any way. Thinking of the physical and social changes, we might say that the people of the Brazilian cities have gone from premodernity to postmodernity in one leap. We might also say that the figures of premodernity (Indians, slaves and gods related to kinship and specific localities) have become free-floating signs in a postmodernist collage. Or we might emphasize the way modernity, in its ideological sense, is celebrated in the ideology of Umbanda, specifically in the idealization of progress and evolution. All of this is true. As for syncretism, the original syncretism of the Afro-Brazilian religions may have provided the precondition for the further development of the religions, and made them ready to adapt new signifiers, which in their turn expands the symbolic universe beyond a syncretism in the traditional sense. The issue of Christianity has almost no importance for the understanding of the contemporary role of the Afro-Brazilian religions. Rather it is a question of how they have managed so successfully to keep real Christian influence out of their practices (although the concept of charity exists in modern Umbanda).[21] The point here is the creative application of cultural signifiers to new meanings, which helps the people in their current complex world in making sense of their surroundings and their destinies.

In Brazil, an interesting and pleasant experience has been to meet anthropological colleagues who not only go to Candomblé or Umbanda to experience an exotic show or an interesting anthropological phenomenon, but who consult their diviners, who relate to and discuss with native protagonists, and who are sometimes initiated themselves. They may do this in a reflexive manner, and perhaps even, though respectfully, slightly tongue in cheek; but they do it, and don't we all? We may not have as vital, colorful and profound a cultural system at our disposal, but if we did, would we not use it? We may be moderns, but are we not still eager to find answers, to know our personal characteristics, public images, horoscopes, destinies, futures? Or, to put the question otherwise, would it not be extremely unwise to limit oneself to an interpretation that is either tradition-modernist or syncretistic in the classic sense, when instead one can take a look into reflexive practices of religions and other belief systems in general? Much of the practice I have witnessed in the Afro-Brazilian religions, both from anthropologists and other intellectual adepts, have been conducted with the reflexivity that comes with the acknowledgment that there are many kinds of truths. This, however, does not deny the existence of superstition in the good old-fashioned sense, implying charlatanry and taking advantage of the weakness of human nature. This exists in the religions as anywhere else, and should not be legitimized by anthropological understanding.

An understanding of a phenomenon as complex as the Afro-Brazilian religions requires a complex set of explanations. I have only been able to touch upon a fringe of the phenomenon. I have tried to show that one explanation for the popularity of the religions in the Brazilian cities may lie in a connection between identity and modernity, i.e., in the need to manifest and define a personal as well as a collective identity in a physical and social world that has changed so fast that radical and special means are required to accommodate, culturally as well as psychologically. Syncretism, in the broad sense of the term, plays a key role in this process. The people of the religions have, in the true sense of the term, bricolaged the raw material of culture, in a dynamic and creative process, which cherishes, mis-reads, invents, recreates, and re-interprets in an ongoing process, of which we have not yet seen the end.

## Notes

1. In 1989 there were about 45,000 Umbanda houses and 3,000 Candomblé houses in the city of São Paulo alone; see Reginaldo Prandi and Vagner Gonçalves, "Deuses Tribais de São Paulo," *Ciência Hoje* 10 (1989), 57.
2. Roger Bastide, *The African Religions of Brazil: Toward a Sociology of the Interpretation of Civilizations* (Baltimore: Johns Hopkins University Press, 1978 [Original 1960]).
3. Charles Stewart and Rosalind Shaw, "Introduction: problematizing syncretism," in *Syncretism/Anti-Syncretism: The Politics of Religious Synthesis*, Charles Stewart and Rosalind Shaw, eds. (London: Routledge, 1994), 2.
4. Stewart and Shaw, *Syncretism/Anti-Syncretism*, 21.
5. Marshall Berman, *All That Is Solid Melts Into Air: The Experience of Modernity* (New York: Penguin, 1988), 22.
6. Frederik Barth, "The Analysis of Culture in Complex Societies," *Ethnos* 54 (1989), 130.
7. Jonathan Friedman, "The Past in the Future: History and the Politics of Identity," *American Anthropologist* 94, no. 4 (1992), 837.
8. Stewart and Shaw, *Syncretism/Anti-Syncretism*.
9. Berman, *All That is Solid*.
10. Stuart Hall, "Old and New Identities, Old and New Ethnicities," in *Culture, Globalization and the World System: Contemporary Conditions for the Representation of Identity*, Anthony D. King, ed. (New York: Macmillan, 1991), 49.
11. Juana Elbein Dos Santos and Deoscoredes M. Dos Santos, "Esu Bara, Principle of Individual Life in the Nàgó System," in *La Notion de personne en Afrique noire* (Paris: Colloques Internationaux du C.N.R.S., no. 544, 1973).
12. Inger Sjørslev, *Gudernes rum: En beretning om ritualer og troi Brasilien* (København: Gyldendal, 1995).
13. Michael Featherstone, "In Pursuit of the Postmodern: An Introduction," *Theory, Culture & Society* 5 (1988), 195-215.
14. The Umbanda religion itself was founded through practice, i.e., by the arrival, at a spiritist seance, of the Caboclo das Sete Encruzilladas. See Diana Brown, *Umbanda: Religion and Politics in Urban Brazil* (Ann Arbor: UMI Research Press, 1986).
15. Stewart and Shaw, *Syncretism/Anti-Syncretism*, 23.
16. James Clifford, "On Ethnographic Authority," in *The Predicament of Culture*, James Clifford, ed. (Cambridge, MA: Harvard University Press, 1988); Inger Sjørslev, "On the Edge of the Text: Three Books on Afro-Brazilian Religion," *Culture & History* 4 (1989): 91-116.
17. Stuart Hall, "The Local and the Global: Globalization and Ethnicity," in King, *Culture, Globalization*, 36.
18. Friedman, "The Past in the Future."

19. The question of ethnographic authority is related to the question of identity in the sense that the authority to define oneself and one's conception of the past and present and the right to acquire acceptance of this definition on the subjective level must be established, at the same time as it must be both possible and right to criticize and discuss it at some other level. If we did not maintain the legitimacy to question and criticize subjective truths about the present and past it would force us to accept any native point of view of history, and this would have disastrous consequences, like accepting some Nazis' denial of the historical facts of genocide.

20. James W. Fernandez, "The Argument of Images and the Experience of Returning to the Whole," in *The Anthropology of Experience*, V. Turner and E. M. Bruner, eds. (Chicago: University of Illinois Press, 1986).

21. Brown, *Umbanda*.

## Chapter 9

# Joana's Story: Syncretism at the Actor's Level

André Droogers

**Introduction**

Syncretism usually is looked at from the supra-individual level. Either the religions from which elements are selected or the religion that is the result of such a syncretic process is at the center of analysis. Even though anthropologists are in the habit of giving due attention to "real people doing real things," rarely do informants speak directly to the reader. The discourse remains almost always on the structural level. Yet if the triangle of signification developed in chapter 1 makes some sense, it would seem useful to pay attention to the way actors deal with structures and how their way of interpreting events and positioning themselves is related to this process. Such a micro-anthropological approach might make visible how an individual engaged in the syncretic process constructs his or her identity, making an effective and strategic use of the repertoires or religious beliefs and other schemas that are available in his or her social environment.

In this chapter such an effort is undertaken. The main character is Joana (not her real name), a Brazilian woman, at the time of the fieldwork in her forties and living in the greater Porto Alegre metropolitan region. Part of her life history is described and analyzed. Taped conversations with her took place in 1990 and 1995, as part of my research on the religiosity of people who do not consider themselves members of a religious institution.

To Joana, the years between 1990 and 1995 had been particularly turbulent. As I will show, her religious beliefs helped her to survive the consequences of a failed marriage with a violent man and the tragic end of a harmonious but impossible relationship with another man. In marshalling all the resources available to her, she showed herself to be doing what anthropologists think of as "syncretizing," without knowing the term. Her case also shows how religion and its mixing may empower a woman when she is confronted by the disadvantages of gender differences. This is not a form of power that necessarily enables her to influence other people's behavior. The prime beneficiary of the syncretic empowerment seems to be Joana herself, because she found a way to manage her life and to survive a deep crisis. Though her problem was partly that there was a difference of power between genders, and her husband exercised his power over her in a violent manner, her form of empowerment did not lead him to change his behavior but gave her the power to live her own life.[1]

I present her story as she told it. No effort was made to verify the events with other people. What use did Joana make of the religious resources she has come into contact with in the course of her life? What are her views on what it is to be a woman, a man (in the south of Brazil where she lived)? The two aspects of power that were mentioned above will be examined in the context of gender and religion: How did Joana manage to survive and to (re)organize her life? And what role did her religious experience play in this syncretic process of empowerment?

An interesting characteristic of Joana's story is that she belongs to the category of persons who do not participate in institutionalized forms of religion. Yet her repertoire of religious models comes to a large degree from institutionalized religion. To facilitate our understanding of the contrast between an actor's free use of repertoires and the institutional aspect of religion, a distinction might be made among three dimensions of institutionalized religion: (a) the internal, (b) the external (both predominantly social structural, but always with a signification aspect) and (c) the supernatural (predominantly cultural or symbolic, but often with a social structural aspect). The social relations existing in the internal and external dimensions are subject to cultural meaning-making. The beliefs concerning God, gods, spirits and saints, on the other hand, imply relations—modeled after the social structure—between them and believers: God is the Father/Mother, etc.

The relations between the opposite categories in each dimension are in fact power relations. Internally, religious specialists and lay people dispute their spheres of influence. Often gender is an essential part of this dimension, as for example when religious specialists are exclusively or predominantly male. Externally all the believers are related in some way to society where a certain religious view may be dominant, perhaps theirs, just as a particular gender definition may predominate. Alternative views and definitions may occur. Supernaturally speaking, power is also present in the relationship between believers and sacred entities, and here too gender notions may be of influence as when God, gods or spirits are explicitly viewed as male or female.

The three dimensions should be viewed in connection with each other. In each concrete case, one should expect idiosyncrasies as a consequence of the particular link or absence of linkage among dimensions. This may include contradictions among dimensions, since it is improbable that the three dimensions will ever be in total harmony and consistency. What is affirmed at one point can be contradicted in another situation. Thus the supernatural dimension has much weight, especially in official ideal versions of religions. Yet, in practice the supernatural dimension may at times be ignored as in the internal dimension—principles being amended under the influence of practice.

An advantage of this inter-dimensional approach is that the usual debate between mechanistic and subjectivist approaches may be avoided. Structure and agency both receive due attention, because the relationships between actors, including supernatural ones, are taken into account. Besides, a focus on the supernatural dimension will help to avoid a one-sided reductionist view on religion, as if the social structural mechanisms explain everything. Important as these latter may be, they cannot be taken as the only factor in the process of religious production, and it seems worthwhile to consider cultural structural processes as well.

Since the focus in this chapter is on one actor, a few remarks should be made with regard to the relationship between agency and structure. Actors can be shown to interpret events and phenomena, appealing to a repertoire of meanings available in structures, both symbolic and social in nature. As was shown in figure 1.1 in chapter 1, signification praxis can be represented within the triangle of signification, connecting events, structures and actors. When events or phenomena cannot be interpreted by an appeal to the available social and symbolic structures, structural changes will occur and new meanings will be added to these structures. On the other hand, events and phenomena are partly formed under the influence of social and symbolic structures. It is within this triangle that actors construct their identity with regard to gender as well as religion.

This may be stated in a different way in terms of the connectionist approach developed recently within cognitive anthropology.[2] The central question in cognitive anthropology is how knowledge is organized culturally. Connectionism takes its name from the connections that are assumed to exist between parallel archives of knowledge in the human mind. Thanks to these connections, these archives can be consulted simultaneously, as it were paradigmatically, just as the conductor of an orchestra, within a split second, in one summarizing view, consults the scores of the different instruments. This approach contrasts with the usual view that people organize their knowledge in the same manner as when they speak or write: i.e., according to so-called sentential logic. One might also call this a syntagmatic approach, just as when a listener to a CD with orchestral music selectively hears the main theme only and is able to sing or whistle along. Now, if people, as was suggested above through the triangle of signification, consult social and symbolic structures in their meaning-making process, they are appealing, in a simultaneous manner, to different but connected archives. Once they reach a conclusion in the paradigmatic manner, they will formulate this in the easier observable syntagmatic manner of sentential logic.

The term "schema" often is used instead of archive. D'Andrade defines schema as "the organization of cognitive elements into an abstract mental object capable of being held in working memory with default values or open slots which can be variously filled in with appropriate specifics."[3] The open slots remind one not only of a computer, but also of an empty bureaucratic form that must be filled in in terms of a concrete case. Religion is packed with schemas that help people to organize and interpret their experience. Again, these schemas are not as eternal as the gods that populate them are said to be: people adapt schemas to their experience, just as their schemas act as constraints on their behavior. Each new situation obliges a person to make a rapid and simultaneous consultation of the available schemas that fit the situation—usually a routine procedure; but if the schemas do not fit the situation or simply have been forgotten, new schemas will be developed, perhaps after some degree of confusion and chaos.

Power, in its aspect of influence on behavior, has the tendency to slow down this process, because it depends in its exercise on the constancy of certain schemas, imposed on the actors that are being influenced. Those in power therefore prefer the verbalized sentential logic over the—to them, risky—connectionist "let a thousand flowers flourish" practice. The politicians do not like subversives. The clergy generally do not like the heretics. Similarly, concrete gender situations can be interpreted and managed with the help of a number of more abstract schemas with regard to maleness and femaleness. Schemas are subject to change, according to changes in the signification process. Changing views on gender refer to alterations in current schemas.

There is one more characteristic of the concept of schema that is worth mentioning. D'Andrade distinguishes among three classes of schemas, organized hierarchically.[4] The first class of schemas is that of the master motives, containing a person's most general goals, acting rather autonomously in instigating behavior (e.g., love, security, play, providing for oneself). Below this is the class of more intermediate goals that help in the realization of the master motives. D'Andrade gives the examples of a job and marriage. The lowest class is that of the schemas that depend on the preceding classes for their motivation. These schemas are often part of daily routine. Thus, if the master motive of marriage is love, marriage in turn motivates the writing of a love letter or the purchase of a bouquet. Behavior is understood by D'Andrade to be the result of hierarchically organized sets of goal-schemas.[5] The motivational force of schemas diminishes according to the hierarchy of the three classes. Each person defines his or her own hierarchy.

Armed conceptually, I turn now to Joana's story.

## Joana's Story

Joana's case illustrates how religion can be a source of power for a woman. When I first met her, in 1990, Joana gave me the impression of being a happy and balanced person. She had been married for almost twenty years. Her husband was employed as a salesman in an international technical firm and spent much of his free time, especially on weekends, performing regional folk music on local stages. The couple had two daughters, then aged seventeen and nine. Joana was a successful professional. With two years of higher education—interrupted by her marriage—she had worked as a secretary and was now teaching a foreign language to children in a commercial language school.

After being introduced to her in 1990 by her brother-in-law, I queried Joana as to what religion meant to her. Perhaps because it was our first contact, she did not tell me at the time about the trouble she already was having with her husband. She also did not speak about the relationship she had with another man.

When we met again in 1995, her situation was radically different. She had gone through years of deep trouble and in the course of our conversation it became clear that in 1990 life had not been as happy and equilibrated as she had presented it. In what follows I will quote mainly from the 1995 interview. Reference will be made to the earlier interview, however, to show the ongoing process of meaning-making.

Between 1990 and 1995 Joana's marriage had ended. The facts are rapidly told. While working as a musician at places where drinks were on the house, her husband had gradually come to drink too much. As a consequence he lost his regular job as a salesman. The family lost friends. At home he became violent to the point of once, shortly before the interview, trying to kill Joana with a butcher's knife while she was ill in bed. She escaped, as she puts it, by a miracle. She then left him and moved with her daughters to another apartment. Her husband then went to Argentina to work as a musician.

In telling me what happened, Joana refers constantly to her religious convictions.

> Many things happened, including a break-up of the family . . . because my husband is a very difficult person. And thanks to my faith, my conviction that God exists, that someone exists who protects us, I am talking with you today. . . . His latest attack was meant to kill me. It was really very difficult.
> 
> He is an alcoholic. He is someone who doesn't have faith in anything. He believes only in himself. He doesn't understand that he needs treatment, that he must have faith in something, that he has to salvage the good things and channel them in a productive manner. . . . For me this was very difficult because I am a very objective person. I have a strong will. I have an ideal in life which is my mission: to obtain security for my daughters . . . to make a harmonious home for them. And all this was falling apart.
> 
> My daughters also have much faith. None of us regularly attends an institutional religion . . . but we never lose contact with God, from where we get our strength, from where strength really comes . . . . You can see that from their and my faith I always succeed in winding up on my feet. . . . I felt as if I were in a deep dark hole from which I was unable to get out. . . . I was unable to rest, I couldn't eat . . . because he always was making trouble, breaking things, threatening us verbally and sometimes physically.

Joana explained that she always confided in her husband, took care of him, devoted her life to him. She was shocked when he started to behave aggressively. She said that she had always believed that when one married it was for life. As she explained, she felt that she had only one card to play because at the time she thought marriage is for eternity. Therefore she was desperate when things began to go wrong. She concluded, "in a very cold manner," that life is a game in which one may win or lose. She emphasized, however, that one need not idly accept things when they start to go wrong. One must have faith.

> Only somebody who has a very great faith is able to live through such a situation. So thanks to my faith, I knew that God would never leave me alone, that he was waiting for an opportunity, that he would give me a chance to get out of this, to breathe anew as a human being deserves to.

Yet at the height of the crisis her daughters had suggested that God did not exist, because if he did he would not permit these things to happen. Why, they asked, do good people have to suffer so? Joana answered them:

> Only God can answer this for us. We do not have the right to judge what he does. He knows why he is doing these things. One day, [however, we will realize that]

all we are going through will enable us to grow and have a marvelous future. Then we will understand why these things happen. Everything in life is a lesson. . . . One should be a warrior and fight the adversities of life. So I think my faith, and my desire to understand what happened, to want to be part of a whole, helped me to be able to talk with you today.

Joana recognizes the role her husband's free will played in destroying him, even though God is the source of this free will. "He [her husband] likes this [the life he leads], so you have to let him live it, isn't that so? It is the free will that God has given him, the right to choose what he wants." Joana is proud, however, to have reacted in time to save herself, after a period in which she took him to a psychotherapist and to Alcoholics Anonymous. When nothing changed she decided that it was time to save herself and her daughters. She believes that she did enough for him and that her conscience is clear.

Joana went on to discuss her belief in guardian angels. She told me about her religious experience as a child, when she was a member of the Assembly of God, a Pentecostal church in which her father, a former Kardecist-Spiritist, was a pastor for some time. She spoke lovingly about her father, telling me, for example, how he always welcomed guests at his table and made hospitality a central value in his house, even though the family scarcely had enough for itself. Her mother was from a Lutheran family. Joana's interest in angels came from neither Pentecostalism nor Lutheranism. "They believed that only God exists and nothing else, no mentor, no guide, it was always God." In 1995, angels had become popular commercially in Brazil and elsewhere. Shops carried statues of them in their windows and sold books about them. With one exception, however, all the books were translations of North American publications.

> . . . a year ago, I got one of those angels as a present. I still keep it in my bedroom. . . . It is not the image that gives me strength. But it makes me feel good when I come into the room, I see the little face of that little angel, . . . and it gives me a kind of strength.

Joana then spoke about God:

> I always talked with God. It was not that I used "ready-made" prayers. . . . I open my heart to him, because I know that he sees everything. I know that better than anyone else God sees everything, he knows all that happens, and why one exists, because I think nothing happens by chance. With me it is like this: I am not an adept of any religion. However, I believe very much in the supreme being, who knows why things happen.

In 1990 Joana did not talk about angels, but the statements she made about the Catholic saints were similar to what she would say five years later about them. The reason why she wanted to be baptized in the Catholic church at the age of eighteen, despite her Pentecostal upbringing, was that she was fascinated by the saints whom she found to be beautiful. As a former Protestant she added that she was aware that the saints in the church were only images before whom she refused to kneel and ask for things. "You don't bargain with God," she insisted. "You may make a request, but then you will have to wait. If you deserve what you ask for, you will get it. I asked a lot from God, and he has helped me and has given me strength." Yet she has her favorite saints, such as St. George and St. Theresa, both of whom, she said, have helped her.

Nevertheless, she does not consider herself to be a typical Catholic and has her difficulties with the institution, its dogmas and especially with its claim to having the absolute truth. "All religions are true, not only the Roman one." Yet she now considers herself to be a Catholic, but of her own making. She refers to Christ and St. Peter as the bringers of the Catholic faith. Yet her view is that faith is much more general and in the end a matter of conscience.

> A person's heart is the church of God. God first came into my heart and then I went to the religion. God always was my friend, the best friend I have. . . . I think the best judgment, the best God we have, is our conscience. We all have faith.

In the 1990 interview Joana was very critical of what she considered to be the commercial activities in the Catholic church, such as baptism and burial being given only after payment. She compares the richness of the church with one of her earliest experiences with religion, when a priest teaching religious education in her class at a public school said that all the rich children would burn in hell. Joana says she then decided not to take part in church life.

Joana referred to a very un-Catholic element in her religious beliefs in our 1995 conversation: reincarnation. "I believe in other lives, and in lives already lived." She linked this to the idea that what a person experiences and suffers from in this life is a consequence of what she or he has done in a previous life. By suffering now you pay, as it were, for what you have done in the past. She used this notion to explain her husband's violence and believes that by now she has fully paid her debt from a former life because "not even Christ would accept what he did to me." The fact that she escaped from his attempt to kill her as by a miracle gives a special meaning to the idea that her life has been saved and that a new phase definitely has begun. She compared herself to a Phoenix risen from the ashes. Yet she still lives with the trauma of her past and almost every night she dreams that she is fleeing from her husband. She says that her prayers are her therapy and when her daughters have nightmares in which their father appears she advises them to pray and to ask God for protection and to take these traumas away.

In 1990 Joana referred to the Kardecist-Spiritist belief in reincarnation when she told me that early in her marriage she had given birth to two still-born babies. She still was grieving for them at the time. Her eldest sister, though not a Kardecist, had told her that she in fact was privileged because God used her womb so that "these spirits of light" could come into her body and move on again.

This helped her overcome the loss of the two children. Treatment by a Kardecist therapist later on helped her with a problem of persistent headaches. Joana also told me about her eldest daughter who suffered from a pain in the leg and who in a dream saw herself being operated on by the spirit of a young doctor who had recently died in a traffic accident in the town where they live. The girl identified herself increasingly with Kardecism. She has intuition, Joana observed, but is afraid to become a medium herself.

In 1993 Joana participated in a Bahai group for about six months, but withdrew because she did not wish to assume the leadership role she was offered. Also, she did not agree with some of the central ideas of Bahai belief, despite finding that faith in general and its prayers in particular beautiful. She had trouble, for example, accepting the belief that Christ, like many other enlightened persons, was merely a "sun ray" from God and that Bahaullah was "almost more divine than God himself." To her Christ is a marvelous figure. Even if he is not the son of God, to her he should be "because he fought, he sacrificed himself for the ideal he had, for the appreciation he had of human beings, for his simplicity and his abnegation."

Talking about these experiences Joana concluded that organized religion always exaggerates and distorts. Its obligations deny free will: "One should see God as a good thing, not as a being that is going to punish us." She prefers to pray by herself, which does not preclude the possibility that now and then she may attend a religious session and enjoy it, be it Bahai or Kardecist-Spiritist or other. "Sometimes I enter a Catholic church when there is nobody there and I pray. It does me good, and it gives me a delicious peace. I feel really better."

Her youngest daughter remained within the Bahai group and even went to international meetings. Eventually, however, she also left, although she did not abandon the faith itself. Joana tells how, at the time she herself was involved with the Bahais, she first attempted to live apart from her husband. The members of the group helped her. The way her youngest daughter, who still identifies as a Bahai, lived through the events, also had religious overtones. The girl had promised to pray a certain number of prayers to Bahaullah in whom she "has very great faith." Though she has distanced herself from the Bahais, Joana says that she supports her daughter's participation: "It is good to have such faith." After Joana escaped the assault by her husband, her daughter pledged to pray to Bahaullah for nine consecutive days in payment of the *promessa* (vow) she had made. Making a vow, usually to a saint, and fulfilling it when one has received what one has asked for are very common in popular Catholicism. This practice had been adopted and incorporataed by her daughter as part of her Bahai faith.

Joana has discovered other sources of strength. She saw a movie about the life of Tina Turner and learned to her surprise that the famous singer had lived through situations similar to what she experienced. One of her daughters then gave her the book the movie was based on. She identified with Turner even more as she read it. She learned from it, she said, not to hold on too long to things that bother you, be it work, or a marriage. "I think this is what I am doing, allowing myself to have a bit of happiness in my way," she added.

"Thanks to the good God," Joana sees her relationship with her daughters as being harmonious and even a form of sisterhood (the Portuguese word for sisterhood, *irmandade*, also is used to refer to a religious order).

Towards the end of the 1995 interview, when she was talking about her belief in reincarnation and in memories from previous lives, Joana offered an example. She spoke about a platonic relationship she had had for eight years with an older man who was not married. It ended with his death in 1993. The relationship according to Joana was characterized by great affection. "I had a very good friend. He was somebody like . . . if I were not married at the time, he would have been the ideal person that I always wanted in my life." It was a case of love on both sides. Yet, they did not get involved sexually because "he understood my situation . . . that I would never want to do something I believed was wrong. I would not feel good about it."

Joana told her husband about the relationship and he did not object to it. She would not leave him for this man. Although they continued to see each other socially, Joana would never visit him at his apartment.

They first met when Joana took a job as a secretary in an office where he was employed. No one else seemed to like him, which made her wonder why she did. "To me he was the sweetest person you can imagine." She was almost certain that she had met him previously somewhere and had been fond of him. Thinking about it, she remembered having dreamt about him when she was a girl. The dream took place in a castle with beautiful lawns surrounding it. The two were together, a couple obviously in love. "It was something very real to me, I even felt his body at my side. He cared for me and liked me." The conclusion she reached was that they had been lovers in a former life who had met again in this one.

Shortly before his death he had telephoned her asking her to come to his apartment. Joana still remembers the exact date. She refused, however, telling him: "You know I will always love you, but I cannot visit you." He countered that some day when she would decide to visit him, it would be too late. Her reaction was to ask whether this was a threat, "that on the day that I would be free, you would not want me anymore?" Two weeks later when she called him at his office, the secretary said that she could not speak with him. Joana felt guilty believing that it was because she had refused to come to his place. She then was transferred to the secretary's boss who told her that her friend had died on the day she had last spoken with him. The official cause of his death was an aneurysm. Joana felt that she had been robbed.

> My God, why this? I live with a very difficult person who tortures me. I am not ashamed of what I thought then: Why did he die and not my husband? Why does somebody die who is good and productive in life. But today I understand that I can't control life. It just happens. It is fate that one has to accept and that happens. It passes, it passed. No other way. Because of what happened, I believe in my previous lives. This immense causality . . .

Joana's presentation of this episode in her life emphasized the contradiction that whereas her friend always was kind and caring with her, to others he was thought of as being nasty and imposing and was not liked because of it. The only explanation she could come up with came from a dream that, she said, may have been a brief rememberance of a former life. "I really expect, and I say this sincerely, that we will have another life together . . . [although] an enormous emptiness remained here. It has marked me." Joana added that one day she read the phrase, "God who made the shoulders also made crosses." She concluded that God knows the size of a person's shoulders and thus also that of the cross the person is able to carry. "And also till when you have to carry it. I think the most difficult part I have finished carrying. I put it down already. It's over." At times she thinks that he is not dead, that one day he will call her and tell her it was all a joke. On the day of our interview, Joana reported having seen someone on a passing bus who could have been his twin. The man had lifted his sunglasses and looked at her. "But of course, it was not him. If it had been, he would have gotten off the bus at the next stop. So it wasn't him. But I was really upset."

## Discussion

Joana's story enables us to examine how one Brazilian woman creatively mobilized pieces from several of the religious belief systems in her culture to find meaning and understanding in a time of personal crisis. It shows syncretism in the making and reveals the process of syncretizing. It also offers us insight into some of the power processes that occur in the construction of gender identities in a religious context. The case is not necessarily representative at the societal level, although it represents a process that may be occurring on a much wider scale. It may be that the Brazilian cultural context is optimal for the combination of ideas and practices that would seem incompatible in other settings.[6] The events in

Joana's married life forced her to find meaning in what had happened to her. With every new event she was obliged to construct her own triangle of signification, drawing on a score of schemas in her repertoire, as it was accumulated and adapted in the course of her life. Strikingly, the schemas she used, including her views on gender, are basically, though not exclusively (Tina Turner!), religious in nature. In maneuvering her triangles of signification she managed to survive, defending herself and her two daughters. The vocabulary she used expressed her struggle and directly referred to power and strength (*força*).

In the course of her life, Joana has become acquainted with a number of religious worldviews. Some of these she knew from her own experience, whereas others were known to her through discussions with friends and relatives. Thus she had learned about Kardecist-Spiritism indirectly and assimilated it through discussions with her sister. Direct participation does not seem to be a precondition for the adoption of ideas. Seen from the perspective of institutionalized religion, some of these views are considered mutually exclusive, but this did not impede Joana from picking and choosing and using them as she liked. Her decision not to actively participate in a religious group put her in what might be thought of as the informal sector of religion. One might say that she did not have a religion, but was very religious. The experiences she has had with a variety of religions in the course of her life have led her to avoid participation. Yet she understands and knows these religions, in their internal and external dimensions, and especially in their supernatural dimension. The way in which she constructs her religious identity is an indirect criticism of rule-directed formal institutionalized religion, which she considers *bitolada*: narrow, limited, short-sighted. The use she made during our conversations of parallel schemas (in connectionist terms) from different religions put her nearer to the paradigmatic comparative pole (the conductor's view of the scores) than to that of syntagmatic sentential logic (the single theme whistled by the listener), which she in fact condemned as dogmatic and too narrow. Her independent position has made it possible for her to apply such a syncretic approach.

Thus, indirectly, the elements she took from different religious sources made her case in a certain way representative of more than one institutionalized religion, though mainly at the symbolic level, more than at the social structural level, which she generally avoided. What she experienced was relevant only to her, yet it was clearly grounded in the repertories of the Brazilian social and cultural context, even though she made her own selection. The Afro-Brazilian religions were virtually absent from her discourse. In 1990 she had talked about Umbanda, saying that she liked "the vivid colors, the music that is theirs," but that she thought of it as a pagan religion. She was not attracted to it, "not even a little bit."

It is the syncretic climate of Brazilian society, it appears,[7] that enabled Joana to construct her religious and gender identity in the way she did. The Brazilian minimal credo seems to be: A person should have faith, it does not matter which one.[8] Joana showed us how in a creative manner the relative freedom of agency (the subjectivist pole) can be combined with structural constraints (the mechanistic pole) in the construction of identity in the course of life's events. She consciously used her freedom to be religious without having to join a religious group, and thus distanced herself from institutionalized settings. When the Bahai group wanted her to take a leadership role, she refused and in the end dissociated herself from the group. On the other hand, she very much depended for her repertoire of religious ideas and meanings on the institutionalized religions she had been in contact with throughout her life. In this process of cultural praxis not only her religious but also her gender identity—and that of her husband!—is very much at stake, primarily because of the failure of their marriage.

When we take a closer look at the cultural repertories of meanings she used, a striking diversity of schemas presents itself.[9] It is striking in comparison with the efforts by most of the institutionalized religions to protect their boundaries and thereby their identities. It is less striking when understood from the viewpoint of the individual actor, as a way of being religious.

At the top of the hierarchy of schemas, a dynamic and heterogeneous concept of God is present as a source of help but also of trial. To Joana He is very much a master motive. The idea is even that He kills her friend and lets her husband live on. Therefore there is also some doubt about the existence of God as a moral and just being as He is conceived of in the Judeo-Christian tradition. It is not clear whether God is outside or inside the person (in the form of moral conscience), or both. God is also the source of the human free will, which Joana mentions as one of the explanations for her suffering. Simultaneously she refers to an inevitable destiny in life.

Christ plays a different role, at the intermediate level of the hierarchy of schemas, because he is a means to a goal of the highest level. To Joana he is an example of perfection, *uma pessoa maravilhosa* (a marvelous person) representing struggle, sacrifice, an ideal, valorizing human beings, simplicity, abnegation, all master motives that to her make him the Son of God, despite what the Bahai faith maintains. Though the difference of opinion led her to leave the Bahai group, Christ is not important to her in her struggle for life. Nor is his mother, the Virgin, who, although she was mentioned in the 1990 interview, was not included in the 1995 conversation.

In a more abstract way faith (*fé*) is an important ingredient, representing optimism and confidence and as such is another master motive. Joana referred to her ex-husband as somebody without faith. Faith is important, as she told her daughter, and it is more important to have faith than to have a specific faith. In this way elements from a variety of religions could be combined in her own faith.

Whereas God seemed to occupy a central place when interpretation of events was needed, this did not exclude an appeal to other schemas for the explanation of affliction. A prominent role was given to the Kardecist belief in reincarnation, which also appeared high in Joana's hierarchy of schemas. To her it explained the death of her still-born babies and also suggested to her that the suffering she endured in her marriage was seen as a form of debt payment carried over from a former life. On the other hand, her belief in reincarnation justified and legitimated her love for her friend and the hope or even certainty that they would be together in the future.

Another source that provided Joana with strength, though more on the intermediate level of schemas, was that of the guardian angel. The image not only made her think of the protection they give, but of their childlike innocence which represented a master motive to her. Next to the angels, also at this intermediate level, certain Catholic saints were a help.

Though the details are not clear from the interview, the Bahai group aided Joana when she first attempted to leave her husband. In offering assistance they also were part of the intermediate level, contributing to a higher goal schema (happiness) through practical third level schemas such as direct counseling.

Clairvoyance, also as an accepted intermediate level schema, provided a way of legitimating and explaining events such as her friend's allusion to his early death. Though not quoted in the fragments above, Joana told me that both she and her daughter have predicted certain events. In the days before her husband attacked her, for example, her daughter had complained that she felt something terrible was going to happen.

Besides these religious schemas, there are secular ones that Joana refers to. At the intermediate level her job provided a source of strength and self-respect. Also at the intermediate level, when trying to explain her husband's alcoholism, she relied on psychotherapy to emphasize his limitation of affect (a master motive) as a reason. Yet when asked whether she herself received treatment, her answer was that her therapy is prayer, thus returning to the intermediate level of the religious field.

It is also striking that certain metaphors were helpful as intermediate schemas. Struggle was a meaningful concept to her and to her daughters. Joana also compared life to a game of cards, in which we have to play the hand we are dealt. When speaking of her relationship with her daughters, sisterhood was mentioned as a source of strength. Phoenix raising from the ashes was the metaphor she used to describe—what she called—her resurrection, again a religious image. There are certain Portuguese words that Joana used to point to situations of bliss: *maravilhoso* (marvelous), *harmonia* (harmony), *lindo* (beautiful), *gostoso* (delicious).

Indirectly, and occasionally directly, Joana presented gender roles in an ideal marriage as parts of a master motive. Her fondness for her father suggests that his behavior was the model of masculinity to her. When she described her critical attitude towards marriage candidates, it is clear that she had certain criteria, and when speaking of her ideal view of a home she mentioned some of these master motives: love, dedication, fidelity, respect. Marriage, for her, comes from God and must be eternal. In a negative sense, her husband's behavior also defined a gender role. In her friend Joana found what was lacking in her husband. In times of crisis, she had to choose between alternative schemas of the intermediate and low level that competed for preference: must she stay with her husband or seek a divorce? Is she to help her husband and believe his promises, or should she leave him? Is she to be faithful to him, or will she opt for a life with her friend? Should she have sex with him or should she abstain, even from visiting him?

Joana claimed to take strength from religion and therefore obtained from it the power to survive. As she put it, "I am now strong enough to put this to an end." Though in a male-dominated society it can be considered as normal for women to accept the alcoholism of their husbands—a common low-level schema in Brazil—Joana refused. As she told her story her moral and personal power, nourished by the master motives of the highest level, was in strong contrast with the physical force of the intermediate and low levels that her faithless ex-husband used against her. Her relationship with her friend is described as sweet (*doce*) and therefore corresponding to a high level gender schema. Yet people did not like him, which suggested that in his relationships with them he applied his own intermediate and low level power schemas. To Joana, the superiority of the sweetness schema was a convincing argument for her love, despite or even because of the fact that he was not amiable to others.

Referring to the two aspects of power we may ask: Is Joana's power of the kind that is capable of influencing other people's behavior? This is not clear from her story. Since her participation in formal bureaucratic structures was minimal—she would not even join religious groups—with the possible exception of her work, she lacked frameworks within which to influence other people.

With regard to her personal relationships, she was not able to modify her husband's attitude or behavior, even though she tried. It seems probable that the training she gave to her daughters, together with the "sisterhood" they shared when the family was in trouble, was a way of influencing them. Her friend respected her, even though in the end he invited her to come to his apartment. Apart from these examples Joana did not seem to have power as a behavior-influencing factor.

Is the power she has then more an illustration of the second aspect of power, survival in life? Her discourse puts a much stronger emphasis on the way she used her relationships with God, angels and saints to obtain power to survive, than on efforts to influence people. The power that Joana has, then, is her strength to survive, as when she escaped from death at the hands of her husband.

## Conclusion

Joana's story was presented for the purpose of examining the syncretic process at the level of the actor. The analytical focus was on relationships among gender, power and religion. Questions were asked with regard to Joana's use of religious resources, her views on gender issues and her ways of exercising power, both as a capacity to influence people and to survive.

From Joana's story a case can be made for defining power not only as the capacity to influence other people's behavior, but also to organize one's life. Though she expresses herself more in terms of strength (*força*) than of power (*poder*), the way she endured the events of her life certainly may be considered empowerment. The most important source of this empowerment, although she did not participate in organized religion and therefore lacked the support of a group, was her "religiosity," which she constructed from a wide variety of religious ideas and practices available in her culture. Since religion, more than any other aspect of—in this case Brazilian—culture, offers answers to questions about life and death, it may come as no surprise that the survival aspect of power has a strong religious component. To a woman, gender is often the primal area where power processes take place. Joana's life phase between interviews was marked by the failure of her marriage. The way she talked about this experience clearly shows her way of living her religiosity and also her views on gender.

The analysis of Joana's story also shows the relevance of a praxis approach and of schema theory. Her account of the events and her interpretation of her life made clear that cultural and social structures, agency and structure, formal and informal behavior, public and private domains should be studied together in a dialectical manner, in an effort to understand how the extremes touch each other and are linked. Schema theory proved to be a useful tool in this regard because it helped us to understand how Joana, as an actor, had her own way of managing the schemas available to her, as she found them in Brazilian cultural and social structures. She did this by defining their importance, rejecting some (Assemblies of God, Umbanda) selecting others (God, reincarnation) and by applying them in her own way in the process of interpreting the events that characterized her life. Though this personal hierarchy of schemas was not consistent nor fully formulated at all times, it helped her to make sense of her life and—to a lesser extent—to influence the people nearest to her.

## Notes

1. I am grateful to Els Jacobs and Marjo de Theije for their insights with regard to power and gender. The first draft of this chapter was read as a paper during a symposium they organized during the BRASA meeting in Cambridge in September 1996. My co-editor was kind enough to help me polish that paper to a publishable article.

2. See Maurice Bloch, "Language, Anthropology and Cognitive Science," *Man* 26 (1991), no. 2: 183-198; Roy D'Andrade, *The Development of Cognitive Anthropology* (Cambridge: Cambridge University Press, 1995), 138-149; Naomi Quinn and Claudia Strauss, "A Cognitive/Cultural Anthropology," in *Assessing Cultural Anthropology*, Robert Borofsky, ed. (New York: McGraw-Hill, 1994), 284-300; Claudia Strauss and Naomi Quinn, *A Cognitive Theory of Cultural Meaning* (Cambridge: Cambridge University Press, 1997).

3. D'Andrade, *The Development*, 179.

4. D'Andrade, *The Development*, 232.

5. D'Andrade, *The Development*, 233.

6. See chapter 3 by Greenfield for elaboration of this point.

7. André Droogers, "Syncretism, Power, Play," in *Syncretism and the Commerce of Symbols*, Göran Aijmer, ed. (Gothenburg: IASSA, 1995), 38-59; André Droogers, "Identity, religious pluralism and ritual in Brazil: Umbanda and Pentecostalism," in *Pluralism and Identity: Studies in Ritual Behaviour*, Jan Platvoet and Karel van der Toorn, eds. (Leiden: Brill), 91-113.

8. André Droogers, "A religiosidade mínima brasileira," *Religião e Sociedade* 14 (1987), no. 2: 62-86.

9. Katherine Ewing, "The Illusion of Wholeness: Culture, Self, and the Experience of Inconsistency," *Ethos* 18 (1990), no. 3: 251-279.

## Chapter 10

## Ragga Cowboys:
## Country and Western Themes in
## Rastafarian-Inspired Reggae Music

Werner Zips

### Introduction

When I first traveled to Jamaica in 1984 my anticipations were (in)formed by years of close attention to Reggae music. This included all available sources exploiting the increasingly international Rastaman vibrations. Most of these representations portrayed Jamaica with standardized images of a righteous and rebellious nation of Bob Marley-likes. The former projections of the "Island in the Sun" had changed to pictures of "Africa in the Caribbean." Most sources of information on the religious/musical aspect of Jamaican culture were rather superficial in content, largely exotizing Rastafari by drawing on the noble savage image attributed to Bob Marley in one way or the other by many outside commentators. In line with this readily available scheme of perception, Marley became epitomized as the authentic representation of Rastafari. And Reggae was accordingly identified as (authentic) Rasta music.

Besides these (distortions of) media constructs there was another source available to me: my first real contact to the music in the late 1970s happened through a Jamaican-born Rastafari, Emsley Smith, who had moved from London to Vienna to open a Reggae record shop in the Austrian capital. Smith was then in his early fifties and therefore to be considered as an elder invested with the cultural (and highly) symbolic capital of knowledge related to the foundations of Rastafari and the origins of Reggae music. Growing up in Kingston during the 1950s and '60s, at the time "when it all started," he knew personally such important figure heads of (modern) Rastafari history as Count Ossie, Prince Emmanuel and Mortimer Planno,[1] as well as most originators of Reggae. He introduced me to the music of Peter Tosh, Burning Spear, Bunny Wailer and Bob Marley and mediated the messages with a rich body of explanations, contextualizations, annotations and so on. In this way I became familiar with Rastafari rhetoric (or *Highalogue*[2]) and "overstandings" of the world in historical context and within a wider political frame.

My actual encounter with Jamaica turned out to differ sharply from expectations nurtured by personal contact with Smith and written sources on Reggae and Rastafari. The first Rasta (or rather Dread[3]) I met (on my first walk into Montego Bay) offered me a ride on his motorbike before he quite convincingly threatened to cut my throat for not paying him the fare for the ride. The second Rasta I met, merely two hours after this disillusioning encounter, invited me to the Nyahbinghi meeting of a large congregation of Rastafari in the vicinity of Mandeville.[4] This *groundation* (as these meetings are also called) celebrated the ninety-second birthday of His Imperial Majesty Emperor Haile Selassie I of Ethiopia with two weeks of nightlong drumming, venerations of Jah Rastafari (identified in H.I.M.) and spiritual death threats to all "Babylonian" forces such as Ronald Reagan, Margaret Thatcher, the South African apartheid regime and, most of all, the Roman Catholic pope who is pictured as the reincarnation of Satan just as Haile Selassie is of god.[5]

The music I experienced at this occasion was quite familiar to me through my preference for spiritual Reggae, so-called Rasta or Roots Reggae which drew heavily on the musical expressions of the Nyahbinghi. In fact this was the form of Reggae I knew best due to its wide distribution on the European market. Like many other international consumers of Reggae I equated the Roots section of the music with the whole musical genre. Such recording artists as Ras Michael and the Sons of Negus, the Mystic Revelation of Rastafari, Israel Vibration, Culture, Burning Spear and others were considered as the true representatives of Reggae when they actually represented textual expressions of Rastafari origin with musical styles combining the drum beats, chants and hymns of the Nyahbinghi with production arrangements geared at the commodification of their aesthetic products for sale on the European, American and Japanese market. Authenticity functioned as one of the best labels for the marketing of Reggae that set the trend for the later commodification of world music.

Just a few days after my unexpected grounding at the Nyahbinghi, I attended the famous yearly Reggae Sunsplash Festival (a goal since I had seen the 1978 film on the first Reggae Sunsplash). Ras Michael and the Sons of Negus were billed as openers for the show. They performed in front of a small crowd of seemingly disinterested Jamaicans and a handful of enthusiastic foreign Reggae fans.[6] The star of the five-day festival, in contrast, was Yellowman, a revered DJ who was at the time preoccupied with the sizes and functions of sexual organs, sending some 50,000 people into a frenzy.[7]

I found myself confused by the apparent contradictions in the social/musical field of Reggae and its relation to other social fields.[8] How could somebody praise the name of Selassie in the same song he talks complete "slackness," as explicit lyrics bordering on pornography are generally referred to in Jamaica? Why would the Rastas I had met participating in the Nyahbinghi be attracted to such performances condemned as filth and Babylonian in most Rastafari reasonings? And what had turned the pure form of (Roots) Reggae into a torn aesthetics owing more to sex and crime entertainment than to the redemption songs promised and delivered by Bob Marley? Rastafarians I talked to in trying to make sense of this paradox would deny altogether the representation of Rastafari through Reggae and declare the music to be "mix up, mix up business"[9]—a doubling notion used to underline the veracity of a mixing in *Jamaica Talk*.[10]

In this essay I wish to unfold the logic of this mixing by use of an extreme example: the abundance of Western film topics, idioms, myths, practices and actual bodily comportment in Jamaican culture. I will focus especially on the field of Reggae which is described by most foreign critics as an Africa-oriented invention.[11] From the outset the guest appearances of Western characters in the African roots format seem to be a paradoxical example for a syncretic process. But the appearance of a Western-structured habitus is not restricted to the aesthetic expressions in musical performances. The incorporation of a set of Western hero-dispositions is also visible in social action, as for example, a multitude of actual everyday practices, be it the rude (boy) style in ordering a drink, approaching a potential sexual partner, by "acting/playing the cool" where and whenever possible, or the readiness to answer the slightest challenge head-on. This social reality organized by a corresponding collective habitus of agents exposed to two divergent sets of philosophical/ideological systems (Rastafari and the Western) is reflected in aesthetic production and reproduction.[12] Yet, the question I am posing goes beyond the mere observation of syncretism (the mixing of these divergent religious/political/mythical systems) and seeks to explain its dynamics in the field studied. To do this I must analyze the logic of practices of concrete agents such as the artists and consumers in the field of Reggae.

In Bourdieu's praxeological fashion, I therefore will turn from the actor's level of (self)explanation to the structural one that determines various practices of Jamaicans with respect to Reggae.[13] At this level actors are assumed to embody dispositions that they need to promote their access to capital in a given field. In this way the dispositions may be thought of as inscribed in what Bourdieu refers to as their *habitus* in such a way that these dispositions are viewed by them as natural and therefore unquestioned. This perspective should restrain us from uncritical acceptance of interpretations of this and other forms of syncretism as deviations from any presupposed original or pure forms.[14] Therefore, while at first I was unable to accept Yellowman's musical and lyrical efforts as Reggae, this approach enabled me to do so. I now understand that my deviation theory negating the relation between DJ, Ragga or Dancehall Reggae and the pure or authentic Rasta or Roots Reggae must have left a great many Jamaicans who discussed it with me puzzled. To them it was as if I lacked any sense of the game, or habitus.[15]

To unfold the logic (of practices) in the field studied, the emanations (i.e., the artistic productions) will not be victimized for an abstract structuralist approach. But, the participatory level alone appears insufficient to uncover the confinements of the individuals who are trapped in all those aspects of social structure of which they are not aware. The theoretical framework provided by Pierre Bourdieu for such a participant objectivation appears to me very useful for the attempt to link the structural conditions to the empirically observed practices by way of revealing the generic processes of habitus formation.[16]

## A Praxeological Approach to the Syncretic Process Studied

In order to account for the construction of such opposite schemata of perception, appreciation and action as the ones embodied in the dominant myth of the Western film and Rastafari with their reflexive postcolonial critique in one and the same artistic field, one must seek to clarify the relation between field (including its relation to other fields, especially the field of power) and habitus as the institution of the social in the individual. Bourdieu's concept of the field accounts for social situations and contexts governed by a set of objective social relations. Any social formation is structured by a hierarchically organized series of fields. Each of the fields (e.g., the economic, political, cultural, educational or artistic field) can be defined as a structured space with its own laws of functioning. Its structure is determined by the relations between the positions that agents occupy in the field.

Habitus is defined or rather openly conceptualized as a system of durable and transposable dispositions that generate and organize practices and perceptions. In other terms it can be described as a practical mastery or a feel for the game that inclines agents to act and react in specific situations in a manner that is not always calculated and even less so a conscious following of the rules.[17] Yet, this sense of the game is socially constituted and therefore mediates a (socially structured) logic to actual practices. The inherent historicity of individual agency must not be confused with a mechanistic objectivist functioning of the individual. Rather, habitus differs radically from habit insofar as the notion conceptualizes the generative (if not creative) capacity inscribed in the system of dispositions as an art (of invention).[18] I will try to show empirically how the inscription of the dominant structures of the Western myth that communicates deep structures of American social belief (through its narratives of a conflict of principles rather than a simple conflict between characters) can also be reflexively questioned.[19]

The conception of habitus as accumulated history enables us to pay attention to the matter of dominance (and cultural imperialism) through its focus on practices generated by the individual and collective history of agents.[20] In this sense social agents in a particular field are the product of history—of the history of the whole social field and of the accumulated experience of a path within the specific subfield.[21] It is in the individual history or social experience of agents that the structures of preference that inhabit them are constituted in a complex temporal dialectic with the objective structures that produced them and which they tend to reproduce.

Artists who have been exposed lifelong (as ordinary agents) to the regularities or principles of White American social beliefs due to the importance of the Western film market in the Caribbean, and at the same time to the Afrocentric and pan-Africanist teachings of Rastafari, will likely show both preferences as structured dispositions in the same aesthetic act. By these acts or performances they also will tend to reproduce the same structures that produced them.[22]

An analysis that seeks to establish the double relation between field and habitus locates the syncretic process in the habitus formation. It aims at mixed or combined expressions in the practices of agents that are structured by the habitus. Syncretic expressions refer in their practical manifestation to a blended, divided or even torn habitus. It depends on the extent of the discrepancy between a particular field and a set of intersecting fields to which the habitus owes its *conditioning*. On the other hand the relation between field and habitus is not only one of conditioning but also a relation of knowledge or *cognitive construction*: "Habitus contributes to constituting the field as a meaningful world, a world endowed with sense and value, in which it is worth investing one's own energy."[23] Therefore, the analytic focus is on the primary experience of the field, or more precisely, the (dynamic) relation between different types of fields and different types of habitus.

It is important to note that the conception of habitus as the socially made body is an *open system of dispositions*. As a (necessary) product of history this system is not the fate of individuals (belonging to a certain class or social category) but rather constantly affected by experience. Consequentially, this experience either reinforces or modifies its structures. This was and currently is, for example, the case due to the flow of Black American films reaching the Jamaican market and substituting for (or counteracting) Western, Karate and Hollywood action movies with bits and pieces of Black American consciousness.[24] Habitus is also not always inhabited by the field of forces, or perfectly adapted to the field without any conscious rational choice. Indeed, the postcolonial experience of alternative cognitive and value systems (which is also the overall frame for our case study) is generally a time of crisis, in which the routine adjustment is brutally disrupted. Then, agents prove in their conscious practices that habitus is not "a conceptual straight-jacket that provides no room for modification or escape."[25]

We will see that the discourses and practices of individuals are situationally specific, with the structures embedded in the habitus influencing them while they in turn transform the structural conditions. Actors are not puppets on the string of social structure. They are not dominated by rules, but rather guided by habitualized regularities. Reflexivity enables them to clarify unconscious structures of domination. Habitus, therefore, always may be viewed as combining or mixing various structures and thus as syncretic. When actors realize or clarify the relationship between the structures of dominance and their own habitus, they may be expected to modify the structures in which they find themselves.[26] Where social dominance is recognized, forms of resistance may develop. Artists may take the initiative because of their privileged position. The reflexive text of Yellowman, in which he questions the unconscious conditioning of Jamaican men exposed to Hollywood films based on mainstream American (white) values, examined later in this paper, is a convincing example.[27]

By controlling what Bourdieu calls symbolic capital, or prestige, artists such as Yellowman occupy privileged positions in the field of Reggae. As a result they are able to recreate meanings that prevail in other fields, as for example in relations of power. Consumers, the audience for the artist's products, of course, are the final arbiters of the artist's efforts at resistance when they accept or reject the artist's work. In Bourdieu's terms, they transform the artist's cultural capital into recognized symbolic capital, and hence power. The social field, also in Bourdieu's terms, might be thought of as a game in which specific patterns, often syncretic regularities rule, such as those taken simultaneously from the oppositional frameworks of Western films and the "livity" of Rastafari. The way the game is played out, however, depends both on the hierarchy of different forms of capital in a concrete field and their dissemination among individual players. In the artistic field of Ragga Reggae[28] such divergent forms of capital as the invincibility of the Western hero and the righteous anger of Rastafari "words, sounds and power" compete with each other through the actions of players (in the game) attempting to acquire and use them as a stake in the struggle for power. Occasionally the apparent conflict of interest between the imperial Western myth and the emancipatory Rastafari philosophy is represented directly in the chosen artistic field. But more often, artists and consumers appear to strive for the safe side through their efforts to combine, or syncretize, both forms of capital. By acknowledging the opposite sources of recognition, or power, the actors seek to maximize the stakes of the game, as rewards of a particular field.[29] I turn next to some examples. In them we will see that Ragga Cowboys at times "saddle Western horses" successfully, thanks to the critical devices acquired from Rastifari reasoning.[30]

## Expressions of the Western Code in the Rude Boy Habitus

When Bob Marley, Bunny Wailer and Peter Tosh started their musical careers, there were not many symbols and expressions of Rastafari to be found in either their artistic output, their representations of everyday life (accessible through innumerable sources) or their bodily comportment in public appearances and performances. They presented themselves as defiant young men, toughened by conditions and experiences of and in the ghetto. "The attitude came to be described as the "rude boy" culture of which the Wailers were masters."[31] Images of the West fitted well into the individualistic rude boy habitus.[32] The Wailers, for example, integrated symbols, maxims and practices of the Wild West in their artistic expressions, if only to deconstruct them. There is no sheriff (to be shot) in Jamaica, much less in Africa.[33] Yet, there are persons who fit the images of sheriffs projected by Western movies. It is against these unjust lawmen, or any other agent of the so-called Babylon system, that the Reggae-Singer takes on the role of the gunman—as exemplified in the album title *Wanted Dread and Alive*[34] and in the cover art showing the portrait of dreadlocks Rastafari Peter Tosh in the style of a wanted poster for dangerous gunmen. But the act is an example of a radical deconstruction: instead of being wanted "dead and alive," Peter Tosh makes a claim to be wanted "dread and alive," meaning as a living Rastafari. Read from the theoretical frame of habitus these examples demonstrate the adequacy of the habitus concept formulated as a generative and even creative capacity inscribed in the system of dispositions as an art of practical mastery and in particular an *ars inveniendi*.[35] The dynamic formation of habitus is not a one-way street for but one set of structures. It could be better characterized as a(n) (individual) battlefield within a large (social) battlefield of divergent interests.

Since they were inexpensive, Western movies were shown almost exclusively in Jamaican cinemas until the 1980s, making them one of the few affordable items of consumption available to many young, predominantly male, Jamaicans.

Whereas other genres of foreign films, such as Karate and equally cheap action films, have displaced the Western in the cinemas, the genre still abounds in TV. Unemployed adolescents might consume more than one of these films per day when they are just killing time. In this way the continual experience of the codes (in the Western) structure the habitus of these individuals side by side with the actual encounters they have with Rastafaris transmitting their philosophy and livity in personal encounters

*Dread and Alive* and *I Shot the Sheriff* are examples of the mixing of dispositions derived from the Western film and Rastafari, whereby the latter critically reverses the former. Images of the Wild West, generally considered repressive of the Black experience, are recreated with the new meanings of resistance against and redemption from dominant structures. Another example is to be found on the album cover of Bob Marley and the Wailers' *Rasta Revolution*, where the Wailers pose with guns in their hands.[36] With the display of their habitus as defiant gunmen, Reggae artists transmit possible strategies for social action. More concretely, when the Wailers pose with guns in their hands they expose dispositions originally inculcated in their habitus by structures of Western media communication.[37] In turn, such artistic practices influence or structure the habitus formations of other social agents sharing similar experiences with the artists.

The incorporation of foreign images, symbols, languages, etc. may subvert their original meaning even more explicitly than in the rude boy deconstruction of the gunslinging outlaw personality performed by the Wailers. Such acts then tend to question the perceived equivalence between different cultural practices. Rasta (influenced) Reggae offers several examples of modes of radical deconstruction. In *Buffalo Soldier* by Bob Marley, for example, the subversive strategy applied to perceived equivalences is heightened. Marley uses the identification of the Buffalo Soldier with the Dreadlocks Rasta to make a political statement for Black (historical) consciousness in general and the acceptance of *Africanness* in particular.

> Buffalo Soldier, Dreadlock Rasta
> There was a Buffalo Soldier
> In the heart of America
> Stolen from Africa, brought to America
> Fighting on arrival, fighting for survival . . .
> If you know your history
> Then you would know where you coming from . . .
> I'm just a Buffalo Soldier
> In the heart of America
> Stolen from Africa, brought to America . . .

Said he was a Buffalo Soldier
Win the war for America . . .[38]

Marley identifies with the (forced upon) position of a Buffalo Soldier to clarify the history of Africans in America. But other artists lacked such a critical (or deconstructive) stance in their identification with Western characters. Some went as far as to name themselves after Wild West heroes or actors who starred in the movies. Many early Sound System-DJs took on the affiliations with these foreign (film) personalities at a time when Reggae was considered by foreign critics as a purely Africa-oriented invention.[39] Clint Eastwood, Dillinger, Trinity, Lone Ranger and John Wayne were among them, some growing dreadlocks and delivering Rastafari content in their songs.[40] On the album cover for *African Roots* the Reggae-DJ Clint Eastwood is pictured forming two pistols with his hands and posing in the well known hexis of the actor Clint Eastwood. The album title *African Roots* signifies the complex process of blending two diverse traditions. Gestures and bodily comportment inscribed in the habitus of the Jamaican Natty (Dread) by Western movies become visible in various modes of expression. This is as true for social agents in the position of consumers in the field of Reggae production as for the recording artists.[41] Together with the philosophical visions of Rastafari (generally called a religion by outsiders), these modes create a new (dynamic) artistic tradition. The rude boy habitus combines the Africanness of Rastafari with the mythologized images of the tough guy (from the Wild West). Its syncretic appearance in various practices and artistic expressions refers to the negotiation of identity among people whose roots were cut in many ways. With the emergence of Raggamuffin, as a somewhat updated (computer age) version of the original rude boy, the orientation to foreign traditions (in social action and music) was on the rise even more. Local media helped to transmit these foreign structures of perception, appreciation and action into local experiences. From all the influences observable in the syncretic formation, I will restrict myself in the following section to the presence of the Wild West motives in Raggamuffin.

## Ragga Cowboys in the Dancehall Rodeo

Dominant metaphors for Dancehall and Raggamuffin culture derive from Western movies. The most important group signifier is the *Posse* which carries a special connotation when used for a group of friends belonging to an organization, a district in Kingston (like Tivoli Gardens, Waterhouse or Dungle), a nation (like in Jamaican Posse, American Posse, etc.) or an ethnic or quasi-ethnic group (like in African Posse or foreign Posse). In all cases it refers to a group that has (or is conceived as having) a certain cohesion. In form it draws on the Western image of a group of men (mostly outlaws) riding together; in content it presupposes a set of informal rules, a code of honor and conduct governing the group. Honor in its specific Posse configuration is at the top of the value system. The hierarchy of these various forms of value are inscribed in the dispositions of social agents by their consumption of hundreds of Western narratives. Jamaican (real life) Posse members take honor in manifesting the most important of these values because of their place in the (fictional) Western Posses. An individual attributed this characteristic by other members of his group qualifies for a position of power. This reveals the structural coincidence between dispositions and positions. In practice the individual may manifest his (symbolic) power by converting it into other forms of capital such as economic or social. He increases his symbolic capital by further investment in the "bank of public opinion" within the Posse.

Another metaphorical notion that signifies the practices of DJing more than anything else is *riding the riddim* (rhythm). The highly competitive practice refers to the ability of the artists to maintain the rhythm with his verbal skills better and longer than competitors.[42] There are thousands of songs that include standardized phrases like *siddung* (sit down) *pon de riddim like a lizzard pon a limb or ride de riddim like a Cowboy on his horse*. Comparable to the Rodeo, the skills and abilities of the (DJ) riders are tested against each other; the artistic competence in riding the riddim is connected in meaning with the musical showdown of the Sounds Clash or DJ Clash when two or more Sound Systems or DJs meet to test their musical and verbal abilities against each other. The weapons of such a duel are, of course, "riddims" and words, but the battle is staged symbolically in terms of the dramat(urg)ical structures known to the actors from the imported Western dramas. At times the performances become real when guns are introduced into the play. The local metaphor for such a situation is *sounds crash*; it means that a sounds clash has ended because violence has broken out. Contrary to interpretations that reduce the violence, sexism and misogyny embraced by some artists (and their audiences) in response to an essentialist notion of blackness, these attitudes and practices, I propose, may be attributed primarily to the values transmitted (inter alia) through Western movies.[43]

Stylistic features of music and everyday practices are connected in intersecting fields and reinforce each other. Both owe their understanding of the appropriate code of honor and conduct partly to the same source: scenes depicting proper (heroic) conduct and images (of gunmen) portrayed by Western motion pictures taken to be real solutions to practical situations in the ghetto. Jigsy King's *Billy the Kid* provides a lyrical example of the inscription of dramatized structures from Western movies in the habitus of Kingstonian rude b(w)oys from areas such as Dungle, Tivoli Gardens or Riverton:

Billy the Kid for the 90s
Watch dis now rude bwoy
An' the new name for all the gunmen
Ah Billy the Kid
You see dat one deh
Down ah Jungle (Dungle) him live
And every day him clean him 'matic
You see dah one deh
An' up ah T.G. (Tivoli Gardens) him live
If you romp with him
You gone six foot six
You see dah on deh
Ah down ah Riverton him live
Him kill 55
And you will be 56 . . .
You see, Junglist man, dem ah Billy the Kid
And T.G. man, dem ah Billy the Kid . . .[44]

Along the same line, Bounty Killer, who has been one of the leading DJs since 1993, tells his audience "how the West was really won" by deconstructing the MGM film. He based his early career mainly on gun talk in which he incorporated in his performances and recorded materials lyrical expressions drawn from Rastafari philosophy and its social critic. He focussed on the typical qualities of the gunslinger: coolness, quickness, dangerousness and a relentless attitude. At *Sting* 1993, the biggest yearly Reggae show in Jamaica, Bounty Killer staged a showdown with his counterpart Beenie Man. This *Clash* crashed when young supporters of the Beenie Man-Posse threw empty bottles at Bounty Killer. The habitus expressed on this occasion (in the aesthetic practices) corresponds to the attitude taken in the song *How the West Was Won* (on the album *Down in the Ghetto*), when the narrator Bounty Killer identifies with the lyrics sung by a fictional master gunman.

You know, riding from Mexico to Alaska . .
Bounty Killer riding through the West . . .
Me no lef' me Winchester . . .
Way down inna de history
Wey the Killer put down the key
Me did murder Billy the Kid
And murder John Wayne
Cowboy come fe test
Me just shot him
How the West was won . . .[45]

Josey Wales, a veteran DJ, named a recent album featuring Western narrations applied to a Jamaican ghetto experiences *Cowboy Style*.[46] The cover pictures the DJ, who gave himself the military title/praise name of Colonel, in a cowboy-like outfit forming a symbolic gun with his hand, the standard gesture used in the Dancehall to signal a symbolic gun salute accompanied by verbal imitations of gun shots.[47] This behavior enables the audience to transform symbols into action. In this way Jamaican rude boys show their structured recourse to the ultimate affirmative expression (of joy) in the Western film genre: the gun salute.

When the highly ritualized showdown of the Western movie is recontextualized into a lyrical showdown in the Dancehall, a syncretic process often referred to as a "localization of the global" takes place. Artistic performances and other social practices appear traceable to intersecting dispositions appropriated from diverse religious and cultural traditions. Values and attitudes inculcated by the continual exposure to Western movies combine with embodied speech patterns of "Black Talk."[48] The motivational themes of the Western outlaw hero are combined with the competitive forms of West Indian *Men of Words* in the performance of Reggae.[49] Young Ragga artists then embody the syncretized structures of Western movies and Caribbean culture as do the consumers of their art. In this way contexts and symbolic codes from Western movies are given meanings that reflect the concerns of actors in Jamaican social situations, both rural and urban.[50] The image of the continually challenged gunman, successfully outcompeting all rivals while taking full responsibility for himself, shapes the habitus in which the game is played.

Wild West images become embodied in the habitus of young (especially male) people in Jamaica even if they are deconstructed. Conscious and unconscious behavior appears in many syncretic acts involving, among other elements, Rastafari consciousness, Bible teachings and gunman fantasies taken from movies about the Wild West. The examples of Reggae texts discussed so far support the suggestion by Stewart and Shaw on the process of syncretism.

> The appropriation of dominance and the subversion of that dominance may be enacted at the same time, in the same syncretic act. Subversion may even be an unintended consequence of a syncretic process in which actors intend to appropriate rather than subvert cultural dominance. These conundrums of agency and intentionality make syncretism very slippery, but it is precisely its capacity to contain paradox, contradiction and polyphony which makes syncretism such a powerful symbolic process.[51]

The final example by DJ Yellowman clearly tends to subvert the dominant cultural imperative of acting cold-blooded as do Clint Eastwood and others in the movies. It questions a syncretic process that I have located analytically in the habitus formation. Yellowman tackles the impact of Western movies on Jamaican men directly in his song *Wild Wild West*, the cover of which pictures Yellowman riding on a wooden horse in an amusement park.

> Listen up guys, this is John Wayne from Texas
> There ain't no gunslingers in Texas
> The Wild Wild West . . .
> Down in the ghetto, I born and grow
> Sufferation is all I know
> I know it from my heart to my toe
> On the microphone is King Yellow . . .
> The Wild Wild West . . .
> Listen now!
> The man in Jamaica have Cowboy mentality
> They watch too much Western movies
> Bonanza, Big Shift and more . . .
> You're going around like John too Bad
> This kind a thing make the world get mad
> You take up your gun
> Walk with your Posse
> All you do is shooting up the country
> I know, you're born to end up in the cemetery
> This is not a joke, this is a sad story
> About the Wild Wild West
> Throw down your gun, throw down your knife
> It's time we all unite
> Please, don't take your brother life
> Whether you're Black, whether you're White
> I'm talking to the brothers in America
> I'm talking to the brothers in South Africa
> I'm talking to the brothers in Jamaica . . .
> Come on everybody, let us live as one
> And help Yellowman to sing this song
> The Wild Wild West . . .[52]

## Conclusion

Because of its affiliation with Rastafari, Reggae became identified as Rasta music. Reggae and Rastafari were intertwined to such an extent that the philosophy and the music were believed by many to be synonymous. The resulting categorization of Reggae as being Rasta music did little, however, for those Rastafari who saw Reggae at best as a possible medium to globalize their philosophy, but who claimed Nyahbinghi to be the authentic Rastafari music.[53] On the other hand, all expressions not consistent with Rasta were discredited or ignored by the media. In some sense Ragga(muffin), the Dancehall style of Reggae, might be interpreted as idiosyncratic and counterhegemonic. It also might be seen as resisting a cultural reductionism by the media that sought to limit variation from the pattern of Bob Marley. The Dancehalls never submitted to these outsiders' expectations. Ragga(muffin)-Reggae did not adhere to any preconstructed ideology of cultural purity. It remained open for diverse patterns, perspectives and modes of perception fueled by the urge of its practitioners to create and recreate continually.

In this paper I have tried to shed light on a process that might be conceptualized as syncretic, even though it does not relate to a purely religious mixing of traditions. In Jamaica young people particularly are presented a range of diverse and often contradictory perspectives. These alternatives become inscribed in their habitus by the media and are then expressed in dispositions to develop specific behaviors, to act, to gesture or to hold one's body in a certain way. Habitus, as the embodiment of social structures and practices of actors in a particular field, I suggest, makes possible empirical access to the site where the integration or mixing of diverse traditions takes place. Reggae, as a culturally expressive form and a field of cultural production governed by its own laws, reveals the syncretic processes of such a habitus formation.

In my view this analysis enables us to avoid the traps in other approaches that see variation as "pollutive" divergence from some original authenticity and purity. The analysis enables researchers at times to unveil patterns of domination that sometimes are not recognized by the actors themselves. If the latter are to become aware of the situation, they must be exposed to an analytic reflection of the inherent logic of their practices, including the ways in which they come to embody the structures and values of the dominant society. Only by such a reflexive stance is it possible to clarify how the general values of mainstream culture provide the norms that are reproduced in popular culture. The roles of gangsters and Western heroes in the movies are examples. They appear in Reggae song texts in reproduced form.[54] But they are not always reproduced uncritically. Some Reggae song texts provide examples as to how dominant structures can become encountered with resistance. This encounter of two oppositional systems in the actual practice (of Reggae artists) was analyzed here as the place for a syncretic process.

Religious and non-religious elements from diverse cultural traditions form the habitus of the Ragga Cowboy. Within what I refer to as a syncretic process, the agents acquire a practical sense that enables to perform a wide range of practices. At one end we have the simple reproduction of the dominant structures, while at the other their critical reversal. Ghetto youths do incorporate the fictional structures, dispositions and corresponding practices learned from Western movies. Acts of violence, both physical and symbolic, may be interpreted as its consequences. The long list of Reggae artists who have been killed tells only part of the story. On the other side emerges the creative transformation of the Wild West image which befits only at first glance the ghetto experience of the survival of the fittest: "Through these modes of deference and presentation, the subtlest nuances of social position, of the sources of prestige, and hence of what is valuable and good are encoded."[55]

As Clifford remarks on the ambiguity inherent in a syncretic process or cultural encounter, there is no need to romanticize such cultural contacts and thereby erase the violence of empire and continuing forms of neocolonial domination.[56] I am not suggesting that the values and standards presented in Western movies are accepted by Jamaican viewers in unmodified form. The syncretism that takes place within them already may lead to forms of resistance. Alien ideas and practices are never simply absorbed wholesale through passive acculturation: "At the very least, their incorporation involves some kind of transformation, some kind of deconstruction and reconstruction which converts them to people's own meanings and projects."[57] Ragga Cowboys, the product of a syncretic process conditioned by diverse structures, may prove to be reflexive critics of the very process that produced them. Accordingly, artistic practices may demonstrate that agency, and even rational agency, may survive the constraining power imposed by foreign systems of thought, such as religion and culture in systems of colonial and postcolonial dominance. Coco Tea's Reggae song *Ruling Cowboy* provides a vivid example.

> Today, you are a ruling Cowboy
> Tomorrow, other men gonna chase you like a boy
> You should be coolin' Homeboy, I say fe cool it off . . .
> Cause everday another Cowboy in the dirt
> So rude boy you gotta be on the alert . . .[58]

## Notes

1. Count Ossie is considered to be one of the originators of a peculiar Rastafari drumming style which he developed with his group, the Mystic Revelation of Rastafari. Prince Emmanuel is the founder of the Ethiopian Africa Black International Congress and one of the strongest advocates of repatriation to Africa; see Yoshiko S. Nagashima, *Rastafarian Music in Contemporary Jamaica: A Study of Socioreligious Music, the Rastafarian Movement in Jamaica* (Tokyo: Tokyo University of Foreign Affairs, 1984), 138-140; and *Black Supremacy in Righteousness of Salvation* (Kingston: publisher unknown, n.d.) Mortimer Planno is widely regarded as a mentor-like influence on Bob Marley whom he introduced to the teachings of Rastafari; he became famous when he welcomed the Emperor Haile

Selassie I at Kingston airport at the occasion of his visit to Jamaica in 1966 (Barry Chevannes, *Rastafari: Roots and Ideology* [Syracuse and New York: Syracuse University Press, 1994], 245) and due to his membership to the official Mission to Africa investigating possibilities for repatriation (see Mission to Africa, *Report of Mission to Africa* [Kingston: The Government Printer, 1961]).

2. Rastafari reasonings deconstruct and reconstruct imperial language by creating an etymology that fits to their own philosophical *overstanding* (instead of understanding). As an example, Rasta speech considered as an act of the celebration of life could not be a diealogue but only a live-alogue or high-alogue; see Alona Wartofsky, "Dread Heads," *Washington City Paper* 9, no. 37 (Sept. 15-21, 1989): 16-17, for the use of such rhetoric devices in international delegations of Rastafari elders globalizing their philosophical overstandings or, as they would also express it, of *spreading the word*.

3. People who sport the symbols of Rastafari, foremost the so-called dreadlocks, without sharing the *livity* (the appropriate way of life and conduct) of Rastafari, are often referred to as Dread. It depends on the context if the notion takes on a pejorative meaning.

4. The 23rd of July, the birthday of Haile Selassie, is usually celebrated with a large Nyahbinghi where Rastafari from all over Jamaica and from other countries congregate for up to several weeks. It also serves the purposes to restrengthen ties between individual Rastafari and groups, to relax from the "pressures of the Babylon system," to clarify and further develop philosophical positions (or more correctly "reasonings") and to practice spiritual warfare (Armagiddeon) against all forces identified as modern expressions of Babylon. See John P. Homiak, "From Yard to Nation: Rastafari and the Politics of Eldership at Home and Abroad," in *"Ay Bobo," Afro-Karibische Religionen, Teil 3: Rastafari*, Manfred Kremser, ed. (Wien: WUV-Universitätsverlag, 1994), 49-76, and Werner Zips, *Black Rebels: African Caribbean Freedom Fighters in Jamaica* (Princeton and Kingston, Jamaica: Markus Wiener Publishers and Ian Randle Publishers, 1998), 179-182, for the meaning and practices of Nyahbinghi. Its music is played on drums and other percussion instruments; the lyrics center among other themes on biblical references, praise songs to Haile Selassie, political claims for repatriation and reparations and protest songs against slavery and *downpression*. See Carole Yawney, "Lions in Babylon: The Rastafarians of Jamaica as a Visionary Movement," unpublished doctoral dissertation, McGill University (1978), 226-240 for a good selection of transcribed Rasta Nyahbinghi songs; on the general character of the music see Peter B. Clarke, *Black Paradise: The Rastafarian Movement* (Wellingborough, Northamptonshire: The Aquarian Press, 1986), 93-94.

5. The reasonings given for the identification of the pope (as an institution) with Satan are manifold. Besides the involvement of the Catholic church in the slave trade, it is the blessing of Mussolini's army before their attack on Ethiopia in 1935 by the pope that is most often referred to.

6. As foreigners, we were looked upon as a strange phenomenon and amusedly noted by most Jamaicans as Rasta wannabees who must have had too much smoke.

7. There is an important distinction between DJs and Singers in the field of Reggae music. DJs, like Rappers, work with the spoken word stylistically in tune with a given rhythm; their style of Reggae is generally specified as Ragga or Ragga-Reggae. The art of "riding the riddim" was developed in the Jamaican dancehalls where the DJs would *lively up* their audience by commenting, interluding, supplying and/or deconstructing the original lyrics of the songs they were playing. Jamaican style DJing depended heavily on the competitiveness of male adolescents sharpening their skills against each other (see Colin Larkin, *The Guinness Who's Who of Reggae* [Middlesex: Guinness Publishing, 1994], 257). Its introduction to New York's Bronx was crucial for the invention of Rap. See Werner Zips, "Let's Talk About the Motherland: Jamaican Influences on the African Discourses in the Diaspora," in *Born Out of Resistance: On Caribbean Cultural Creativity*, Wim Hoogbergen, ed. (Utrecht: ISOR Publ., 1994), 57-58.

8. The notion of field as one of the organizing concepts of Bourdieu's work is an open concept just as the other central concepts of habitus and (forms of) capital. The Reggae field studied here could be seen as a subfield to the whole artistic field relatively autonomous to other subfields like the literary field or theater production.

9. For example, interview with Ras Winston, 10.9.1985.

10. Cassidy referred to the Jamaican idiom of African English as "Jamaica Talk" to analyze it as a national language. See Frederic G. Cassidy, *Jamaica Talk: Three Hundred Years of the English Language in Jamaica* (London and Basingstoke: MacMillan, 1982).

11. For example, Dick Hebdige, *Subculture: The Meaning of Style* (New York: Methuen and Co., 1979), 31-39.

12. There are of course more influences on the habitus like other religious expressions, political interests and social meanings that I can not focus on for reasons of limited space. The two I am paying attention to in this context appear to be symbolically dominant.

13. Pierre Bourdieu, *Outline of a Theory of Praxis* (Cambridge: Cambridge University Press, 1977).

14. André Droogers, "Syncretism: The Problem of Definition, the Definition of the Problem," in *Dialogue and Syncretism: An Interdisciplinary Approach*, Jerald D. Gort et al., eds. (Grand Rapids, Michigan and Amsterdam: Eerdmans and Rodopi, 1989), 7 and 24-25.

15. A number of my Austrian Reggae-loving friends likewise are surprised by my willingness to select records with "slack," violent, and even cowboy lyrics in addition to so-called conscious Reggae when working as an amateur DJ in a Viennese Reggae Club.

16. Pierre Bourdieu, *Outline of a Theory; The Logic of Practice* (Cambridge: Polity Press, 1990); *The Field of Cultural Production: Essays on Art and Literature* (Cambridge: Polity Press, 1993); "Concluding Remarks: For a Sociogenetic Understanding of Intellectual Works," in *Bourdieu: Critical Perspectives*, Craig Calhouhn et al., eds. (Cambridge: Cambridge University Press, 1993), 273-274; and Pierre Bourdieu and Loic J. D. Wacquant, *An Invitation to Reflexive Sociology* (Cambridge: Polity Press, 1992), 68.

17. Randal Johnson, "Editor's Introduction to Pierre Bourdieu on Art, Literature and Culture," in *The Field of Cultural Production: Essays on Art and Literature*, 5-6.

18. Bourdieu and Wacquant, *An Invitation to Reflexive Sociology*, 122.

19. For an analysis of the conceptualizing structures of the Western myth in Western filmic narratives see Will Wright, "The Structure of Myth and the Structure of the Western Film," in *Cultural Theory and Popular Culture: A Reader*, John Storey, ed. (New York: Harvester Wheatsheaf, 1994), 118.

20. Bourdieu, *Outline of a Theory*, 182; and Pierre Bourdieu, "The Forms of Capital," in *Handbook of Theory and Research for the Sociology of Education*, John G. Richardson, ed. (New York: Greenwood Press, 1986), 241.

21. Bourdieu and Wacquant, *An Invitation to Reflexive Sociology*, 136.

22. Cf. Bourdieu, *Outline of a Theory*, 164; and Bourdieu and Wacquant, *An Invitation to Reflexive Sociology*, 123.

23. Bourdieu and Wacquant, *An Invitation to Reflexive Sociology*, 127.

24. One such film with tremendous impact on the habitus of many Jamaicans was Spike Lee's *Malcolm X*.

25. Henri Giroux, "Power and Resistance in the New Sociology of Education: Beyond Theories of Social and Cultural Reproduction," *Curriculum Perspectives* 2, no. 3 (1982), 90.

26. Bourdieu and Wacquant, *An Invitation to Reflexive Sociolgy*, 113-140.

27. I chose this text because in 1984 I misinterpreted Yellowman's work by viewing it as a deviation from pure Rasta *livity* and as an inscription, in Bordieu's sense, of the (dominant) American way of life. By livity Rastafarians refer to an overall way of life and mode of thinking. It might be translated as a specific form of habitus.

28. Ragga is the shortened form of Raggamuffin (meaning wild, unruly, streetwise, etc.) which came to refer to the DJ or Dancehall form of Reggae since the introduction of computerized beats to the music and the concurrent hit song "Ragamuffin Soldier" (1985) by Lloyd Hemmings on one of the first popular albums promoting the computer age in Reggae.

29. Cf. Bourdieu and Wacquant, *An Invitation to Reflexive Sociology*, 98-99.

30. Bourdieu differentiates three main forms of capital (economic, cultural and social) which all can take the form of symbolic capital through their recognition by other agents. (See Bourdieu, "The Forms of Capital," 242-252.)

31. Malika Lee Whitney and Dermont Hussey, *Bob Marley: Reggae King of the World* (London: Plexus, 1984), 59.

32. See for instance the cover picture on the album *Rasta Revolution* that portrays the Wailers (Bob Marley, Peter Tosh and Bunny Wailer) in the typical poses of Western gunslingers.

33. I refer to the song *I Shot the Sheriff* written by the Wailers (LP: Burnin' Island Records, Ltd., 1973) but ironically made popular by rock star Eric Clapton.

34. Peter Tosh, *Wanted Dread and Alive* (LP: Wanted Dread and Alive. EMI. Electrola, 1981).

35. Cf. Bourdieu and Wacquant, *An Introduction to Reflexive Sociology*, 122.
36. Bob Marley and the Wailers, *Rasta Revolution* (Trojan Records, n.d.).
37. On the album cover of Bob Marley and the Wailers, *Rasta Revolution*.
38. On the album *Confrontation* (Island Records, 1983).
39. See Hebdige, *Subculture*, 31-39; and Howard Johnson and Jim Pines, *Reggae: Deep Roots Music* (London and New York: Proteus Books, 1982).
40. Cf. *Real Clint Eastwood* re-released on the album *African Roots* by Clint Eastwood (Esoldun, 1992).
41. The artistic expression is so close to everyday life that most consumers will occasionally perform as DJs, but only at a private party.
42. Werner Zips, "To Make War with Words: Soziale Organisation und Widerstand in afrikanischer-karibischer Oralliteratur," in Kremser, *"Ay Bobo,"* 119-148.
43. See bell hooks, *Outlaw Culture: Resisting Representations* (New York and London: Routledge, 1994), 118.
44. Jigsy King, *Billy the Kid*, CD: *Have to Get You* (V.P. Records, 1993).
45. Bounty Killer, *How the West Was Won*, CD: *Down in the Ghetto* (Greensleeves, 1994).
46. Josey Wales, *Cowboy Style*, CD: *Cowboy Style* (Greensleeves Records, 1994).
47. The gun salutes become real at ghetto dances in many instances when members of the audience draw real guns and fire into the air.
48. Ben Sidran, *Black Talk* (New York: Da Capo Press, 1981).
49. Roger D. Abrahams, *Man of Words in the West Indies: Performance and the Emergence of Creole Culture* (Baltimore and London: The John Hopkins University Press, 1983), 3.
50. An excellent description of this process is to be found in the film *The Harder They Come* by Perry Henzell, 1972; see Michael Thelwell, *The Harder They Come* (London: Pluto Press, 1980), 148-149, and Stephen Davis and Peter Simon, *Reggae Bloodlines: In Search of the Music and Culture of Jamaica* (London: Anchor Press, 1979), 2-4.
51. Stewart and Shaw, *Syncretism/Anti-Syncretism*, 21.
52. Yellowman, *Wild Wild West*, LP: *Yellowman Rides Again* (Ras Records, 1988).
53. See Homiak, "From Yard to Nation," 49-57; and Werner Zips, *Schwarze Rebellen: Afrikanisch-karibischer Freiheitskampf in Jamaica* (Wien: Promedia Verlag, 1993), 219-222.
54. See hooks, *Outlaw Culture*, 117, for her critical analysis of the politics of hedonistic consumerism which perpetuates and maintains these values by reinforcing the embodiment of violence, sexism and misogyny.
55. Charles Taylor, "To Follow a Rule," in Calhoun, *Bourdieu*, 58.
56. James Clifford, *The Predicament of Culture: Twentieth-Century Ethnography, Literature, and Art* (Cambridge: Harvard University Press, 1988), 15.
57. Stewart and Shaw, *Syncretism/Anti-Syncretism*, 20-21.
58. Coco Tea, *Ruling Cowboy*, CD: *Various Artists: Twin City Spin 2* (Greensleeves Records, 1991).

## Chapter 11

# Polyvocality and Constructions of Syncretism in *Winti*

Ineke van Wetering

### Women: Guardians of Suriname Creole Culture

Whether *Winti*, or Suriname Creole Religion, is syncretic or not has been hotly debated both in academic circles and in the arena of religious politics. Calling Winti syncretic has been dismissed by some, both as lacking in heuristic value and as a denial of its authenticity. Yet, the matter of what concepts may be useful in the analysis of cultural exchanges remains open.

Most Creoles are wholeheartedly devoted to the Christian faith, Roman Catholic or Protestant.[1] Through a long-term involvement with the slaves and their descendants, the Moravian Brethren or Herrnhut Society has put an imprint on Creole religiosity. Many Creoles simultaneously accept the African heritage as a marker of their identity. For the believers, the situation does not create problems. Over the years and generations, a code has been developed to deal with diverse religious understandings. Whenever Christians also participate in Winti rituals, they do entertain ideas about the interrelations between the two religious idioms with which they are conversant. If these notions often remain implicit and do not regularly find expression in words, they surface in practices. This essay explores the interrelation between the two religious traditions as it is made manifest in the celebration of birthday anniversaries, an important institution in Creole social life. The data on Winti is taken from the religion as it is practiced in the diaspora, by women in Amsterdam in the 1980s.[2]

Creole women, the guardians of the African American heritage in Suriname since Herskovits and Herskovits[3] drew attention to their cultural role in the 1920s, regard their religion as authentic, "their culture" (*Wi Kulturu*), their way of life.[4] In the Netherlands, where many Surinamese have settled since the 1970s when the one-time Dutch colony attained political independence, many Creole women, particularly of the elder generation, make it a point to consciously maintain and promote what they see as their traditions. Although the women who pursue such politics are fully aware that they live in a globalizing, modern world, accepting this as a normal state of affairs, even participating in it with gusto, they will insist that when all is said and done it is their own culture that matters. We will investigate what cultural resources women draw upon to construct "their culture" and what terms we can apply to the mixture.

## A Classical Study

In a volume of more than 600 pages, Herskovits and Herskovits[5] discuss birthday celebrations and Winti, which makes their work a starting point from where to look for continuities and changes. It is quite striking that the notion of syncretism does not appear in *Suriname Folk-Lore*.[6] Also, their enthusiasm for Winti as a testimonial of Africa in the New World may have kept these pioneers from going into the relation between Christian culture and Winti. Yet, this aspect deserves more attention than it received from them.

Since 1936 when this ethnography appeared, new interpretations have been added which do not necessarily contradict these earlier findings. It has been argued that Winti rituals have played a substantial role in the processes of ethnic mobilization. It unites Creoles, people who trace descent in some, often rather complex, way to African ancestors. In the face of mass migration, it underpins the survival of a Creole group in Suriname and beyond.[7] Simultaneously, Winti or *Kulturu* is also a boundary-marker. Winti, like similar movements in the Caribbean,[8] is part of an ethnic and a nationalist project. Popular religion plays a double role in both separating and integrating social classes.[9] Most adepts come from the residual sectors of the population that have not moved ahead socially or economically. Middle-class Creoles, although often keenly looking for their roots, are highly ambivalent towards the tradition. Yet birthday celebrations, often sanctified with Christian and non-Christian rituals, are occasions that bridge social distinctions by bringing together persons related by kinship who occupy different stations in life. The birthday party, as celebrated in Amsterdam's Bijlmermeer in the 1980s, will be juxtaposed to that described by Frances Shapiro Herskovits in Paramaribo in the 1920s, to see what conclusions can be drawn, particularly regarding cultural mixing.

## Cultural Encounters

Debates on syncretism—popular in Herskovits' days as part of the study of acculturation—have been re-opened at present after a period of relative neglect. Arguments critical of the general theoretical outlook need not be repeated here, as they have been amply dealt with elsewhere.[10] Discontent with Herskovits' culturalist bias was voiced in the 1960s by students of the Caribbean and, as a result, the concept fell into disuse. Horowitz,[11] however, would grant Herskovits, the pioneer of African American studies, that though failing in the field of economy and politics, his approach had been relatively successful in music, dance and religion. Mintz[12] did not even accept this more modest claim, insisting that a clear distinction be made between society and culture, and that culture is used as a resource in a social arena. Far from denying the importance of African retentions and survivals, Mintz and Price[13] advocated a subtle, in-depth, historically informed approach. As these authors have argued,[14] the Africans transported to the Caribbean as slaves were drawn from diverse societies and did not form groups or share a culture. The holistic concept of culture implied in it has the effect of masking the processes implicit in both the continuities and discontinuities between Africa and the Americas. The slaves' need to create institutions that articulate culture was stressed, and the term "syncretism" was evaded at all costs. Even when the concept was applied to its *locus classicus*, the merging of Catholic saints with African gods, Mintz[15] prefers to call the religious result "synthesized." This stance does not prevent Mintz and Price[16] from acknowledging that all culture is syncretic. What they repudiate is the concept's heuristic value. They opt for a different research strategy.

The Caribbeanists' outlook generally is shared in modernist social science. Mintz' view that culture is made and remade while human beings are engaged in coping with the demands of everyday life is echoed, for instance, in Berger and Luckmann's work.[17] The significance of institutions, though, is contested at present. Marcus, for instance, questions the claims of realism in representations of an uncertain world. The ethnography privileged in postmodern anthropology would "seek to convey the quality of its subjects' experiences, free of the mediation of customs and institutions, concepts that carry an embedded bias toward seeing order, where on the level of experience such order is not felt or imagined to the same degree."[18] In the same volume, Tyler went so far as to assert that natives do not have an idea of an integrated whole.[19]

Where the appreciation of concepts is concerned, there are revolutions and cyclical movements. Concepts that once were basic for anthropology have been dismissed, only to have their potential re-assessed later.[20] This has also happened to syncretism.

Stewart and Shaw[21] have recast the term "syncretism" for use in the present day by focusing on political processes. They shift attention from culture to the politics of religious synthesis and constructions of authenticity. Whereas Herskovits had looked for cultural borrowings and reinterpretations, new generations of anthropologists would speak of appropriation and agency.

Aijmer allows for these objections against the implications inherent in the term "syncretism."[22] Yet, he seems to remain closer to Herskovits' original program, focusing on culture. Aware of the political dimension, as the volume's title *Syncretism and the Commerce of Symbols* indicates, he stresses cultural exchanges: What do people take from others, under what circumstances? The editors of the present volume stress that syncretism, once proposed as a dimension of reinterpretation, is concerned with "the mixing and merging of cultures." By underlining common understandings, they hope to steer clear of some of the pitfalls earlier students of syncretism fell into.

It is generally accepted, for instance, that it is impossible to speak of culture as an integrated cultural whole in an allegedly Durkheimian sense.[23] The term "group" is equally suspect. The assumption that current globalizing processes result in boundaries being crossed or becoming blurred holds *a fortiori* for migrants. In the case of Creoles and Winti, we are well advised to follow Aijmer in thinking of "agglomerations of people around particular activities" rather than groups. This is certainly true of the women's group discussed here. These women belong to a Creole subculture, and their activities are part of cultural and communal politics.

No less than "syncretism," "culture" and "group," the concept "community" also has come under scrutiny. As Baumann observes, it is often reified and used by actors in a political arena.[24] Nevertheless, it is relevant when understood in Anderson's sense as an "imagined community."[25] Also, it is taken for granted that participation in activities implies the endorsement of some guiding ideas. A community implies boundaries[26] and symbols that are to some extent communal. Ideas need not be completely shared, as the author points out; individuals associating themselves with groupings or activities may attach different meanings to cultural symbols. This implies politicalization: "In the face of this variability, the consciousness of community has to be kept alive by the manipulation of its symbols."[27]

The forms of entrepreneurship required to mobilize a community affect the exchange of cultural meanings. This brings us to the question raised by

Droogers: "When we speak of syncretism, what is actually mixed: culture, ideology, religion?"[28] As Stewart and Shaw[29] observe "What appeared to be important religious phenomena at a given point in time may later be reinterpreted as merely 'cultural' phenomena and vice versa." This issue was not raised in Herskovits' days, but has to be addressed today.

## Cultural Politics in Suriname

Outside of academia, the quest for authenticity implied a move towards anti-syncretism. The impact of nationalism, one of the forces behind this movement,[30] was manifest in Suriname's political arena beginning in the 1950s. A nationalistic cultural movement, *Wi Egi Sani* (Our Own Things), had emerged as an active force in nation-building.[31] The guiding idea was to liberate a society from imposed biases against their own background and promote self-respect and pride in the African American heritage. Until 1971, the practice of Winti rituals was prohibited by law in Suriname. Rituals used to be performed in secret, often on remote plantations. Winti was distrusted, looked upon as idolatrous and backwards by respectable citizens. Few would publicly acknowledge being well acquainted with either its beliefs or practices, let alone to take part in its rituals. These attitudes have been challenged, but have not completely disappeared. Still, a nationalist endeavor to "lift the taboo on Winti" is manifest in both Suriname and the Netherlands.

## Winti Theology

Winti found a staunch advocate in Wooding, a university-trained anthropologist and native speaker. His doctoral dissertation, which first appeared in 1972, met with great acclaim both among his colleagues[32] and with the Suriname Creoles in general. As a detailed ethnographic account of a functioning religious system in the Para district, a rural area known as a Winti hotbed, his study provided welcome information to a middle class estranged from its roots and has served as a source book. Winti was described as an autonomous, self-sufficient religious system that meets the demands of its adherents and their communities. Wooding denies syncretism: Winti is boldly represented as African, untainted by the creed of a dominant power.[33]

Wooding's inside view, his personal involvement and his stand in defense of a religion despised for a long time by colonialists and post-colonialists alike were one cause of the work's popularity. His covering of ethnographic detail makes clear that this is a totalizing effort, an authoritative overview of beliefs and customs that provides norms and a canon of truth. Critics have pointed out that the image he creates of a rural community as a *Gemeinschaft*, supported by communal rituals, has romantic or nostalgic overtones.[34] This feature, however, has contributed to the book's success. Creole middle classes respond positively to this idealization; the exposition of a hallowed past is cherished as a myth.

The presentation of Winti religion in written form was new. Until the appearance of Wooding's dissertation, control of the dissemination of religious knowledge rested mostly with the elderly heads of kin groups. Their authority on Winti lore was based on experience (*Ondrofeni*), which, in their view, only a life-long participation in ritual life could bring. Wooding's codification of beliefs not only challenged a skeptical outside world, but the hard core of adepts as well. Yet, he could rest his claim to the right to speak about Winti on his position as a believer.

Wooding has done more than highlight popular religion's positive sides. His acclaim as a practitioner and expert who has published on his therapeutic work[35] has contributed to the warm reception his writings have received and as proof of their authenticity. To a growing middle class it was important that he had demonstrated his ability to meet academic standards. In order to straddle the class line and to legitimate his aspirations to the rank and file of Winti adherents he had to speak as an adept. So Wooding became the first and perhaps main theologian of his religion. His definition of Winti brings this out. Winti, he writes, "is an Afroamerican religion which centres round the belief in personified supernatural beings, who take possession of a human being, eliminate his consciousness, after which they unfold the past, the present and the future, and are able to cause and cure illnesses of a supernatural origin."[36]

The supernatural is presented here as a category *sui generis* that is present "out there." Wooding does not conform to the liberal methodological standards to abstain from truth claims common in the social sciences. This position befits a believer and a theologian, but not necessarily the scholar. The same may be said of his conception of illness in which some symptoms are claimed to be induced metaphysically as part of another reality rather than being an emic, social construction. When speaking with spirit mediums, for example, Wooding accepts their messages as unmediated by human vessels. He not only conducts interviews with people, but also with gods.[37] What mediums in trance divulge about their West African origin then is treated as historically valid information and introduced as evidence in academic debate.[38]

In the field of religious studies, controversies on such issues are of long standing. Sociologists and believers have different points of view. Berger and Luckmann accepted the tendency to objectify as natural in humans as social beings.[39] Codification in written form contributes to the process of objectification. As Clifford warned, freezing the ongoing processes of cultural exchanges into texts brings in the dangers of reification and raises questions of textual authority.[40]

Contests between meaning-producers, as Berger and Luckmann[41] observe, are not decided by conceptual considerations. Social power is needed to have legitimations accepted. Wooding took up the cudgels for Winti at a moment power relations in the world were changing, and discussions about ethnographic representation and practice were opened in anthropology. Reflexivity has become a focus of interest, and the indigenous ethnographer has been privileged. "Insiders studying their own cultures," as Clifford argues, "offer new angles of vision and depths of understanding. . . . Their accounts are empowered and restricted in unique ways."[42] The acceptance of polyvocality creates opportunities to realize an ideal of a "dialogic anthropology," an exchange between systems of meaning.[43]

A basis for the reorientation was laid in the 1960s when Castaneda challenged received anthropological viewpoints. Like Castaneda, Wooding showed himself willing to defy academia. Not merely as an anthropologist-outsider, but as a sorcerer's apprentice, a native voice and ritual expert he could claim authority. As a cultural broker, Wooding was well prepared for a struggle on two fronts: with anthropologists basing their views on conventional methodology, and with other indigenous voices to whom he could boast academic credentials.

This complicates the issue of a possible dialogue. Not merely an exchange between believers and outsiders is at issue. Diversity in meaning production among Suriname Creoles is as characteristic of Winti as of other religions in complex societies where many natives speak or produce written accounts. Wooding's reliance on the testimonies of spirit mediums precludes a dialogue with skeptics, whether native or not. A reduction of the cross-cultural communication processes to discussions between an outsider-anthropologist and a native speaker is an unwarranted simplification.[44] In brief, there really is no such thing as a native point of view.

Wooding's message was responded to positively by a new Creole middle class, but less so by lower-class adherents. Since the view of culture Wooding used was that of a text, like any text, it is a construction that is debatable. Consequently, Wooding found himself fighting on two fronts. As a result the issue of religious legitimacy is still pending.

This also is brought out in discussions about syncretism. The debate, therefore, is waged not between anthropologists and believers, as might be expected, but between diverse native voices.

## Winti and Christianity

Other anthropologists who study Winti support Wooding's view that syncretism is not the most appropriate term to use to characterize the symbiotic relationship between it and Christianity.[45] This may be based on other grounds, as these authors do not, or as in Voorhoeve's case no longer, directly take part in Suriname's cultural politics.[46] No representation of the matter is neutral, but at times it is difficult to ascertain what politics are implied in anthropological writings.

Yet many observers have noted that attempts are made to bridge what is experienced as a gap between the two religions. The High God in Winti, *Anana*, for instance, is put on a par with the Christian God by many believers,[47] although there are differences in the way these deities are approached in ritual.[48] Jesus Christ is referred to as "the highest Winti" by some.[49] Winti are compared by many with Lucifer and other fallen angels.[50] The chief Winti in the pantheon, Mother Earth or *Aisa*, is honored with Christian hymns.[51] Various accommodations have been noted, such as a rule not to perform Winti rituals on Christian feast days.[52] Such views and practices are not standardized, however, and remain contested. Schoonheym notes that the lower echelons in the Christian churches entrusted with death rituals, the *dinari*, promote such syncretisms.[53] As members of congregations with wide-ranging contacts throughout the Creole population, they have an institutional basis and forum to disseminate their views. Their authority, however, is apparently contested, as these syncretisms remain informal and are not publicly legitimated.[54] The question of to what extent the two religious systems have influenced each other is still open.[55]

A general preference is expressed for the term "complementarity," implying that the two religions co-exist but do not merge. It is good to remember that even Herskovits, the archetypical syncretist, did not postulate that syncretism would be omnipresent. As Jackson observes, for example, Herskovits did not speak of merging in the case of Haitian Vodun, and looked upon Haitian culture as an unstable, partial amalgam of African and French elements, characterized by "socialized ambivalence."[56]

Why complementarity has remained an ingrained feature of religious practice, and the attempts to make the two religions merge are blocked, remains an issue. Like nationalism, ethnicity and multiculturalism have been singled out as factors that favor authenticity and obstruct syncretism. However, as Stewart and Shaw note, neither nationalism, ethnicity nor regionalism are necessarily anti-syncretic.[57] In the case of Winti, the effects of cultural nationalism and multiculturalism were found to be contradictory.[58] On the one hand, moves towards accommodation are made mostly in public while "authentic worship" is conducted in the private sphere. The latter, however, feeds upon unconscious forces, dream messages for instance, that bring in symbolism derived from daily life, thus making for syncretism.[59]

Ethnicity prompts solidarity between kinsmen of different class backgrounds. Whereas Christian churches promote individualism, Winti congregations value communalism, thereby emphasizing different forms of economic ethics. Conflicts between these guidelines for action are difficult to bridge. As a consequence, such class-linked differences encoded in religious practices are underplayed in discourse, and people behave contextually by "code-switching."[60] By not resolving the contradiction, ethnic pursuits tend to constrain syncretism.[61]

## Polyvocality in Winti

Multicultural societies present new challenges and opportunities. Ethnic strategies do not lose their relevance. Mass migration threatens to slacken kinship ties, and both migrants and relatives back home, most of them economically insecure, have an interest in maintaining relations. In a multicultural society such as the Netherlands, for example, government funds are allocated for cultural purposes. New migrants who lack familiarity with large-scale bureaucracies and institutions create opportunities for go-betweens. There is scope for ethnic brokerage in health care, welfare work, education and religion. Moreover, religion is a marketable commodity in modern society. Winti adherents have not been slow in responding to this situation; ethnic entrepreneurship and brokerage are markedly present.[62]

In order to bring across to the world at large what the Creole worldview entails and the problems in cross-cultural communication that present themselves, some publications supplying information have been issued. These accounts, written for the public at large, have no academic pretensions. Yet, like Wooding's major work, they construct a native view. If Wooding's exposé covered a whole range of relevant ethnographic detail, the new renditions offer concise summaries of the main aspects, providing glimpses into the Winti world. Stephen, for instance, not only hopes to enhance sympathy for and eliminate misunderstandings about Winti, he also includes a call for spirituality in a secularized world aimed at agnostics, Creole and non-Creole.[63] His publications are meant to be used as manuals for religious self-help; they contain condensed ritual and theological information, schematic descriptions of the major deities and their attributes, a few myths and texts of songs, some concise accounts of divinatory procedures, anecdotes about personal experiences and a few "magical" recipes for home use. For illustrative case material, Stephen relies to a great extent on his experience as a guardian in a psychiatric ward in one of Amsterdam's main hospitals. His books not only cater to a Creole public that has not been reared in Winti-practicing communities, but also to an esoteric market. Trance, for instance, is mentioned as a pan-human possibilty. Some descriptions of ritual include mention of children unacqainted with the tradition, and even white people, usually women, unexpectedly falling into a trance state. Such "miracles" are presented as "proof" that there is more between heaven and earth than is usually assumed in a rationalistically biased world. Like Wooding, Stephen claims truth value for mysterious messages and happenings.[64] The entrepreneurial mode inherent in ethnic mobilization appears to favor an attempt to advance into a cosmopolitan field of occultism.

Although his outlook is no less nationalistic than Wooding's, Stephen takes syncretism for granted.[65] He mentions several instances including the equating of the Christian God and the Supreme Being in Winti as noted above, the importance of candles, holy water, incense and crucifixes in both and the use of the Bible for divination and defense against evil forces. Stephen not only records the mixing and merging of Christianity and Winti, but also has an open eye for the effects of cultural encounters between the diverse ethnic groups in Suriname, a much-neglected topic. Without referring to contemporary anthropological discourse, he notes interesting developments. From his descriptions we can infer that a neat separation of constitutive cultural elements, whether European, African or other, is impossible.

## Birthday Celebrations in the Past

Apart from those who write, there are native voices that speak out in ritual. A birthday is one of the cultural traits that are hard to trace to specific cultural sources. African elements are manifestly present. Almost any book on Winti supplies a list of "day names" of West African origin.[66] In Ghana these are personal names linking the individual to one of the seven days of the week on which he or she was born. In Suriname, not surprisingly, this part of the cultural heritage was kept from outsiders along with other "hidden scripts." The day names were attached to the inner, hidden self, the soul, the *kra* or *yeye*. Incorporated into the Winti complex, these names were called upon in ritual settings. African culture was sacralized and reconstituted as religion.[67] A case for European derivation also can be made. The role of a flower bouquet as a main gift and partly recast symbol—rivals trample upon each other's flower gifts, as Frances Herskovits[68] mentions—is telling. European culture was appropriated and reconstituted. Religious as well as secular meanings have been attached to the constructed event, according to group allegiance and personal taste. Processes of convergence have taken place from an early date.

The first ethnographers to draw attention to the significance of the ceremonial surrounding a birthday were Melville and Frances Herskovits,[69] who discussed them in a description of the lives of mati, the local variety of female homosexuals.[70] They note the appropriation—without using the term—of European cultural items to construct a culture and underline the importance of women's initiatives for Creole social life. They explicitly state that the birthday festivities have no religious implications. The interpretation of the case described is probably correct; the detailed observations betray a vivid interest in what was witnessed and heard and guarantee, with due regard to the limitations inherent in all fieldwork reports, the validity of the work. This, however, does not imply that birthday celebrations have changed over time, carrying religious meanings now that were absent at the time. An assumption to that effect in my judgment would be unwarranted; the outcomes of the processes of cultural mixing must have been as variable in the past as they are now and different according to context. An apparently secular event may have connotations of the sacred for the inner circle that pass unnoticed by others.[71] Moreover, the Herskovits couple did not claim to have given a complete report of Creole life.

## Birthday Celebrations Today

Schoonheym has noted that birthday parties contribute to the reproduction of Creole culture.[72] Although they do not necessarily have religious overtones, they are believed to enhance the soul of the celebrant. Whereas many writers highlight the *prey*, a large-scale ritual, as the defining Winti event, the birthday party is even more important in maintaining Winti culture because of the contribution it makes in publicly marking the life crises of individuals.

A birthday encompasses a string of rituals, a range of possibilities that may vary according to circumstances and the preferences of the celebrant. The opening part usually is for the intimate circle, giving the individual whose birthday it is a personal New Year's Eve. It takes place on the night before the feast day, and is dedicated to the purification and strengthening of the self or soul. The person being honored takes an herbal bath which is regarded as part of the Winti complex. The next morning, or in the afternoon of the feast day, a church service in the home begins the festivities. A pastor, chaplain or church elder of either the Roman Catholic or Moravian denomination is invited to conduct the ceremony. This may be interpreted as an appropriation of Christianity; by carrying over the service into the home, women maintain ties with the church while still remaining in control. The celebrant selects the hymns to be sung. The pastor usually makes reference to her or him in his brief sermon. The psalms and hymns are the most enjoyed elements. Many of the older women know them by heart. Elements derived from Roman Catholic and Protestant worship are intermingled; denominational differences do not have intrinsic meaning here. The Christian service provides respectability to the occasion. Afterwards, live instrumental music often adds luster to the party. The band hired for the event always starts with a few well-known Christian hymns and gradually shifts to a combination of secular and Winti songs. These often are intertwined, making it difficult to determine when the Winti part actually begins. Winti rituals then open the festivities and often also end them.

As the rites and their interrelation with secular festivities have been described elsewhere,[73] we will turn in the next section to the so-called "morning" or "afternoon blessing" (*morgen- of middagzegen*) to make clear the Christian themes that appeal to Creole women. This will suggest that although Christian and Winti rituals are highly compartmentalized, to speak of syncretism is not inappropriate.

## Ma Nolda's "Morning Service"

As a household head, mother of grown-up daughters, active member in women's groups and dignified personality, Ma Nolda commands respect among Winti adepts. Her birthday receives due attention, particularly because she celebrates a *bigi jari*, a jubilee year; she will be sixty-five. She has saved money for a long time and her children assist her in making the event a success.

A group of guests arrives around twelve o'clock noon, the appointed time. Most women wear a costume inspired by tradition, or at least a starched cotton kerchief as a headdress. Some wear matching colors, and make it clear that way that they belong to the same organization, in this case, a burial society. Suriname's national flag is pinned to the wall. A certain studied slowness marks the procedures. Haste is modern, undignified and uncalled-for. Those present intimate that they are not involved in the bustling outside world, although this may be quite unrealistic. An odor of fried fish reaches us from the kitchen, and now and then the cook puts her head around the door to ask for or say something. Our earthly needs are not put below those that are more uplifting. Toddlers and phone calls also cause some slight disruptions, to partly undermine the solemnity of the occasion, which is otherwise maintained, with stern remonstrations, if need be. This belongs to the pattern of play with social relations. Men with middle-class connections are the proper figures to play a leading role, but are also relativized and discretely challenged.

Chairs have been placed in ordered rows, like in a church. The parson is seated in front, opposite the day's central figure who wears a beautiful traditional koto misi costume. The theme of the sermon is Bethania, a popular topic, as the brother-sister relation between Martha, Maria and Lazarus is central in this biblical episode. This has its echoes in the Creole situation, where the consanguineal family rather than the procreative one is the unit of worship. Suspicion would arise if affines would be directly involved.[74] Hymns about cleansing and life-giving water, not rare in the Herrnhut hymnal, have been selected. The symbolism is shared with that in Winti, with its characteristic herbal ablutions. Another hymn that is a favorite is one dedicated to Mary. Whether the service is Protestant or Roman Catholic, this one is frequently heard, as the stress on the female element in the world of the sacred, the Earth Mother *Aisa*, is important and familiar in Winti. The selection of Christian themes is guided by elective affinities.

After the service, congratulations are offered. An enormous bouquet is carried in, a tribute of one of the women's groups Ma Nolda belongs to. In it is an envelope that contains money, regarded not as an evil but as a life-supporting force. The traditiona' feature—the offering of the bouquet—has been retained.[75] The members gather around Ma Nolda, resting their hands on hers, her shoulders and on each others' backs. She is surrounded by a warm, living circle that radiates its strength and supports her.

The guests make toasts, sing women's club songs, and share a meal in Suriname style. All this happens simultaneously. On one occasion I was caught with a plate in hand when I had to rise for a hymn. Hurriedly, I put the plate under my chair since I saw no other empty spot in the room crowded with people, flowers, handbags. There was a great outcry, unequivocal proof of a genuinely shared culture. I had committed an outrage, and was to be reprimanded: food for humans should never be placed on the floor. That is good for dogs, not for human beings. This sentiment conceivably originated in slavery days as a reaction to them being treated as less than human.

## Conclusion

The convergence of culture traits of African and European origin in Winti origin is marked and, although lacking in explanatory power, the term "syncretism" has descriptive value; it refers to what happens concretely. There is a culture, authentic but not pure.[76] There obviously is a shared culture, a sedimentation of historical experience that marks boundaries.[77] Contrary to what Tyler[78] postulated, Creole women's rituals communicate a vision of a shared, integrated whole. Obviously, a selective process among possible symbols has been at work. Many but not all symbols of modern life-ways are claimed as belonging to the culture.

Winti has been partly sacralized: the sacred is looked upon as the quintessence of culture. Birthday celebrations as secular events have their roots in sacred, covert culture. As an institution they have served as a lynch-pin around which a culture has crystallized. Women, as active agents, have made an imprint, but not in isolation. They share aspirations with other participants. The signs of ideologies—ethnicity, nationalism, etc.—that are flaunted in ritual bear this out.

Contrary to some postmodernist assertions, there is no merging in a void. Although there is ample scope for bricolage and blurring of genres in Creole practices, constraints are conspicuous. The world of the subject, as defined in ritual, is anchored in experience shared with others. Within these bounds, the ritualized cultural complex is naturalized and uncontested.[79] Participation in institutions like birthday celebrations brings home to those involved where boundaries and restrictions lie.

## Notes

1. R. A. J.Van Lier, *Bonuman* (Leiden: ICAU Publication 60, 1983); Peter Schoonheym, "Het Gebied van Boven-Para en de Synthese tussen Christendom en Creoolse Religie," in *Winti-Religie: een Afro-Surinaamse Godsdienst in Nederland*, F. E. R. Derveld and H. Noordegraaf, eds. (Amsterdam/Leuven: De Horstink, 1988), 52-72.

2. The research, conducted between 1984 and 1987, was sponsored by ZWO, now NWO (Netherlands Foundation for the Advancement of Science) in the Hague.

3. Melville J. Herskovits and Francis S. Herskovits, *Surinam Folk-Lore* (New York: AMS Press, 1969 [Original 1936]), 9.

4. Another term in use is *Afkodrey*, literally *Afgoderij*, or idolatry. For the adherents, this has no pejorative meaning. Yet, many of the young people prefer to speak of *Kulturu*.

5. Herskovits and Herskovits, *Surinam Folk-Lore*.

6. The reason for this is that Melville Herskovits did not develop the notion of syncretism as part of his conceptualization of acculturation until several years after the research in Surinam was completed and the book on it written and published. Therefore, it is not surprising at all to find that the corpus of data was not analyzed in terms of the concept.

7. Henri M. J. Stephen, *Winti: een Afro-Surinaamse Religie en Magische Rituelen in Suriname en Nederland* (Amsterdam: Karnak, 1983); Yuri Banna and Yok Moy, *De Voorouders en haar Winti* (Paramaribo/Amsterdam, 1991).

8. Cf. Thomas H. Eriksen, *Us and Them in Modern Societies: Ethnicity and Nationalism in Trinidad, Mauritus and Beyond* (Oslo: Scandinavian University Press, 1992).

9. W. Van Wetering, "Informal Supportive Networks: Quasi-kin Groups, Religion and Social Order Among Suriname Creoles in the Netherlands," *The Netherlands Journal of Sociology* 23, no. 2 (1987):92-101.

10. For references see André Droogers and Sidney M. Greenfield, "Recovering and Reconstructing Syncretism," in this volume.

11. Michael M. Horowitz, *Peoples and Cultures of the Caribbean* (Garden City, NY: Doubleday, 1971), 8.

12. Sidney W. Mintz, "Forward," *Afro-American Anthropology*, Norman E. Whitten and John F. Szwed, eds. (New York: Free Press/London: Collier Macmillan Ltd., 1970), 1-16.

13. Sidney W. Mintz and Richard Price, *The Birth of an African American Culture: An Anthropological Perspective* (Boston: Beacon Press, 1992 [Original 1976]), 55.

14. Mintz and Price, *The Birth of an African American Culture*, 7, 14ff.

15. Mintz, *Caribbean Transformations*, 18.

16. Mintz and Price, *The Birth of an African American Culture*, 62.

17. Peter L. Berger and Thomas Luckmann, *The Social Construction of Reality* (Harmondsworth: Penguin, 1976), 59.

18. George E. Marcus. "Contemporary Problems in Ethnography," in *Writing Culture*, James Clifford and George E. Marcus, eds. (Berkeley: University of California Press, 1986), 190ff.

19. Stephen A. Tyler, "Postmodern Ethnography: From Document of the Occult to Occult Document," in Clifford and Marcus, *Writing Culture*, 131.

20. Sherry B. Ortner, "Theory in Anthropology Since the Sixties," *Comparative Studies in Society and History* 26, no. 1 (1984), 126-166.

21. Charles Stewart and Rosalind Shaw, eds., *Syncretism/Anti-Syncretism: The Politics of Religious Synthesis* (London/New York: Routledge, 1994).

22. Göran Aijmer, ed., *Syncretism and the Commerce of Symbols* (Göteborg: IASSA, 1995).

23. Aijmer, *Syncretism and the Commerce of Symbols*, 3.

24. Gerd Baumann, *Contesting Culture: Discourses of Identity in Multi-Ethnic London* (Cambridge: Cambridge University Press, 1996).

25. Benedict Anderson, *Imagined Communities* (London/New York: Verso, 1989 [Original 1983]).

26. Anthony P. Cohen, *The Symbolic Construction of Community* (London/New York: Routledge, 1992 [Original 1985]), 13.

27. Cohen, *The Symbolic Construction*, 14-15.

28. André Droogers, "Syncretism: The Problem of Definition, the Definition of the Problem," in *Dialogue and Syncretism*, J. Gort et al., eds. (Grand Rapids, MI: Eerdmans, 1989), 13.

29. Stewart and Shaw, *Syncretism/Anti-Syncretism*, 10.

30. Stewart and Shaw, *Syncretism/Anti-Syncretism*, 6ff.

31. Jan Voorhoeve and Ursy M. Lichtveld, *Creole Drum* (New Haven/London: Yale University Press, 1975).

32. Richard Price, "Review of Winti: een Afroamerikaanse Godsdienst in Suriname, by Charles J. Wooding," *American Anthropologist* 75 (1973): 1884-86.

33. Charles J. Wooding, *Evolving Culture: a Cross-Cultural Study of Suriname, West Africa and the Caribbean* (Lanham, MD: University Press of America, 1981 [Original 1972]), 1, 271 ff., 290.

34. Peter Schoonheym, *Je Geld of . . . Je Leven* (Utrecht: Instituut voor Culturele Antropologie. ICAU Mededelingen 14, 1980), 81.

35. Charles J. Wooding, *Geesten genezen* (Groningen: Konstapel, 1984).

36. Wooding, *Evolving Culture*, 137.

37. Wooding, *Evolving Culture*, 86.

38. J.G. Platvoet, *Comparing Religions: A Limitative Approach* (The Hague: Mouton, 1982).

39. Berger and Luckmann, *Social Construction*, 15.

40. James Clifford, "On Ethnographic Allegory," in Clifford and Marcus, *Writing Culture*, 115ff.

41. Berger and Luckmann, *Social Construction*, 126.

42. Clifford, "On Ethnographic Allegory," 9.
43. George E. Marcus and Michael M. J. Fisher, *Anthropology as Cultural Critique* (Chicago: University of Chicago Press, 1986), 30.
44. Obeyesekere observes that there is no "native point of view" since differences of opinion are to be found everywhere (Gananath Obeyesekere, *The Work of Culture* [Chicago: University of Chicago Press, 1990], 219). Similarly Sanjek reminds us that one of the chief defining characteristics of the ethnographic method is the recording of "speech in action" and not a reduction of recorded texts (Roger Sanjek. "The Ethnographic Present," *Man* 26 [1991]: 609-628).
45. Jan Voorhoeve, "The Obiaman and His Influence in the Moravian Parish," *Bijdragen tot de Taal-, Land- en Volkenkunde* 139, no. 3 (1983), 411-420; Van Lier, Bonuman, 15; Schoonheym, *Je Geld of... Je Leven*, 78-79; Peter Schoonheym, "Het Gebied van Boven-Para en de Synthese tussen Christendom en Creoolse Religie," in Derveld and Noordegraaf, *Winti-Religie*, 53; Tijno Venema, 1992 *Famiri nanga Kulturu: Creoolse sociale verhoudingen en Winti in Amsterdam* (Amsterdam: Het Spinhuis, 1992), 83-84, 171; W. Van Wetering, "Some Thoughts on Syncretism in Suriname Creole Migrant Culture, as Reproduced by Migrant Women in the Netherlands," in *New Trends and Developments in African Religions*, Peter Clarke, ed. (Westport, CT: Greenwood Press, 1998), 223-243.
46. Voorhoeve, a Christian studying Creole language for the purpose of translating the Bible in the late 1950s, was among the first to defend popular culture publicly.
47. Schoonheym, "Het Gebied van Boven-Para. . . . ," 53; Van Lier, *Bonuman*, 15; Venema, *Famiri nanga Kulture*, 66, 88, 140.
48. Wooding, *Evolving Culture*, 86.
49. Venema, *Famiri nanga Kulture*, 140.
50. Schoonheym, "Het Gebied van Boven-Para. . . . ," 53; Wooding, *Evolving Culture*, 86.
51. Schoonheym, "Het Gebied van Boven-Para. . . . ," 57; Henri M. J. Stephen, *De Macht van de Fodoe Winti* (Amsterdam: Karnak, 1986), 46.
52. Schoonheym, *Je Geld of... Je Leven*, 78-79, "Het Gebied van Boven-Para . . . ," 57; Van Lier, *Bonuman*, 62.
53. Schoonheym, *Je Geld of... Je Leven*, 62.
54. W. Van Wetering, "Ethnicity's Constraints on Syncretism: Suriname Creole Religion in the Netherlands," in press.
55. Schoonheym, *Je Geld of... Je Leven*.
56. Walter Jackson, "Melville Herskovits and the Search for Afro-Amerrican Culture," in *Malinowski, Rivers, Benedict and Others*, George W. Stocking, ed. (Madison, WI: The University of Wisconsin Press, 1986), 113.
57. Stewart and Shaw, *Syncretism/Anti-Syncretism*, 8-9.
58. Van Wetering, "Some Thoughts on Syncretism."
59. Fisher has drawn attention to the significance of dreaming and transference processes in the invention and reinvention of ethnicity. See Michael M. J. Fisher,

"Ethnicity as Text and Model," in Marcus and Fisher, ed., *Anthropology as Cultural Critique*, 173 ff.

60. Van Wetering, "Some Thoughts on Syncretism."

61. Van Wetering, "Ethnicity's Constraints on Syncretism."

62. W. Van Wetering, "Women as Winti Healers," in *Illness and Healing Alternatives in Western Europe*, Hilary Marland, ed. (London: Routledge, 1997), 243-261; "Some Thoughts on Syncretism"; "Ethnicity's Constraints on Syncretism."

63. Stephen, *Winti*, 18; *De Macht van de Fodoe Winti*, 17.

64. Comparable genres and styles may be found in other contemporary insiders' accounts of African American diaspora religion. See for example Stephan Palmié, "Making Sense of Santería: Three Books on Afro-Cuban Religion" (review article), *New West Indian Guide* 70, no. 3/4 (1996): 291-300.

65. Stephen, *Winti*, 19 & 29, *De Macht* . . . , 13.

66. Herskovits and Herskovits, *Suriname Folk-Lore*, 45; Wooding, *Evolving Culture*, 72; Stephen, *Winti*, 37.

67. Voorhoeve and Lichtveld noted the process of sacralization of various other cultural elements. See Voorhoeve and Lichtveld, *Creole Drum*.

68. Herskovits and Herskovits, *Suriname Folk-Lore*, 33.

69. Herskovits and Herskovits, *Suriname Folk-Lore*, 32ff.

70. It is to Frances Shapiro Herskovits that we owe the first description of social entrepreneurship by women. As Stephan Palmié informed me in a personal communication based on his examination of the Herskovitses' diaries and field notes, the couple were in Surinam for only a short time during the summers of 1928 and 1929. Melville spent much of the period in the interior collecting the data published in his *Rebel Destiny* (Melville J. Herskovits, *Rebel Destiny: Among the Bush Negroes of Dutch Guiana* [New York: McGraw Hill, 1934]). He concludes that Frances was the one who obtained the data on women's life in Paramaribo.

71. An example would be the *Kra tafra*, the dinner party for the soul (see Schoonheym, *Je Geld of . . . Je Leven*, 62; Wooding, Evolving Culture, 71). This ostensibly is a secular affair, but the guest may infer from details—i.e., the type of food and drinks served, the color scheme of clothes worn, the music played, etc.—that the sacred is involved. Covert worship of this type might be cited as an example of the mask or cloak covering Africanisms as intended by Melville Herskovits in his "African Gods and Catholic Saints in New World Negro Belief," *American Anthropologist* 39 (1937).

72. Schoonheym, *Je Geld of . . . Je Leven*, 83.

73. W. Van Wetering, "Informal Supportive Networks: Quasi Kin Groups, Religion and Social Order Among Surinamese Creoles in the Netherlands," *The Netherlands Journal of Sociology* 23, no. 2 (1987): 92-101, and W. Van Wetering, "Transformations of Slave Experience," in *Slave Culture and Cultures of Slavery*, Stephan Palmié, ed. (Knoxville, TN: University of Tennessee Press, 1995), 271-304.

74. Cf. Venema, *Famari nanga Kulturu*, 134.

75. Herskovits and Herskovits, *Suriname Folk-Lore*, 33.

76. Stewart and Shaw, *Syncretism/Anti-Syncretism*, 7.
77. Cf. Stewart and Shaw, *Syncretism/Anti-Syncretism*, 18; Sidney W. Mintz, "Enduring Substance, Trying Theories," *Man* 2, no. 2 (1996), 289-311.
78. Tyler, "Postmodern Ethnography," 131.
79. Stewart and Shaw, *Syncretism/Anti-Syncretism*, 18.

## Chapter 12

## Seeking Syncretism: The Case of Sathya Sai Baba

Morton Klass

In 1957, Michael M. Horowitz and I conducted research in Martinique among descendants of indentured laborers who had been brought to that island from South India during the nineteenth century. Our East Indian informants had all been raised as Roman Catholics—that is, all had been baptized and many had learned their catechism; if they were married, the ceremony had been performed by a Catholic priest; and when eventually they would die, the funeral rites would be those of the church.

Meanwhile, however, they all repaired periodically (in some cases weekly) to a structure, known popularly in Martinique as *la chapelle coolie*, in front of which goats and sheep were sacrificed to beings with such names as *Maldevidan* and *Mari-Amma*. Maldevidan, our informants advised us, was simply the Indian name for *St. Michel* (as proof, it was pointed out that both were represented as being on horseback). Mari-Amma is familar to Indologists as the south Indian goddess of fearful mien and practice who presides over smallpox and other afflictions. Our informants insisted, however, that the name simply represented the Tamil pronunciation of *Marie-aimée*, the mother of Jesus Christ—that, in fact, Mari-Amma and Marie-aimée were one and the same divine personage.[1]

How could this be?

The explanation customarily offered for such seemingly bizarre and contradictory fusions is of course that they represent examples of the phenomenon known as syncretism—a term, as Droogers and Greenfield demonstrate in chapter 1 of this volume, that has many definitions and is subject to much conflict reflective of differences in approach and theory. I begin, to keep it simple, with the usual dictionary definition: the attempt or tendency to combine or reconcile differing beliefs, as in religion or philosophy.[2]

In 1985, I undertook a study, this time in the West Indian nation of Trinidad and Tobago, of the devotees of a South Indian holy man, Sathya Sai Baba.[3] His claim, accepted by all his devotees whatever their original faith, is that he is God —the only God there is or has ever been. Specifically, he teaches that, no matter what the name or term used for God in any religion on this planet, he—Sathya Sai Baba—is really the one to whom all prayers go, for there is none other. Is this then another example of the phenomenon of *syncretism,* so frequently described in the literature on the West Indies? Or is it in fact perhaps something even more: is the religion of Sathya Sai Baba the *ultimate* syncretism, an assertion that all religions are one, and that oneness is personified by Sathya Sai Baba?

In my effort to probe the nature and significance of Sai Baba's message I have, almost inevitably, gone back to the issue of syncretism, and the perceptions and problems it presents. Two excellent collections of interdisciplinary papers on aspects of syncretism have contributed much to my current understanding of the topic and the problems.[4]

Putting firmly to one side the suggestion that syncretism originated as a Plutarchian pun ("the coming together of Cretans") on the earlier Greek term *synkrasis,*[5] we may still observe that the term (and the subject) have had a rather checkered career over the centuries. According to Stewart and Shaw, theologians and other students of religion have shifted back and forth a number of times about whether syncretism is a good or bad thing—whether, for example, it constituted "a positive achievement which strengthened and enriched Christianity" or "an entirely unprincipled jumbling together of religions."[6]

The underlying problem may be, as André Droogers has suggested, that the term "syncretism" has come to reflect both objective and subjective meanings:

> The basic objective meaning refers neutrally and descriptively to the mixing of religions. The subjective meaning includes an evaluation of such intermingling from the point of view of one of the religions involved. As a rule, the mixing of religions is condemned in this evaluation as violating the essence of the belief system.[7]

I hope to demonstrate later in this paper that one may also examine syncretism as a possible violation of the "essence of the belief system" even when adhering to the objective meaning.

In any event, it was in its objective meaning that the term was introduced into the anthropological discourse by Melville J. Herskovits, the first anthropologist to study extensively the descendants of people enslaved in Africa and brought to the New World.[8] Herskovits eschewed judgment, using the term only to denote "one form of reinterpretation": "the process by which old meanings are ascribed to new elements or by which new values change the cultural significance of old forms." More specifically, he used the term to signify the "reinterpretation" that took place when (in his view) conjoined or fused elements deriving from disparate sources and therefore once unrelated to each other were now somehow "reconciled."[9]

Whatever its problems or shortcomings, it is nevertheless certain that the approach to syncretism introduced by Herskovits generated a large body of still-important data and interpretation produced by Herskovits himself and by those who followed his lead. Through their efforts, many of the mechanisms of culture change have been illuminated, and of course the work of Herskovits and his followers have provided the argument that made possible the original formulation of what the so-called Afro-Catholic belief systems of the Caribbean and Latin America were and how they came to be:

> The argument offered is that people were brought from Africa carrying with them their natal religions: names and attributes of deities, details of rituals, explanations of the universe. They were stripped (often forcibly) of some of these religious elements and acquired (again, often forcibly) a new set deriving from European (usually Roman Catholic) Christianity. The result in many cases was the emergence of a new and syncretic religion (such as Haitian Vodun, Trinidad Shango, and Brazilian Candomblé) in which the various traits are sufficiently discrete that provenience is easily determinable.[10]

Many scholars, however, deriving from other theoretical schools began to reject the very notion of syncretism. E. R. Leach, for example, noted that the worship of the god *Pulleyar* by Buddhists in Ceylon—unquestionably derived from the Hindu *Pillaiyar* (or *Ganesha*), the elephant-headed son of Siva—would appear to be a clear example of syncretism. He embarks, however, on a structural analysis in which he argues that Hindu Shiva (potent) and Ganesha his son (sexless) are equivalent to the seemingly reversed Sinhalese Buddhist Lord Buddha (sexless) and his servant Pulleyar (potent). This leads him to the following challenge:

Is this usefully considered a situation of syncretism at all? Are we concerned here with a merging of religious ideas or is it just one particular manifestation of a complex of ideas which appears in a great variety of religious systems?[11]

Few scholars have joined Leach in concluding that there may be no such thing as syncretism and that what we observe as such is actually "one particular manifestation" of something common to many religions. Indeed, much more widespread is the belief that it is syncretism itself that is the universal phenomenon:

> Virtually every culture or religion is synthetic; they have all changed over time, adopting and incorporating exogenous elements and ideas along the way . . . creolization, hybridization, interculturation, or whatever one wishes to call it, is now the rule not the exception. I would only add that it has probably been this way for a very long time, not just since colonization or the emergence of global capitalism.[12]

One conclusion to be drawn from the foregoing might be that one scholar's syncretism is another's something-very-different, and this observation should not be dismissed as flippant. Droogers observes:

> The change of meaning is almost by definition prominent in situations of contact. The recipient of a message does not necessarily understand that message in the same way as the person sending it meant to be understood. This alone can mark the start of syncretism. Since communication between cultures and religions takes place in the context of doubled sets of symbols, patterns, and meanings, reinterpretation, misunderstanding, and distortion will be the more probable.[13]

Droogers' insights, it will be seen, have contributed considerably to the following examination of the syncretic nature of Sathya Sai Baba's teachings. What do those teachings mean to the giver of them? How are they understood by the recipient?

The worship of the South Asian holy man Sathya Sai Baba, who claims to be God incarnate, has within recent decades spread rapidly among Indo-Trinidadians; that is, among those citizens of the West Indian nation of Trinidad and Tobago who are of South Asian descent.[14] Since the new faith derives from South Asia, and more specifically from India, the land from which Indo-Trinidadians originally derive, one might easily approach it as a typical example of a Herskovitsian syncretic religion.

There are problems, however. To begin with, let us observe that there has been considerable divergence of opinion among scholars as to how "Indian" this India-derived population actually remains after more than a century and a half of residence in the New World. Some anthropologists and sociologists have long argued that the people of South Asian derivation in the New World have lost or turned away from the culture of their ancestors and have merged inextricably into the dominant Creole or West Indian culture with its roots in Europe and Africa.[15] Others, myself included, have challenged this view, arguing that important dimensions of South Asian social structure, values and ideology were reconstituted among Indo-Trinidadians.[16]

Whichever position is held on the degree of creolization experienced by Indo-Trinidadians, it is generally agreed that they are not, from any cultural perspective, "Indians of India." As Indo-Trinidadians they are very much part of the West Indian matrix, in terms of language, educational background, leisure-time activities and much much else. A significant, though small, percentage is now Christian, and the Hinduism practiced by the majority reflects both the long separation from India and the effects of contact with Christianity.

Given, therefore, the undeniable differences between Indo-Trinidadians and present-day inhabitants of South Asia, one may reasonably inquire as to why Indo-Trinidadians were attracted to the worship of a South Asian holy man who, among other things, spoke a language (*Telegu*) that was as unintelligible to all Indo-Trinidadians as it was to all Afro-Trinidadians.

Indeed, as it turned out, if *Indo*-Trinidadians were attracted by the teachings of Sathya Sai Baba, *Afro*-Trinidadians were at first seemingly equally attracted! The first gathering of Sai Baba devotees in Trinidad, in 1974, was made up of equal numbers of Indo- and Afro-Trinidadians, who determined to proselytize equally in both ethnic communities.

Let us observe that this was not an unusual phenomenon for the Sai Baba movement, for—despite its South Asian origins—it has attracted devotees all over the world, from Thailand to Italy, to Argentina, to the United States. The very logos of the movement is as sharp and definitive an example of religious syncretism as Melville Herskovits could ever have imagined: a six-petaled lotus, with each petal containing a symbol identified with a specific world religion (a cross for Christianity, the word "OM" in Devanagri script to represent Hinduism, the six-pointed Star of David for Judaism, the wheel of Buddhism, the star and crescent of Islam, and the cup of fire representing the Parsee or Zoroastrian faith). In the center of the logos is the identifying symbol of Sathya Sai Baba, a lotus on a vase; but the entire logos is one, representing not just ecumenicism but what Sathya Sai Baba insists is the unity—the identity of message—of all faiths, which is what, in fact, he claims he has come to preach.

We must conclude, therefore, that the religion of Sathya Sai Baba is not a simple (or Herskovitsian) syncretism of Trinidadian and Indian elements. Indeed, as I proposed earlier in this paper, it must be approached as an effort—in fact, a conscious effort!—to merge and encompass all existing religions into one.

Putting to one side, then, the attraction the teachings of Sathya Sai Baba have for educated, upper class Indo-Trinidadians, let us focus on the issue raised by Sathya Sai Baba's central message: that all religions teach the same thing, that all names of God and all prayers represent the same God and the same prayer. In other words, how syncretic in fact is this most syncretic of all faiths?

His worshippers, particularly those who derive from other parts of the world and from faiths other than Hinduism, are clearly quite convinced of the syncretic nature of his teachings; indeed, it is one of the things they find most appealing about those teachings. Thus, Samuel Sandweiss, a psychiatrist and American Jewish devotee, writes of the conflict first experienced by his wife, concluding:

> The conflict between Baba and Judaism was gradually resolved, however, as Sharon began to discover the universality in Baba's message . . . when she learned that he encourages people to follow their own familiar religion and teaches that since God is behind all names and forms, everything is a manifestation of God.[17]

Elsewhere, Sandweiss writes:

> To me, the most mind-blowing event of all regarding Baba's relationship to Christ happened Christmas Day, 1972. He told a group of people: Christ said, "He who has sent Me will come again." To my amazement he said that he himself was the one to whom Christ was referring.[18]

Another Western devotee, Howard Murphet, whose writings on Sai Baba and his teachings are among the most popular books of the movement, notes:

> After her first visit to Prasanti Nilayam [Sai Baba's ashram] a woman of Germany, a devout and earnest seeker on the path, said, "Baba is the incarnation of purity and love." Later, after spending more time with him, she wrote in a letter: "I get more and more convinced from within that he is Jesus Christ who has come again, in the fullness of Christ, as Satya Sai Baba."[19]

And Murphet himself is clearly aware of the identification of Sathya Sai Baba with Jesus ("Sai Baba has many similarities to Christ, not only in the miracles but in the style of his presentation").[20]

To be fair to these non-Hindu devotees, Sai Baba himself encourages such identifications, and alludes to them frequently himself in his sermons and speeches. Thus, according to Murphet:

> Baba puts it this way: "The Lord can be addressed by any name that tastes sweet to your tongue, or pictured in any form that appeals to your sense of wonder and

awe. You can sing of him as Muruga, Ganapathi, Sarada, Jesus, Maitreyi, Sakti, or you can call on Allah or the Formless, or the Master of all Forms. It makes no difference at all. He is the beginning, the middle and the end; the basis, the substance and the source."[21]

Put simply, but I think fairly, Sai Baba teaches that all religions present what is fundamentally the same message—turn to peace and love and thus achieve salvation for your soul—because the voice behind the universal message emanates from the same divine presence, the same "God" whatever the name and attributes assigned by the particular religious group. Sathya Sai Baba himself, he says, is simply a current manifestation of the universal divinity, engaged in the task of making fully apparent to all people everywhere the universality of both divinity and divine message. Indeed, the foregoing is but a paraphrase of his own words. For example, in 1968, in a visit to Nairobi, Kenya, Sathya Sai Baba preached the following to all who came to hear him:

> I have come to light the Lamp of Love in your hearts, to see that it shines day by day with added lustre. I have not come to speak on behalf of any particular Righteousness like the Hindu Righteousness. I have not come on any mission of publicity for any sect or creed or cause; nor have I come to collect the followers for any doctrine. I have no plan to attract disciples or devotees in My fold or any fold. I have come to tell you of this Universal unitary faith, the Inner Self principle, the Path of Love, this Righteousness of Love, this Duty of Love, this Obligation to Love.
> 
> All religions teach one basic discipline; the removal from the mind of the blemish of egoism, of running after little joys. Every religion teaches man to fill his being with the Glory of God and evict the pettiness of conceit. It trains him in the methods of detachment and discrimination, so that he may aim high and attain liberation. Believe that all hearts are motivated by the One and Only God, that all Names in all languages and all Forms man can conceive, denote the One and only God; His adoration is best done by means of Love. Cultivate that attitude of Oneness between men of all creeds, all countries and all continents. That is the Message of Love, I bring. That is the Message I wish you to take to heart.[22]

Thus, then, the ultimate syncretism: *all* names of God are one; *all* theological teachings are fundamentally the same; *all* religions, all *religion*, constitutes an identity. In short, if the teachings of Sathya Sai Baba of Puttaparthi do not represent religious syncretism, it is hard to imagine what else possibly could.

Nevertheless, I would now argue, a closer examination of the teachings of Sai Baba do indeed make questionable the assertion of their syncretic nature. Sathya Sai Baba claims, we have seen, that the Messages of all religions resolve into one universal Message: would theological representatives of the various branches of, say, Christianity, Islam, Judaism and Buddhism agree; or would they be likely to insist that *they* perceive many most fundamental and profound differences between their respective teachings and those of Sathya Sai Baba? Go on to question the advocates of all the other religious systems of the world—with one exception—and the responses, I am convinced, would be equally negative.

The exception, of course, is Hinduism. This faith, known on the South Asian subcontinent as *Sanatan Dharma,* the ancient and everlasting doctrine, is most complex and intricate, exhibiting an enormous corpus of theological and ritual literature, and I certainly do not mean to imply that it is a unitary faith in any way. Nevertheless, there are certain fundamental assumptions and perceptions held in common by all who subscribe to it, which serve to set the religious system off from other faiths. Among these, I would particularly note the following:

a. The souls of individual humans are immortal though the humans themselves are mortal: thus, the soul of any living human is a sojourner—it existed in another human before the present one was born and will pass to still another after death.
b. The goal of every human should be to live so as to end this transmigration of the soul, immediately after death if possible or in some proximate rebirth.
c. There is a universal law—the Law of Karma—which determines the fate of each soul: certain kinds of behavior and thought lead inevitably to continuing rebirth and miserable future lives, and other kinds of behavior and thought lead to both happier rebirths and the possibility of total cessation.
d. Neither divinities nor human teachers can contravene the universal law, but both can help people find the paths to salvation, meaning a more favorable Karma. Given this, an identification of "teacher" (Guru) with "divinity" is often asserted by Hindus.
e. There is a "veil" (Maya)—reflecting the deceptive nature of reality itself—that obscures or distorts both the divine message and the ability of humans to receive it. Thus, all religions, insofar as they reflect the divine message, contain truth (advice leading to Karmic salvation) but they also inevitably exhibit error. This is even true, inevitably, of the Sanatan Dharma, though it exhibits less error and more truth than any other faith.[23]

Though some of the above are shared with faiths other than Hinduism,[24] the totality of assertions is reflective exclusively of Hinduism. Any analysis of Sathya Sai Baba's sermons will swiftly demonstrate his adherence to all of the above. Thus, his message is the common message of Hinduism: how best to end or ameliorate the burdens of rebirth. Here are just a few samples chosen from some of Sai Baba's sermons:

> *Moksha* [Hindu salvation—the end of rebirth] is attained when the Atma shines in its own glory . . . when delusion is shed, grief gets destroyed; joy is established . . . The manas or mind is the villain; it is another name for desire; the texture of the mind is just desire. . . . If desire goes, the mind disappears.[25]
>
> Whichever the book, whoever the guru, whatever the peetam or institution, the goal is the same . . . you can picture it as a four storeyed [sic] mansion, the ground floor being karmayoga [the behavior ordained by one's karma] and the succeeding ones—bhakti [devotional prayer], jnana [wisdom] and vairaga [detachment].[26]
>
> Only through karma can liberation be effected . . . without karma, progress is difficult. The jnani [one who has chosen the path of wisdom] too has to do karma, but . . . karma will not affect them at all. They do it with no ego, with no desire.[27]
>
> India has been announcing this Truth to the world since ages; this is the land where holy personages, divine personalities, saints and sages, avathars, carrying the authentic stamp of God, have demonstrated that nothing else can give man the peace and joy that the contemplation of the universal Atma can give.[28]
>
> You must tread the spiritual path with an uncontrollable urge to reach the Goal [ending of rebirth]; you must cultivate the yearning for liberation from all this encumbrance. Remember that you have to dwell in a house built on four stout pillars: Dharma, Artha, Kama, and Moksha.[29]

It could be argued, of course, that most of these sermons are preached before Hindu audiences, and so Sathya Sai Baba must of necessity couch his message in terms intelligible to them. While this is true, it is nevertheless quite clear from his sermons that Sathya Sai Baba's message derives from, and reflects, the specific body of religious teachings known to its adherents as the Sanatan Dharma and to others as Hinduism: "Nor is the message I bring anything new! It is the message of the Vedas, tested by time and guaranteed by the experience of many who put it into practice."[30]

Indeed, there is little in his teachings that most Hindu gurus would find either objectionable or even novel—including, it could certainly be argued, the statements that he himself is an avatar of God and that all names of God are in the end references to the same universal divinity.

Now, the Western devotee, as we have seen, is convinced that Sai Baba's teachings are truly syncretic, that is, encompassing and even fusing the teachings of all other religions. But if I am correct in my conclusion that Sai Baba preaches what are essentially the views of non-syncretic Hinduism alone—and, further, that any assertion of syncretism serves only to mask the total absence of any actual structural or ideological syncretism—what then is the actual belief system of the Western devotee?

I would argue that there is in fact nothing significantly objectively syncretic about the Western devotee's belief system. Whatever he or she might think—

whatever Sathya Sai Baba might argue, the Western devotee's belief system is recognizably a descendant or development of *one and only one* of its supposed ancestors—just as English, despite the incorporation of large amounts of French (and other) linguistic elements (phonological, grammatical, lexical) remains indisputably a Germanic language. Thus, I would argue, the Western devotees of Sathya Sai Baba become in fact Hindus in all respects but that of self-identification. That is, they have in essence relinquished whatever belief system they formally held and have replaced it with that of the Sanatan Dharma; but at the same time they remain convinced they actually do continue to maintain both sets equally, because (so *they* believe) both sets, indeed all religious systems, are identical.

Howard Murphet (a Western devotee and official spokesman for Sai Baba) writes:

> God is formless, yet he has form. He is that which lies beyond all forms yet he creates, maintains and destroys everything that exists. God is really in every form, but in Man more than in anything else, and in some men more intensely and completely than in others. A few men in the world's history have been one hundred per cent God.[31]
>
> The fact is that every man is a spark of divinity; every man is potentially God —not God as we usually think of him, with form, but the formless God, the divine ocean from which comes all existence. Baba states this plainly: "If you realise the *Atma*-principle you become God himself. . . . Each one of you can become God by merging your separate individual souls in the ocean of the universal *Atma*."[32]
>
> Man is essentially the *Atma*. . . . He is not the body and must never identify himself with the body which is merely a temporary vestment.[33]

Though Murphet may believe that the above teachings of Sathya Sai Baba are identical to those of Christ and Mohammed and the founders of all other faiths, I think most devotees of non-Hindu faiths, and most students of comparative religion, would disagree with him. Nevertheless, this belief in the universality, the supposed syncretic nature, of Sai Baba's teachings is of central importance to his Western devotees. Thus, Samuel H. Sandweiss responds to the question of relationships between Hinduism on the one hand and Judaism and Christianity on the other with the following assertion:

> I see more similarities than differences when I investigate these spiritual doctrines. The idea of *karma*, that we reap what we sow, that we create our future with the slightest of our actions in each moment of the present, is akin in spirit to the golden rule: "Do unto others as you would have them do unto you."[34]

Indeed, Sandweiss goes even further, asserting that even the teachings of Western medical science are congruent with those of Sathya Sai Baba:

> I have come to realize that through love both the therapist and the patient can grow in the realization that our basic identity is *Atma*—that we in fact extend beyond time and space. . . . The ultimate goal of psychiatry, I feel, is the same as that of religion: to find the God or *Atma* within, through the experience of love. Reflecting my fervent hope that psychiatry awaken to the reality of Sai Baba, I myself would rather call this still young science "Sai-chiatry," the Sai-chiatry of Atma consciousness, the Sai-chiatry of love.[35]

Some cynics may suspect that assertions by devotees of Vodun or Shango or Maldevidan that their beliefs are truly a blend of two faiths are dissembling, perhaps for the purpose of deflecting criticism. Whatever the validity of that suspicion, I do not hold it about the devotees of Sathya Sai Baba: I am satisfied that they do indeed believe in the syncretic nature of their belief system. But honest conviction is not enough: objectively, analytically, the teachings of Sathya Sai Baba do not constitute *syncretism*.

And yet, having said that, I must admit there is at least one other arena in which a syncretic dimension to the Sai Baba movement might be noted. Sathya Sai Baba's teachings, I noted earlier, have proved particularly attractive to people of South Asian descent who live in the West Indian nation of Trinidad and Tobago. Let us also note that, among this population, the people most attracted to Sathya Sai Baba have been, overwhelmingly, the educated, the professional, the wealthy—in short, the most westernized and cosmopolitan segment of the Indo-Trinidadian community.

Elsewhere, I have endeavored to explore some of the sources of this attraction; I have argued for example that their devotion to Sathya Sai Baba frees the Indo-Trinidadian elite from what many of them have experienced as a chafing and uncomfortable dependence on poor and parochial village Brahmans for religious needs.[36]

Here, however, let me focus, as I conclude this chapter, on still another attraction Sathya Sai Baba has for this segment of the Indo-Trinidadian population: I would argue that his message—overtly syncretic but fundamentally and unchangingly Hindu—is remarkably similar in both dimensions to the elite Indo-Trinidadian's perception of self. Westernized and cosmopolitan in language, education, clothing, economic aspirations and much else, the Indo-Trinidadian overtly represents a *cultural* syncretism, and in fact sees himself as one.

And yet, on another level, the identification with India—with its philosophy, its social system, its fundamental values—remains pervasive in the society, despite all change.[37] The educated, westernized Indo-Trinidadian, therefore, accepts the teachings of Sathya Sai Baba at one and the same time as both syncretic (a cosmopolitan amalgam like himself) and as a summons to pure and unadulterated Hinduism.

Is it possible, then, that when the East Indian of Martinique (whom we met in the first paragraph) asserts that Mari-amma, the fearful South Indian goddess, and Marie-aimeé, the gentle mother of Christ, are one and the same, he is really expressing his perception of himself: a baptized Roman Catholic Christian merged inextricably with a Tamil Hindu?

Syncretism, we have seen, has objective and subjective meanings; it is arguably universal and non-existent; and it may be found in the eye of the beholder or the mind of the believer. One begins to see why the term has precipitated frustration and confusion over the centuries since Plutarch first foisted it upon us—and also why, despite all, it remains ever stimulating, ever useful.

## Notes

1. Michael M. Horowitz and Morton Klass, "The Martiniquan East Indian Cult of Maldevidan," *Social and Economic Studies* 10, no. 1 (1961): 93-100.

2. *The American Heritage Dictionary of the English Language*, William Morris, ed. (Boston: American Heritage and Houghton Mifflin, 1969), 1304.

3. Morton Klass, *Singing with Sai Baba: The Politics of Revitalization in Trinidad* (Boulder, CO: Westview Press, 1991). [Reprinted 1996 Waveland Press.]

4. Charles Stewart and Rosalind Shaw, eds., *Syncretism/Anti-Syncretism: The Politics of Religious Synthesis* (London & New York: Routledge, 1994), and J. D. Gort et al., eds., *Dialogue and Syncretism: An Interdisciplinary Approach (Currents of Encounter: Studies on the Contact between Christianity and other Religions, Beliefs, and Cultures)* (Grand Rapids, Michigan: Wm. B. Eerdmans Publishing Co., 1989).

5. Stewart and Shaw, *Syncretism/Antisyncretism*, 3.

6. Stewart and Shaw, *Syncretism/Antisyncretism*, 4.

7. André Droogers, "Syncretism: The Problem of Definition, and the Definition of the Problem," in Gort, *Dialogue and Syncretism*, 7.

8. Melville J. Herskovits, *The Myth of the Negro Past* (Boston: Beacon Press, 1941).

9. Melville J. Herskovits, *Man and His Works: The Science of Cultural Anthropology* (New York: Alfred A. Knopf, 1949), 553.

10. Morton Klass, *Ordered Universes: Approaches to the Anthropology of Religion* (Boulder, CO: Westview Press, 1995), 143.

11. E. R. Leach, "Pulleyar and the Lord Buddha: An Aspect of Religious Syncretism in Ceylon," *Psychoanalysis and the Psychoanalytic Review* 49, no. 2 (1962): 101.

12. Charles Stewart, "Syncretism as a Dimension of Nationalist Discourse in Modern Greece," in Stewart and Shaw, *Syncretism/Anti-Syncretism*, 127.

13. Droogers, "Syncretism," 19.

14. See Klass, *Singing with Sai Baba*.

15. See, for example, Daniel Crowley, "Plural and Differential Acculturation in Trinidad," *American Anthropologist* 59 (1957): 817-819; and "Cultural Assimilation in a Multiracial Society," in *Social and Cultural Pluralism in the Caribbean*, Vera Rubin, ed., *Annals of the New York Academy of Sciences* 83, no. 5 (1960), 850-854; R.T. Smith and Chandra Jayawardena, "Hindu Marriage Customs in British Guiana," *Social and Economic Studies* 7 (1958): 178-194; Chandra Jayawardena, *Conflict and Solidarity in a Guianese Plantation* (London: London School of Economics Monographs on Social Anthropology, No. 25, 1963); Barton M. Schwartz, "The Failure of Caste in Trinidad," in *Caste in Overseas Indian Communities*, B. M. Schwartz, ed. (San Francisco: Chandler Publishing Company, 1967), 117-147; and Joseph Nevadomsky, "Economic Organization, Social Mobility, and Changing Social Status among East Indians in Rural Trinidad," *Ethnology* 22, no. 1 (1983): 63-79.

16. See, for example, Morton Klass, *East Indians in Trinidad: A Study of Cultural Persistence* (New York: Columbia University Press, 1961) [Reprinted 1988 Waveland Press]; Colin Clarke, *East Indians in a West Indian Town: San Fernando, Trinidad, 1930-1970* (London: Allen & Unwin, 1986); John G. LaGuerre, ed., *Calcutta to Caroni: The East Indians of Trinidad* (Trinidad and Jamaica: Longman Caribbean Limited, 1974); and Mahin Gosine, *East Indians and Black Power in the Caribbean: The Case of Trinidad* (New York: African Research Publications, 1986).

17. Samuel H. Sandweiss, *Sai Baba: The Holy Man . . . and the Psychiatrist* (New Delhi: M. Gulab Singh & Sons (P) Ltd., 1975), 219.

18. Sandweiss, *Sai Baba*, 176.

19. Howard Murphet, *Sai Baba: Man of Miracles* (Delhi: The Macmillan Company of India Limited, 1971), 206.

20. Murphet, *Sai Baba*, 191.

21. Murphet, *Sai Baba*, 193.

22. Grace McMartin, ed., *A Recapitulation of Satya Sai Baba's Divine Teaching* (Hyderabad: Avon Printing Works, 1982), 25-26.

23. It is always difficult (if not, indeed, impossible) to encapsulate the principal teachings of any faith. There is much more to Hinduism than this, but I think it fair to say that this, too, is there, and may therefore legitimately be contrasted with the equivalent beliefs of other religions (see Klass, *Singing with Sai Baba*).

24. Reender Kranenborg, after a lengthy examination of the many attempts to absorb the notion of reincarnation into Christianity, concludes: "This combination proved impossible: because of the context in which reincarnation was found, the church saw it as something incompatible with and essentially foreign to the Christian faith" (Reender Kranenborg, "Christianity and Reincarnation," in Gort, *Dialogue and Syncretism*, 185). The question he does not pursue is why, then, people who consider themselves Christians appear to have no difficulty in absorbing reincarnation into their belief system.

25. N. Kasturi, *Sathya Sai Speaks: Discourses of Bhagavan Sri Sathya Sai Baba* [Vol. IV] (Bangalore: Sri Sathya Sai Books and Publications, 1981), 91.

26. Kasturi, *Sathya Sai*, 111.

27. Kasturi, *Sathya Sai*, 133-134.
28. Kasturi, *Sathya Sai*, 187.
29. Kasturi, *Sathya Sai*, 316.
30. Kasturi, *Sathya Sai*, 325.
31. Murphet, *Sai Baba*, 193.
32. Murphet, *Sai Baba*, 192.
33. Murphet, *Sai Baba*, 191.
34. Sandweiss, *Sai Baba*, 174.
35. Sandweiss, *Sai Baba*, 190.
36. Klass, *Singing with Sai Baba.*
37. Cf. Gosine, *East Indians and Black Power*; Clarke, *East Indians in a West Indian Town*; La Guerre, *Calcutta to Caroni.*

# Index

Abimbola, Wande, 53
Abiodun, Rowland, 50, 53
Abrahams, Roger D., 181
academia, 27, 187, 189
acculturation, 10, 24, 26-27, 38, 57, 88, 109, 177, 185, 196, 213; process 26
*Acossi-Sakpata*, 94
actor(s), 13, 17, 22, 30, 32-33, 36-38, 128, 145-148, 151, 153, 155, 157, 159-161, 166, 168-169, 171-172, 174, 176, 186
adaptive strategies, 56
Adejanu, Henry, 49, 53
Admiral Balão, 108, 110
*adugbo*, 118
African: purity, 88, 102; religious, 44, 90, 92, 101, 115, 125; survivals, 114
Africanisms, 114-115, 199
Africanness, 76, 80-81, 90, 170-171
Afro-Brazilian religions, 16, 74, 80, 83, 87, 89-90, 91, 97, 99-103, 105-107, 109, 111, 114-115, 143

agency, 16-17, 132, 139, 147, 157, 160, 167, 174, 177, 186
Aijmer, Göran, 29, 40, 161, 186, 197
Ainlay, Stephen C., 67
*Aisa*, 190, 194
Alaafin, 118
alcoholism, 158-159
*aldeias* (villages), 73-74
Allada, 90
Alvares, Diogo, 111
ambiguity, 30, 177
Amerindian, 16, 63, 74, 92, 100-101, 104, 106-109; identity, 74
Amerindians, 18, 100, 105
Amsterdam, 17, 184-185, 191
*Anana*, 190
Anastácia Lúcia dos Santos, 104
Anchieta, Father José de, 107
Anderson, Benedict, 186, 197
Angola, 76, 90, 100, 103; traditions 100
anthropological writing, 139

anthropologist(s), 10-12, 14, 21, 24, 26-27, 36, 46, 68, 79, 87, 93, 95, 113-114, 125, 139, 142-143, 145-146, 186-187, 189, 197, 199, 203, 205, 213
anti-syncretism, 30, 39, 133, 143, 181, 187, 197-198, 200, 212
Apter, Andrew, 116-119, 126
Arensberg, Conrad M., 69
asceticism, 74
Assembly of God, 151
assimilation, 11-12, 30, 213
Aubey, Robert T., 41
authentic, 15-16, 71, 76, 81, 113-115, 117, 120, 163-164, 166, 176, 184, 190, 195, 209
authenticity, 18, 30, 37-38, 76, 79, 81, 101, 114, 136, 139, 141, 165, 176, 183, 186-188, 190
authority, 16, 51, 66, 117-118, 132, 139-140, 143-144, 188-190
Awolalu, J. Omosade, 122, 128
*axé,* 76, 114, 116, 134, 137
Azevedo, Thales de, 59, 61, 68, 83, 120, 127
Azzi, Riolando, 68, 127

*babalawo,* 14, 43, 50
Babylon, 169, 178
Bahai, 153-154, 157-158
Bahaullah, 153
Bahia, 16, 62, 73, 77-79, 82, 84-85, 89, 101-103, 109, 116, 119, 124-125, 128, 132, 137
Baird, Robert D., 39
Bakhtin, Mikhail, 97
Banna, Yuri, 196
*Bantu,* 76, 100-103
Barnes, Sandra, 43-44, 52
Barreto, Maria Amália Pereira, 109, 124
Barth, Frederik, 133, 143
Bastide, Roger, 38, 42, 59, 67-68, 82, 84-85, 89, 101, 109-111, 114, 116, 120, 125-127, 139, 143
Bateson, Gregory, 44
Baumann, Gerd, 186, 197
Beier, Ulli, 117, 126
bell hooks, 181
Benin, 76, 90, 124-125
Berger, Peter L., 14, 32, 40, 64, 67, 69, 71-72, 81-82, 84, 185, 188-189, 196-197
Berman, Marshall, 143
Berry, Philippa, 41
Beyer, Peter, 41
Bible, 174, 192, 198
Bijlmermeer, 185
birthday anniversaries, 17, 184
Black movements, 79
Bloch, Maurice, 34, 41, 161
Boas, Franz, 24-25, 27, 39, 84
body, 45, 48, 51, 75, 79, 93, 131-132, 135-136, 153-154, 164, 168, 176, 203, 209-210
*boiadeiros,* 103
Borofsky, Robert, 40-41, 161
boundaries, 18, 26, 30, 52, 66, 82, 96, 157, 186, 195
Bourdieu, Pierre, 17, 32-33, 40, 166, 168, 179-181
Brazil, 14-16, 42, 55-59, 61-69, 71-85, 88-90, 95, 99-101, 103-111, 113, 115-116, 119-125, 127-128, 134, 140, 142-143, 146, 151, 159, 161
Brazilian: Catholicism 120, 124; Paradox, 15, 71, 79-81; Umbanda, 38
bricolage, 90, 132, 195
Brown, Diana, 77, 83-84, 128, 143-144
Bruner, E. M., 144
Burdick, John, 69
burial society, 194
Burning Spear, 164

Cabinda 100; traditions, 100
*Cabocla Mariana,* 104

*Caboclo(s)*, 63, 73-74, 77-78, 81-83, 92, 99-110, 105, 131, 143
*cachaça* (raw rum), 73
Calhouhn, Craig, 180
candles, 61, 127, 192
Candomblé, 16, 36, 40, 42, 73-77, 79-85, 89, 92-93, 95, 102-104, 109, 113-116, 118, 122-126, 131-133, 136-140, 142-143, 203; de Caboclo, 77, 82, 100
*capangueiros,* 103
Cape Verde, 90
capital, 17, 57, 85, 89, 100, 102-104, 107, 117-118, 164, 166, 168-169, 172, 179-180
Caramuru, 111
Cardoso, Fernando Henrique, 58
Caribbean, 89, 163, 167, 174, 178-179, 184-185, 196-197, 203, 213
Carneiro, Edison, 82, 84, 89, 101, 109, 125-126
Carter, William, 68
Carvalho da Costa, Valdeli, 85, 109
*Casa Branca,* 116
Casa das Minas, 16, 87-88, 92-97, 106, 109
Casa das Minas-Jeje, 92, 106-107
Casa de Nagô, 89, 106-107, 111
Cascudo, Luis da Câmara, 100, 108, 110-111
Cassidy, Frederic G., 179
Castro, Yêda Pessoa de, 109
Catholic: church, 14, 62, 64, 69, 72, 80-81, 91, 113, 123, 137, 152-153, 179; saints, 61, 63-65, 90-93, 115, 122, 132, 152, 158, 185, 199 (*see also* saints)
Catimbó, 73-75, 77, 81-83
Catimbozeiros, 73, 82
chapelle coolie , 201
Charlemagne, 16, 104, 108-110
*Cheganças,* 104-105, 108
Chevannes, Barry, 178

child spirit, 136
Christ, 10, 90, 135, 152-153, 157, 190, 202, 206, 210, 212
Christian, 28, 46, 78, 85, 90-91, 110, 142, 183-184, 190, 192-194, 198, 205, 212-213; churches, 85, 190; God, 190, 192
Christianity, 9-10, 14, 17, 28, 30-31, 35, 44, 47, 52-53, 67, 69, 72, 77, 88, 97, 110, 114-115, 121, 132, 142, 189, 192-193, 202-203, 205, 208, 210, 212-213
Christians, 104-105, 183, 213
church, 14, 25, 59, 62, 64, 67-69, 72-73, 76, 80-81, 91, 93, 96, 113, 120, 123, 127, 137, 151-153, 179, 193-194, 201, 213
clairvoyance, 158
Clarke, Peter B., 39, 97, 125, 178, 198, 213-214
class, 75, 88, 100, 103, 148-149, 152, 168, 184, 187-190, 206
Clifford, James, 40, 43-44, 52, 88, 143, 177, 181, 188-189, 196-198
code, 169, 172, 183
codification, 188
cognitive construction, 167
Cohen, Anthony P., 197
collage, 132, 141
communalism, 190
complementarity, 190
complexes, 25
concepts, 11-13, 22-24, 27-28, 30, 32, 39, 45, 51-52, 85, 91, 125, 132, 139-140, 179, 183, 185-186
Congo, 76, 90, 100, 103; traditions, 100
connectionist, 17, 34, 147-148, 156; logic, 34
constraints, 36, 148, 157, 195, 198-199
consumer market, 71
consumers, 17, 72, 79, 81, 84, 164, 166, 168-169, 171, 174, 181

contradictions, 30, 147, 165
contradictory perspectives, 176
convergence, 16, 18, 42, 83, 90-92, 94, 96, 113-115, 120, 122, 124, 192, 195
counterhegemonic, 176
Count Ossie, 164, 177
cowboy spirits, 103-104
creative, 43, 104, 139, 142, 157, 167, 169, 177; capacity, 167, 169
creativity, 16, 132, 139, 141, 179
Creole, 17-18, 44, 52, 181, 183-184, 186, 188-195, 197-199, 205; culture, 52, 181, 183, 193; identity, 18
creolization, 14, 43, 132, 204-205; theory, 43
Crowley, Daniel, 213
crucifixes, 192
Cuban *Santeria*, 47
cult of the saints, 59
cultural: capital 168; contact, 11; ecologists, 32; imperialism, 167; nationalism, 190; politics, 187, 190; production, 176, 180; purity, 176; reductionism, 176; traits, 18, 25-27, 57, 195

Da Costa Eduardo, Octávio, 109
Da Costa Lima, Vivaldo, 84, 124, 128
Da Matta, Roberto, 15, 88, 97, 108-109
D'Andrade, Roy, 33, 38, 41, 148-149, 161
Dantas, Beatriz, 110, 114-115, 125-126
Da Silva, Arthur Augusto, 110
Davis, Stephen, 181
D'Azevedo, Warren L., 53
de-africanization, 136
Dealy, Glen C., 123, 128
death rituals, 190
deconstruction, 169-170, 177
de-ethnicization, 79, 81
Della Cava, Ralph, 69
Derveld, F.E.R., 196, 198
Desroche, H., 109
de-syncretizing, 137

dialogic anthropology, 189
diaspora, 179, 184, 199
dimensions of institutionalized religion, 146
discourse(s), 11-13, 16, 27, 29, 31, 38, 77, 101, 106-107, 117, 132-134, 136-139, 141, 145, 156, 159, 168, 179, 191-192, 197, 203, 212-213
dispositions, 17, 165-170, 172, 174, 176
distribution of wealth and the national income, 58
divinatory procudures, 191
dominance, 29-30, 123, 136, 138-139, 167-168, 174, 177
Dom João, 105
Dona Zeca, 105, 110
Dos Santos, Anastácia Lúcia, 104
Dos Santos, Deoscoredes M., 143
downsizing, 57
dreadlocks, 169-171, 178
dream, 153-155, 190
Droogers, André, 7-8, 17, 19, 21, 39-40, 56, 67, 88, 145, 161, 179, 187, 196-197, 202, 204, 212
dual morality, 123
Durkheim, Emile, 28

East Indian, 201, 212
eclecticism, 32
economic: development, 36, 41, 82; ethics 190
education, 89, 100, 149, 152, 180, 191, 211
*eguns,* 101
Elbein dos Santos, Juana, 84, 114, 116, 124-126, 128, 143
Elie, Paul, 69
Ember, Melvin, 42
emic, 37, 42, 188
empowerment, 146, 160
Emsley Smith, 164
enchanted forest, 104

## Index

EngenhoVelho, 76, 101, 104-105, 107, 116
entrepreneurship, 35-36, 38, 41, 82, 186, 191, 199
Erasmus, 27
Eriksen, Thomas, H. 196
Esu, 121, 143 (*see also* Exu)
ethical religion, 74
ethics, 74, 140, 190
Ethiopia, 164, 179
ethnic: brokerage, 191, entrepreneurship, 191; identity, 15, 71, 140; mobilization, 184, 192; strategies, 191
ethnicity, 15, 71, 79, 81, 140, 143, 190, 195-196, 198-199
ethnographic: authority, 16, 132, 140, 143-144; representation, 189
ethnography, 76, 181, 184-185, 196-197, 200
etic, 37, 42
Etkin, Nina, 53
Evans-Pritchard, E. E., 45, 52
evil, 49, 66, 128, 192, 195
evolutionary: paradigm, 25; thinking, 25
Ewing, Katherine, 161
exchange, 13, 17, 57, 59, 61-63, 65, 74, 77, 96, 121, 186, 189
Exu, 82-83, 134-136 (*see also* Esu)

Fadipe, N. A., 124
faith, 18, 48, 61, 64, 150-154, 156-157, 183, 202, 204-205, 207-208, 213
Fanti-Ashanti House, 102-104, 110
*favelas,* 58
Featherstone, Michael, 41, 143
Fernandez, James W., 38, 40, 144
Fernhout, R., 67
Ferrabrás of Alexandria, 16, 104, 108-110
Ferretti, Mundicarmo, 15-16, 66, 68-69, 97, 99, 108-111
Ferretti, Sergio, 15, 66, 68-69, 87, 97, 124, 129

field, 11, 13, 17, 22, 25, 27, 38, 102, 140, 158, 165-169, 171, 176, 179-180, 185, 188, 192, 199
films, 168, 170
Fisher, Michael M. J., 198-199
Flanagan, Kieran, 41
*flecheiros,* 103
food, 195, 199
Foster, George, 68, 83
Freyre, Gilberto, 15, 72, 82
Friedman, Jonathan, 41, 143
Fry, Peter, 72, 82

Gambia, 90
game, 49, 61, 150, 158, 166-169, 174
Ganesha, 203
Gantois, 76, 101, 116
Geertz, Clifford, 40, 43-44, 52, 88
*Gemeinschaft,* 188
gender(s), 146-148, 155-161
Giddens, Anthony, 32, 40, 126
Ginzburg, Carlo, 88, 97
Giroux, Henri, 180
globalization, 26, 35, 38, 41, 143
globalizing processes, 186
glocalization, 35
God, 18, 59-61, 64-65, 68, 74-75, 90-91, 118, 120-122, 124, 127, 134-135, 146-147, 150-155, 157, 159-160, 164, 190, 192, 202-204, 206-207, 209-211
Goffman, Irving, 44, 52
Gomes, Alexandre, 109
Gonçalves, Vagner, 143
Good, Charles M., 53
Gort, Jerald D., 39, 67, 179, 197, 212-213
Gosine, Mahin, 213-214
Gottschall, Carlota, 124
great traditions, 44
Greenfield, Sidney M., 14-16, 19, 21, 39-42, 55, 66, 68-69, 82-83, 85, 88, 113, 125, 161, 196, 202
Gross, Daniel, 68, 83, 107, 127

Guanche, 110
guardian angels, 151
Guerreiro, Ana Maria, 124
Guine, 90
Gypsy, 73, 109, 136

habitat, 32
habitus, 17, 32-33, 165-174, 176, 179-180; formation 166-167, 174, 176
Haile Selassie, I 164, 178
Haiti, 128
Hall, Stuart, 134, 143
hallucinogen, 73
Hannerz, Ulf, 41
healer, 14, 43, 45-47, 49, 51, 53, 73, 75, 77, 79, 81, 83, 85, 105, 108
healing, 14, 45, 51, 53, 69, 73, 89, 108-109, 120, 199
health care, 45, 51, 53, 191
Hebdige, Dick, 179, 181
Heelas, Paul, 41
hegemony, 29, 118-119, 122-123, 138-140
herbalists, 46-47, 50
hermeneutics of power, 117, 119, 126
Herrnhut Society, 183
Herskovits, Frances S., 196
Herskovits, Melville J., 15, 24, 26-29, 38-39, 56, 88, 97, 114, 126, 184-187, 190, 193, 196, 198-199, 203, 205, 212
High God, 118, 190
Hinduism, 205-206, 208-210, 212-213
Hobsbawm, Erik, 93
Holanda Ferreira, Aurélio Buarque de, 108
Holland, 14
Holland, Dorothy, 38
Holy Ghost, 64, 94
holy water, 192
Homiak, John P., 178, 181
homosexuals, 192

Hoogbergen, Wim, 179
Horowitz, Michael M., 185, 196, 201, 212
Hunter, James Davison, 67
Hussey, Dermont, 180
Hutchinson, Bertram, 68
hybridity, 132

identitophagy, 15, 72, 80-81
identity politics, 16, 131
ideology, 31, 40, 77, 88, 141, 176, 178, 187, 205
*idile,* 118
Ifá, 121, 127-128
Ijexa, 76
Ilé Axé Apô Afonjá, 114
Ile-Ife, 118
illness, 45, 53, 59, 188, 199
*ilus,* 117, 119, 122
imagined community, 186
incense, 192
Indian, 14-15, 18, 71, 73, 78, 83, 100-101, 105-108, 111, 131, 140, 174, 199, 201-202, 204-205, 211-213
indigenous, 43-44, 53, 89, 99-108, 117, 189; ethnographer, 189
individualism, 134, 190
individuality, 133, 135-136
individual religiosity, 17
Indo-Trinidadians, 204-206
industrialization, 14, 55-59, 61, 63, 65, 67, 69, 85
initiation, 77, 91, 95, 115, 122, 137
institutionalized religion, 146, 156
interculture, 132
internal migration, 55
interpenetration, 9, 11, 42, 82, 91-92, 96
*irmandade,* 154
Islam, 9-10, 14, 31, 44, 53, 205, 208
*iwà,* 46, 49-50, 52-53
*iwarefa,* 117
Iyá Nassô, 116

# Index

Jackson, Walter, 39, 190, 198
Jacobs, Els, 161
Jahoda, 50, 53
Jamaica, 17, 163-165, 169, 173-176, 178-179, 181, 213
Jayawardena, Chandra, 213
Jeje, 76, 83, 92-94
Jesus Christ, 10, 90, 135, 190, 202, 206
Johnson, Howard, 181
Johnson, Randal, 180
Judaism, 95, 205-206, 208, 210
Jupp, Peter C., 41
*jurema,* 73, 104

Kadt, Emanuel de, 61, 68, 121, 127
Kardec, Allan, 63, 77-78, 81
Kardecist-Spiritism, 60, 62, 77, 92, 156
Kardecist-Spiritist, 96, 151, 153
Karma, 208
Kasturi, N., 213-214
Ketu, 76, 125
Kikongo, 90
Kinbundo, 90
King Agonglo, 92
King, Anthony D., 143
kin groups, 128, 188, 199
King Sebastian, 103
kinship ties, 191
Klass, Morton, 18, 66, 201, 212-214
Kranenborg, Reender, 213
Kremser, Manfred, 178, 181
Kuhn, Thomas, 13, 21-25, 38, 124

LaGuerre, John G., 213
Landes, Ruth, 84, 108-109, 126
Larkin, Colin, 179
Latin America, 68, 74, 111, 123, 127, 203
Lawson, E. Thomas, 127-128
Leach, E.R., 203-204, 212
Leacock, Ruth, 109
Leacock, Seth, 109
Leers, Bernardino, 68

Légua-Boji-Buá, 104
Leite S.I., Serafim, 111
Lett, James, 42
Levinson, David, 42
Lewis, Ioan, 74, 83
Lichtveld, Ursy M., 197, 199
life crises, 193
*Lisa,* 90
little traditions, 44
livity, 168, 170, 178, 180
Lody, Raul Giovanni, 109
logic of practices, 166
LogunEde, 136
Lord Buddha, 203, 212
Lourdes B., Maria de, 109
Lucifer, 190
Luckmann, Thomas, 32, 40, 185, 188, 196-197
Lutheran, 151

MacLean, Una, 50-51, 53
Mãe Andreza, 106
Mãe Aninha, 114
Mãe Stella Azevedo, 114
Magalhães, Elyette Guimaraes de, 122, 128
Magnani, 61, 68
Maldevidan, 201, 211-212
Malthus, Th. R., 66
Manoel Teus Santos, 105, 110
Maranhão, 15, 87-90, 92-93, 95-96, 100, 102-106, 108-110
Marchant, 67, 127
Marcus, George E., 185, 196-199
Margolis, Maxine, 68
Mari-Amma, 201-202, 212
Marland, Hilary, 199
Marley, Bob, 163-165, 169-171, 176, 178, 180-181
Martin, Grace Mc, 213
Martinique, 201, 212
Marxism, 29

Marxist, 30
Marx, Karl, 66-67, 85
Mary, 194
mass migration, 184, 191
McCarthy Brown, Karen, 128
McClelland, E. M., 127
meaning-making, 17, 32, 146, 148-149
meaning production, 189
mechanistic, 147, 157, 167
media, 58, 95, 164, 170-171, 176
Medina, 127
medium(s), 63, 73, 77, 99-101, 103, 108, 135-137, 141, 153, 175, 188-189
mestizo, 100
Mestres, 73-74, 78, 81
metaphor, 15, 22, 25, 28, 38, 158, 172
micro-anthropological approach, 145
middle class, 184, 187-189
Mina, 15, 59, 62, 76, 83, 87, 89-96, 99-110, 116; coast, 116
Mina-Jeje, 89
minimum wage, 57
minorities, 11, 27, 36
Mintz, Sidney W., 185, 196, 200
miracle, 60, 69, 149, 152
missionaries, 9, 62, 90
mixing of diverse traditions, 176
Moçambique, 76
models, 22-23, 30, 37-38, 70, 102, 114, 125, 146
modernity, 16, 35, 41, 66-67, 80, 85, 131-135, 137, 139, 141-143
modernization, 10, 29, 35-36, 56, 58, 65-67, 80; theory, 29, 35-36, 56, 65
modernized, 56, 65, 78, 80-81
Moksha, 209
Moloye, Olu, 46, 52-53
Moore, Sally Falk, 32, 40
Moors, 104-105, 110
Moravian Brethren, 183
Mortimer Planno, 164, 178

Mother Earth, 190
Motta, Roberto, 15, 66, 68-69, 71, 82, 84, 97, 124-125
Moura, Carlos Eugenio Narcondes de, 110
Moy, Yok, 196
multiculturalism, 11-12, 190
Murphet, Howard, 206, 210, 213-214
Murphy, Joseph M., 47, 52
music, 17, 26, 36, 52, 94, 125, 148-149, 156, 163-165, 171-172, 175-179, 181, 185, 193, 199
myth(s), 17, 76-78, 92-93, 102, 106-108, 117-119, 121, 126, 138, 165-167, 169, 180, 188, 191, 212

Na Agontime, 92
nação, 76, 84, 101
Nagashima, Yoshiko S., 177
nagô, 76, 78, 82-84, 89, 100, 102, 106-107, 110-111, 113-116, 124-126
Nagô-Ketu, 89, 92
nation, 18, 37, 57, 67, 76, 78, 80, 104-105, 107, 111, 163, 171, 178, 181, 202, 204, 211; -building, 187; -state, 35-36
nationalism, 41, 81, 187, 190, 195-196
national religion, 78
native discourse, 16, 134
Negrão, Lísias, 68
Netherlands, 18, 184, 187, 191, 196, 198-199
Nevadomsky, Joseph, 213
Nigeria, 14, 19, 43-46, 51-53, 90, 115, 125-126
Nisbet, Robert, 25, 39
Nochê Sepazim, 94
Noordegraaf, H., 196, 198
Norris, William P., 67
Nyahbinghi, 164-165, 176, 178
Nzambi, 90

*oba,* 46, 117-118, 122, 126, 128
Obeyesekere, Gananath, 198
objectification, 188
objective view, 31
Oduduwa, 118
*ogan,* 95
Ogbomosho, 46
Ogboni, 46
Ogboni society, 46
Okwu, A.S.O., 53
Old Oyo, 116, 118
Oliveira, Pedro Ribeiro de, 60, 127
Olodumare, 118, 121-122
Omolú, 103
oppression, 29-30
*orixás,* 63, 74, 78, 80, 99, 101, 105, 114-115, 123
orthodoxy, 76, 95, 133, 136, 138-139
Ortiz, Renato, 72, 82, 84-85
Ortner, Sherry B., 32, 40-41, 197
Oyo, 76, 116, 118, 125

Pai Euclides, 102, 104, 107, 110-111
*pajé,* 105, 108
*pajelança,* 89, 108-109
Palmié, Stephan, 199
pan-Africanist, 167
Panikkar, R., 88, 97
paradigm(s), 12, 22-25, 27-29, 41, 49, 69-70, 82, 139; replacement, 23
paradigmatic, 27, 32, 59, 148, 156
paradox(es), 15, 69, 71, 79-81, 132, 134, 139, 165, 174
parallelism, 90-92, 94, 96, 115, 124
Paramaribo, 185, 196, 199
patron-client exchanges, 14, 56, 59, 61
patterns, 17, 25-28, 39, 119, 168, 174, 176, 204
Pearson, Harry W., 69
Peel, John D. Y,. 126
Pentecostal, 60, 63, 151-152; groups, 63

performances, 38, 136-137, 165, 167, 169, 172-174
Peter Tosh, 164, 169, 180-181
philosophical thought, 44
Pierson, Donald, 125
Pike, Kenneth, 37, 42
pilgrimages, 59
Pillaiyar, 203
Pines, Jim, 181
Platvoet, Jan G., 161, 197
Plutarch, 18, 27, 212
Polanyi, Karl, 69
political economy, 14, 56
politicalization, 186
polyvocality, 17, 183, 185, 187, 189, 191, 193, 195, 197, 199
popular: Catholicism, 59-60, 62-63, 68, 74, 80, 83, 120, 127, 154; culture, 17, 176, 180, 198; religion, 14, 30, 67, 83, 85, 184, 188
Porto Alegre, 62, 67, 146
Posse, 171-172, 175
possession, 16, 63, 77, 99, 101, 121-122, 124, 131-133, 135-137, 139, 141, 143, 188
postcolonial, 166, 168, 177
postmodern anthropology, 185
postmodernism, 34-35, 41
postmodernity, 41, 80
power, 14, 16-17, 29-31, 33, 35-37, 43, 45, 47-48, 51-52, 60, 64, 68, 75, 77, 116-117, 119, 122-123, 126, 128, 132-134, 136-139, 141, 146-149, 155-156, 159-161, 166, 168-169, 172, 177, 180, 187, 189, 195, 213
practices, 9-10, 14-17, 26, 35-36, 39, 44-46, 57, 59-60, 62, 67, 73, 76-77, 80, 87-90, 92-96, 101, 108-109, 113-115, 120, 122-124, 132, 136-137, 139, 142, 155, 160, 165-174, 176-178, 184, 187, 190-191, 195
Prandi, Reginaldo, 125-126, 143

praxis theories, 32-33
pre-modernity, 141
prestige, 51, 74, 92, 168, 177
*Pretos Velhos* (Old Black People), 63, 78-79, 103
Price, Richard, 196-197
Prince Doctor, 14, 43, 46-52
Prince Emmanuel, 164, 177
Princess Floripes, 108-109
Príncipe, 90
private, 10, 95, 123, 134, 160, 181, 190
process, 11, 14, 21, 23, 26, 29-32, 34-37, 41, 43, 51, 53, 67-69, 77, 80-81, 84, 91, 122, 136, 139-140, 142, 145-149, 155, 157, 160, 165-167, 171, 174, 176-177, 181, 188, 195, 199, 203
production and reproduction of structures and meanings, 33
*promessa,* 61, 65, 127, 153
Protestant, 17, 63, 152, 183, 193-194
Prust, Russell, 83, 85
public, 27, 38, 81, 92-95, 123, 128, 136-137, 142, 152, 160, 169, 172, 190-191
publication(s), 13, 32-33, 35, 76, 126, 138, 151, 191, 196, 213
purification of Umbanda, 137
purity, 15, 30, 37, 71, 79, 88-90, 102, 114, 136, 138-139, 176, 206
puzzle solving, 22

Quinn, Naomi, 38, 41, 161

Radcliffe-Brown, A. R., 28
Ragga, 17, 163, 165-167, 169, 171, 173-177, 179, 181; Cowboys, 17, 163, 165, 167, 169, 171, 173, 175, 177, 179, 181
Raggamuffin, 171, 177
Ramalho, João, 111
Ramos, Arthur, 84, 88-89, 97, 114, 126
Ranger, Terence, 93, 97, 171
Rastafari, 163-171, 173-178

rationality, 74, 77, 138
re-Africanization, 114, 123
reflexive approach, 13
reflexivity, 16, 34, 132-133, 141-142, 168, 189
reggae, 17, 36, 163-166, 168, 170-171, 173-177, 179-181; music, 17, 36, 163-164, 179
reification, 82, 188
reincarnation, 53, 91, 135, 152-154, 157-158, 160, 164, 213
reinterpretation, 15-16, 26-28, 34, 42, 56, 77, 83, 88, 113, 115, 117, 119, 121-123, 125, 127, 129, 186, 203-204
religion, 9-11, 14-18, 26, 28, 30-31, 34-35, 40-41, 44, 47, 52-53, 56, 59, 62-70, 72-76, 78-81, 83-85, 87, 89-92, 94-97, 99-103, 105-107, 109, 111, 113-121, 123, 125, 127, 132, 136-137, 139-141, 143, 145-153, 156, 159-160, 171, 177, 183-185, 187-188, 191-192, 196, 198-199, 202-207, 210-212
religious: authenticity, 114; dogmas, 44; market, 14, 56, 64-65, 71-72, 79-80, 84; marketplace, 14, 56, 64-65, 79; mixture, 88; pluralism, 56, 64-65, 69, 161; purity, 114; self-help, 191; texts, 140
repertoire(s), 17, 132, 145-147, 156-157
Ribeiro, René, 60, 82, 85, 127
Richardson, John G., 180
ritual, 15-16, 18, 35, 42, 50-52, 60, 65, 67-68, 71, 73, 75-78, 81-83, 87-89, 91-97, 99-106, 108-110, 113-123, 125-128, 131-141, 161, 183-184, 187-195, 203, 208; praxis, 131-132, 136-137; system, 117
ritualistic trance, 99
Robertson, R., 35, 41
*roças,* 116
Rodrigues, Nina, 89, 114, 125-126
Rolim, Francisco C., 68

Roman Catholic, 14, 17, 47, 62, 64, 72, 81, 113-114, 164, 183, 193-194, 203, 212; Church, 14, 62, 64, 72, 81
Roman Catholicism, 14, 56, 59, 61, 65, 73, 75, 79, 114
Roniger, Luis, 66, 68
Roots Reggae, 164-166
Rosenau, Pauline Marie, 34, 41
Rubin, Vera, 213
Rudolph, Kurt, 39

sacred, 18, 65, 69, 75, 81-82, 84, 101, 105, 108, 118, 126, 147, 193-195, 199
sacrifices, 46, 74, 91, 94, 121, 128, 136
Sahlins, Marshall, 40-41
saint(s), 14, 44, 59-61, 63-65, 69, 72, 74, 78, 80-81, 90-94, 114-115, 120-123, 127, 132, 137, 146, 152, 154, 158-159, 185, 199, 209
Salamone, Frank, 14, 43, 53
salvation religion, 75
Sanatan Dharma, 208-210
Sandweiss, Samuel, 206, 210-211, 213-214
Sanjek, Roger, 198
*San-eria,* 47
Santos, A., 66
São Paulo, 62, 66-68, 84-85, 97, 103, 109-111, 116, 125, 129, 132, 136-137, 139, 143
São Tomé, 90
Sapequara, 101, 105, 108
Satan, 164, 179
Sathya Sai Baba, 8, 18, 201-211, 213
Sayers, Raymond, 68, 83, 127
schema, 17, 33, 148, 158-160
Schoonheym, Peter, 190, 193, 196-199
Schumpeter, Joseph, 36, 41
Schwartz, Barton M., 213
scientific: community, 22-23; hegemony versus native conceptions, 140
Scott, R. Parry, 97

secularized world, 191
self, 17, 134-136, 140-141, 161, 166, 192-193, 207, 211
*Senhores,* 102
sentential logic, 33-34, 148, 156
separation, 48, 90-91, 94, 96, 101, 120, 192, 205
sexism, 172, 181
Shango, 47, 118, 203, 211
Shaw, Rosalind, 30, 39-40, 132, 143, 174, 181, 186-187, 190, 197-198, 200, 202, 212
Sidran, Ben, 181
Sierra Leone, 90
signification, 32, 37, 145-148, 156
Simon, Peter, 69, 181
sisterhood, 154, 158-159
Siva, 203
Sjørslev, Inger, 16, 66, 68, 131, 143
slavery, 10, 78, 103, 106, 178, 195, 199
Smith, M. Estelle, 67, 83
Smith, M. G., 119, 126-127
Smith Omari, Mikelle, 116, 125-126
Smith, R. T., 213
Smith, T. Lynn, 127
social: agenda, 27, 29; class, 75, 88; drama, 32
sociologists, 79, 188, 205
song(s), 73, 92-93, 103, 165, 171-173, 175-179, 180, 191, 193, 195
South Asian: social structure, 205; ideology, 205; values, 205
spirit(s), 16, 41, 46, 48, 52, 59, 62-63, 73-74, 77-79, 81, 83, 94, 99-102, 111, 121-122, 124, 128, 131-133, 135-141, 143, 146-147, 153, 188-189, 210; of light, 153
St. Anthony, 90
St. Barbara, 47
St. Benedict, 90, 93
Stephen, Henri M. J., 67, 69, 181, 191-192, 196-199

Stewart, Charles, 30, 39-40, 132, 143, 174, 181, 186-187, 190, 197-198, 200, 202, 212
St. George, 90, 114, 152
Stocking, George W., 25, 39, 198
Storey, John, 180
St. Peter, 61, 152
Strauss, Claudia, 41, 161
Strickon, Arnold, 41, 68, 82
structural-functional theory, 28
structuralism, 29, 88
structure(s), 13, 17, 21, 32-33, 35-36, 38, 42, 44, 67-68, 75, 80, 117-119, 122, 124-125, 145-148, 159-160, 166-172, 174, 176-177, 180, 201, 205; of Scientific Revolutions, 21, 38, 124; of dominance, 168
St. Theresa, 152
subaltern classes, 15, 88
subjective view, 31
subjectivist, 147, 157
suffering, 48, 59, 61, 120, 152, 157-158
supernatural, 45, 48, 60, 62-63, 65, 68, 74, 80, 115, 121-122, 146-147, 156, 188
superstition, 134, 142
Supreme Being, 115, 120-122, 151, 192
Surinam(e), 17, 183-184, 187, 189-190, 192, 194-199; Creole Religion, 183, 198
*surrupira*, 104, 107-108
symbol(s), 29, 32, 34, 37, 40, 42, 72, 101, 133-135, 141, 161, 169-170, 174, 178, 186, 192, 195, 197, 204-205
Symbolic Anthropology, 29
symbolic studies, 83, 88
syncretic, 11, 14-15, 17-18, 31, 36, 43, 45, 47, 49, 51, 53, 73, 75, 77, 79, 81-83, 85, 87, 90, 95-96, 132, 140, 145-146, 156, 160, 165-168, 171, 174, 176-177, 183, 185, 203-204, 206-207, 209-211; process, 11, 31, 145-146, 160, 165-167, 174, 176-177
syncretism(s), 7-9, 10-12, 14-18, 21, 23-33, 35, 37, 39-44, 46-47, 49, 52, 56-57, 62-63, 67, 71-72, 83, 87-97, 99, 101-102, 104, 107-108, 113, 122, 124, 131-135, 137-139, 141-143, 145, 147, 149, 151, 153, 155, 157, 159, 161, 165-166, 174, 177, 179, 181, 183-187, 189-205, 207, 209, 211-213
syntagmatic, 148, 156
Szwed, John F., 196

Tabajara, 100-101, 107
*tambor de choro*, 91
Tambor de Crioula, 90, 97
Tambor de Mina(s), 15, 59, 83, 87, 89-96, 99-110
Telegu, 205
terreiros, 75-77, 82, 84, 91, 109, 115-116, 131, 139
textual authority, 188
Theije, Marjo de, 161
Thelwell, Michael, 181
therapeutic, 59, 120, 188
Thompson, Robert Farris, 43-44, 52-53
Thornton, John K., 90, 97
traditional healing practitioners, 45
traditional religious practices, 15
trance, 74, 80, 99, 101, 110, 136, 188, 191
transnational corporations, 57
trickster god, 134
Trinidad, 14, 18, 196, 202-205, 211-213; and Tobago, 18, 202, 204, 211
Troeltsch, Ernst, 77, 85
truth claims, 188
Tunde Lawuyi, 47
Tupã, 100
Turkish spirits, 102, 104-108
Turner, Tina, 154, 156
Turner, Victor, 37, 40, 42, 74, 83, 88, 144, 154, 156
Tyler, Stephen A., 185-186, 197, 200

Umbanda, 16, 38, 60, 63, 76-85, 99, 101-103, 109, 131-133, 136-144, 156, 160-161; Branca, 77, 84, federations, 138
University of Ibadan, 46, 52
University of Ife, 46
urbanization, 56, 65

Van der Toorn, Karel, 161
Vandezande, René, 83
Van Lier, R.A.J., 196, 198
Van Wetering, Ineke, 8, 17-18, 183, 196, 198-199
Velez, Claudio, 68
Venema, Tijno, 198-199
Verger, Pierre, 92, 97, 125-126, 139
Villas Boas Cancone, Maria Helena, 84
violence, 66, 152, 172, 177, 181
Virgin, 59, 120, 157
Vodun, 90, 190, 203, 211
*voduns,* 89, 91-94, 96-97, 99, 101, 109
Vó Missã, 105
Voorhoeve, Jan, 190, 197-199
vow, 66, 74, 153-154
Vroom, H. M., 67

Wach, Joachim, 73, 83
Wacquant, Loic J.D., 180-181
Wafer, Jim, 123-124, 129
Wailer, Bunny, 164, 169, 180
Wales, Josey, 174, 181
Wallace, Anthony, 39
Warren Jr., Donald, 53, 83
Wartofsky, Alona, 178
water, 58, 118, 192, 194
Weber, Max, 52, 74-75, 77, 83, 85
Weingaertner, Lindolfo, 85

welfare work, 191
Wernick, Andrew, 41
Wessels, A., 67
westernization, 35
Western movies, 169-172, 174-175, 177
Whitney, Malika Lee, 180
Whitten, Norman E., 196
wholeness, 139, 141, 161
Winti, 17-18, 183-199; theology, 187
women, 17-18, 45, 58, 69, 84, 89, 94, 100, 108-109, 116, 159, 183-184, 186, 191-195, 198-199
Wooding, Charles J., 187-189, 191-192, 197-199
Woodward, Kenneth L., 69
world economy, 35-36, 57
world religions, 9, 43
Worsley, Peter, 53
Wright, Will, 180

Xambá, 76
Xangôs, 59, 62, 73-74, 115
Xapanã, 103

Yawney, Carole, 178
Yellowman, 165-166, 168, 174-175, 180-181
Yoruba, 14, 16, 43-49, 51-53, 63, 73-77, 79, 81, 83, 85, 89, 92, 100, 114-122, 124, 126-128; epistemology, 14; *orisa,* 44, 118
Young, Alan, 53, 211

Zaluar, Alba, 127
Zips, Werner, 17, 36, 41, 163, 178-179, 181

# About the Contributors

**André Droogers** (co-editor)
 is professor of the anthropology of religion at the Vrije Universiteit, Amsterdam. He has done fieldwork in Zaire and Brazil, and also has held academic positions in both countries. His doctoral dissertation on boys' initiation among the Wagenia (in Zaire) was published under the title, *The Dangerous Journey* (The Hague: Mouton, 1980). He is the author of numerous articles, several books and co-editor of a number of volumes. His recent publications include *More than Opium: An Anthropological Approach to Latin American and Caribbean Pentecostal Praxis* (Lanham, MD and London: Scarecrow Press, 1998), co-edited with Barbara Boudewijnse and Frans Kamsteeg, and *The Popular Use of Popular Religion in Latin America* (Amsterdam: CEDLA, 1993), co-edited with Susanna Rostas. His research interests include syncretism, popular religions, Pentecostalism and play. His e-mail address is: af.droogers@scw.vu.nl.

**Mundicarmo Maria Rocha Ferretti**
 is a professor in the department of social sciences at State University of Maranhão in the city of São Luís, Brazil, where she teaches and conducts research on popular culture and Afro-Brazilian religion. She holds a Ph.D. from the University of São Paulo. Since 1992, her work has focused on the representations of non-African spiritual entities who embody in mediums at an Afro-Brazilian religious center while they are in

ritual trance states. Her more recent publications include *Desceu na guma: o caboclo do Tambor de Mina no processo de mudança de um terreiro de São Luís—A Casa Fanti-Ashanti* (São Luís: SIOGE, 1993), *Terra de caboclo* (São Luís: SECMA, 1994) and "Rei da Turquia, o Ferrabrás de Alexandria? A importância de um livro na mitologia do Tambor de Mina," in Carlos Eugínio Marcondes de Moura, *Meu sinal está no teu corpo: escritos sobre a religião dos orixás* (São Paulo: EDICON/EDUSP, 1989). Her e-mail address is: mundicarmo@prof.elo.com.br.

## Sergio Ferretti

is adjunct professor of anthropology in the department of sociology and anthropology at the Federal University of Maranhão in the city of São Luís. A Ph.D. from the University of São Paulo, he teaches and does research on Afro-Brazilian religions and popular festivals as the symbolic productions of subordinate classes. He is interested in syncretism and the contribution religious festivals make in the construction of social identities. His publications include *Querebentã de Zomadonu: Etnografia da Casa das Minas* (São Luís: EDUFMA, 1996), *Repensando o Sincretismo* (São Paulo/São Luís: EDUSP/FAPEMA, 1995) and *Tambor de Crioula: Ritual e Espectáculo* (São Luís: SECMA/CMF/LITHOGRAF, 1995) of which he was the editor. His e-mail address is: ferretti@elo.com.br.

## Sidney M. Greenfield (co-editor)

is Professor Emeritus at the University of Wisconsin-Milwaukee. He has conducted ethnographic research in the West Indies, New Bedford, Massachusetts and Brazil and ethnohistorical and historical research in Portugal and the Atlantic Islands on problems ranging from family and kinship, patronage and politics, the history of plantations and plantation slavery and entrepreneurship to Spiritist surgery and healing and syncretized religions in Brazil. Author and/or editor of five books, as well as producer, director and author of five video documentaries, he has published more than 100 articles and reviews in books and professional journals. Among his more recent works are *Cirurgias do Além: Pesquisas Antropológicas Sobre Curas Espirituais.* (Petrópolis, RJ: Editora Vozes, 1999), a book in Portuguese about his studies of Spiritist healing; "Recasting Syncretism . . . Again: Theories and Concepts in Anthropology and Afro-American Studies in the Light of Changing Social Agendas," in Peter B. Clarke, ed., *New Trends and Developments in African Religions*, Westport, CT: Greenwood Press, 1998, pp. 1-15, and *Spirits, Medicine, and Charity: A Brazilian Woman's Cure for Cancer* (Media Resource Department of the University of Wisconsin-Milwaukee, 1995, 39.36 Min.), a video documentary. His e-mail address is: EGreenf222@aol.com.

## Morton Klass

Professor Emeritus of Anthropology at Barnard College, Columbia University, has conducted research on Overseas South Asians in Trinidad and Tobago on cultural persistence and on the worship of the Indian Godman Satya Sai Baba. In India he studied industrialization and village-level Hinduism. His numerous publications include: *East Indians in Trinidad* (New York: Columbia University Press, 1961; Reprinted by Waveland Press, 1988), *Caste: The Emergence of the South Asian Social System* (Philadelphia: Institute for the Study of Human Issues, 1980), *Singing With Sai Baba: The Politics of Revitalization in Trinidad* (Boulder, CO: Westview Press, 1991) and *Ordered Universes: Approaches to the Anthropology of Religion* (Boulder, CO: Westview Press, 1995). His e-mail address is: mk153@columbia.edu.

## Roberto Motta

is professor in the department of social sciences at the Federal University of Pernambuco in Recife, Brazil. He has studied and taught in France, Italy and the United States in addition to his native Brazil. Much of his extensive research has focused on Afro-Brazilian cults, but he also has worked on social change, race relations and social thought. He has published extensively in Portuguese, French, Italian and English. His many publications include *Sobrevivência e Fontes de Renda* (Recife: Editora Massangana, 1983), with R. Parry Scott; *Cidade e Devoção* (Recife: Edições Pirata, 1980); "Ethnicité, Nationalité et Syncrétisme dans les Religions Populaires Brésiliennes," *Social Compass* (International Review of Sociology of Religion), vol. 41 (1994), no. 1; and "The Churchifying of Candomblé: Priests, Anthropologists, and the Canonization of African Religious Memory in Brazil," in Peter B. Clarke, ed., *New Trends and Developments in African Religions* (Westport, CT: Greenwood Press, 1998). His e-mail address is: rmotta@elogica.com.br.

## Frank Salamone

is professor of anthropology at Iona College in New Rochelle, New York. He has conducted fieldwork in Nigeria, Kenya, Ghana and the United States and published more than 150 articles and chapters in books. Among his recent edited books are *Explorations in Anthropology and Theology* (Lanham, MD: University Press of America, 1997), edited with Walter Adams; *The Yanomami and Their Interpreters* (Lanham, MD: University Press of America, 1997); and *Bridges to Humanity: Narratives on Anthropology and Friendship* (Prospect Heights, IL: Waveland Press, 1995), with Bruce Grindal. His e-mail address is: fsalamone@iona.edu.

## Inger Sjørslev

is an Associate Professor at the Institute of Anthropology of the University of Copenhagen. She has done ethnographic research on Candomblé and Umbanda in Bahia and São Paulo, Brazil and has done museology in Brazil and India. She also has worked with indigenous issues and politics as director of The International Work Group for Indigenous Affairs (IWGIA). Her publications include *Gudernes rum: En beretning om ritualer og tro i Brasilien* (Copenhagen: Gylendal, 1995) which has been translated into German as *Glaube und Besessenheit. Ein Bericht über die Candomblé-*

*Religion in Brasilien* (Gifkendorf: Merlin Verlag, 1999). Her e-mail address is: inger.sjoerslev@mail1.anthro.ku.dk.

## Ineke van Wetering,

who is affiliated with the Amsterdam School for Social Science Research, has had a long-standing interest in African culture in the diaspora. After conducting anthropological fieldwork among the Ndyuka, a Maroon group in Surinam, she has been studying the rituals of Surinamese Creole women in Amsterdam. She has written extensively on Maroon witchcraft, religious movements and other aspects of the lives of Creole women in Amsterdam. She co-authored *The Great Father and the Danger: Religious Cults, Material Forces and Collective Fantasies in the World of the Surinamese Maroons* (Leiden: KITLV Press, 1991). Her e-mail address is: thoden@wxs.nl.

## Werner Zips

is assistant professor at the Institute for Social and Cultural Anthropology (Ethnology) of the University of Vienna who has done research in Jamaica, Ghana, Tanzania and Botswana. His many publications include *Sovereignty, Legitimacy, and Power in West African Societies* (Hamburg: LIT, 1998), co-edited with van Rouvery van Nieuwaal, and *Ethnohistorie. Rekonstruction und Kulturkkritik* (Wien: Promedia, 1998), co-edited with Karl R. Wernhart. He also has directed the documentary films: *Power is Like an Egg: Ghana Land of Kings* (about chieftancy in Ghana) and *Accompong; Black Freedom Fighters of Jamaica* (a social history of the Maroons). His current interests focus on questions of legal pluralism and the anthropology of law in Jamaica. His e-mail address is: werner.zips@univie.ac.at.